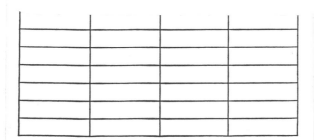

DID JESUS EXIST?

The Historical Argument for Jesus of Nazareth

BART D. EHRMAN

HarperOne

An Imprint of HarperCollins*Publishers*

HarperOne

FIRST EDITION

Library of Congress Cataloging-in-Publication Data is available upon request.
ISBN 978-0-06-220460-8

12 13 14 15 16   RRD(H)   10 9 8 7 6 5 4 3 2 1

Contents

ACKNOWLEDGMENTS

I WOULD LIKE TO THANK a number of people who selflessly helped me in the writing and editing of this book: my brother, classical scholar at Kent State University, Radd Ehrman; one of my closest friends in the field or out of it, Jeffrey Siker at Loyola Marymount University; one of my other closest friends in the field or out of it, Judy Siker at San Francisco Theological Seminary; my esteemed colleague at crosstown rival Duke University, Mark Goodacre; my student and research assistant extraordinaire from the graduate program at Duke, Maria Doerfler; my student and research assistant extraordinaire from the graduate program at the University of North Carolina–Chapel Hill, Jason Combs; my unusually perceptive daughter, Kelly Ehrman; and my industrious and sharp-eyed editor and friend at HarperOne, Roger Freet. All of these have carefully read my manuscript and suggested that I make (innumerable) changes. When I have listened to them, the manuscript is much improved; when I have not, the fault is all mine. I would also like to thank the other members of the HarperOne team who have made this book possible, especially Julie Burton, Claudia Boutote, and Mark Tauber. It's an amazing ensemble and I'm privileged to work with them.

I would also like to thank the attendees of the CIA—the Christianity in Antiquity reading group of faculty and graduate students in New Testament/Early Christianity at both UNC and Duke—for a lively evening of conversation on two of the chapters.

New Testament translations throughout the text are my own; I have taken translations of the Hebrew Bible from the New Revised Standard Version.

INTRODUCTION

For the past several years I have been planning to write a book about how Jesus became God. How is it that a scarcely known, itinerant preacher from the rural backwaters of a remote part of the empire, a Jewish prophet who predicted that the end of the world as we know it was soon to come, who angered the powerful religious and civic leaders of Judea and as a result was crucified for sedition against the state—how is it that within a century of his death, people were calling this little-known Jewish peasant God? Saying in fact that he was a divine being who existed before the world began, that he had created the universe, and that he was equal with God Almighty himself? How did Jesus come to be deified, worshipped as the Lord and Creator of all?

I have to admit that I am eager to write the book, as these are among the most pressing questions in the entire history of religion. But I have continually been forced to put the book off as other writing projects have taken precedence. It will, however, be my next book. In the meantime, something more pressing has come up, a prior question that I have to address first. This book deals with that prior question.

Every week I receive two or three e-mails asking me whether Jesus existed as a human being. When I started getting these e-mails, some years ago now, I thought the question was rather peculiar and I did not take it seriously. Of course Jesus existed. Everyone knows he existed. Don't they?

But the questions kept coming, and soon I began to wonder: Why are so many people asking? My wonder only increased when I learned that I myself was being quoted in some circles—misquoted rather—as saying that Jesus never existed. I decided to look into the matter. I discovered, to my surprise, an entire body of literature devoted to the question of whether or not there ever was a real man, Jesus.

I was surprised because I am trained as a scholar of the New Testament and early Christianity, and for thirty years I have written extensively on the historical Jesus, the Gospels, the early Christian movement, and the history of the church's first three hundred years. Like all New Testament scholars, I have read thousands of books and articles in English and other European languages on Jesus, the New Testament, and early Christianity. But I was almost completely unaware—as are most of my colleagues in the field—of this body of skeptical literature.

I should say at the outset that none of this literature is written by scholars trained in New Testament or early Christian studies teaching at the major, or even the minor, accredited theological seminaries, divinity schools, universities, or colleges of North America or Europe (or anywhere else in the world). Of the thousands of scholars of early Christianity who do teach at such schools, none of them, to my knowledge, has any doubts that Jesus existed. But a whole body of literature out there, some of it highly intelligent and well informed, makes this case.

These sundry books and articles (not to mention websites) are of varying quality. Some of them rival *The Da Vinci Code* in their passion for conspiracy and the shallowness of their historical knowledge, not just of the New Testament and early Christianity, but of ancient religions generally and, even more broadly, the ancient world. But a couple of bona fide scholars—not professors teaching religious studies in universities but scholars nonetheless, and at least one of them with a Ph.D. in the field of New Testament—have taken this position and written about it. Their books may not be known to most of the general public interested in questions related to Jesus, the Gospels, or the early Christian church, but they do occupy a noteworthy niche as a (very) small but (often) loud minority voice. Once you tune in to this voice, you quickly learn just how persistent and vociferous it can be.

And the voice is being heard loud and clear in some places. Even a quick Internet search reveals how influential such radical skepticism has been in the past and how rapidly it is spreading even now. For decades it was the dominant view in countries such as the Soviet Union. Yet more striking, it appears to be the majority view in some regions of the West today, including some parts of Scandinavia.

The authors of this skeptical literature understand themselves to be "mythicists"—that is, those who believe that Jesus is a myth. Rarely do mythicists define what they mean by the term *myth,* a failure that strikes real scholars of religion as both unfortunate and highly problematic, since in technical scholarship the term has come to mean many things over the years. When mythicists use the term they often seem to mean simply a story that has no historical basis, a history-like narrative that in fact did not happen. In this sense Jesus is a myth because even though there are plenty of ancient stories told about him, they are not historical. His life and teachings were invented by early storytellers. He never really lived.

Those who do not think Jesus existed are frequently militant in their views and remarkably adept at countering evidence that to the rest of the civilized world seems compelling and even unanswerable. But these writers have answers, and the smart ones among them need to be taken seriously, if for no other reason than to show why they cannot be right about their major contention. The reality is that whatever else you may think about Jesus, he certainly did exist. That is what this book will set out to demonstrate.

I hardly need to stress what I have already intimated: the view that Jesus existed is held by virtually every expert on the planet. That in itself is not *proof*, of course. Expert opinion is, at the end of the day, still opinion. But why would you not want to know what experts have to say? When you make a dental appointment, do you want your dentist to be an expert or not? If you build a house, do you want a professional architect or your next-door neighbor to draw up the plans? One might be tempted to say that in the case of the historical Jesus it is different since, after all, we are just talking about history; experts have no more access to the past than anyone else. That, however, is simply not true. It may be the case that some of my students receive the bulk of their knowledge of the Middle Ages from *Monty Python and the Holy Grail,* but is that really the best place to turn? So too millions of people have acquired their "knowledge" about early Christianity—about Jesus, Mary Magdalene, the emperor Constantine, the Council of Nicaea—from Dan Brown, author of the aforementioned *The Da Vinci Code.* But at the end of the day, is that such a wise choice?

Serious historians of the early Christian movement—all of them—have spent many years preparing to be experts in their field. Just to read the ancient sources requires expertise in a range of ancient languages: Greek, Hebrew, Latin, and often Aramaic, Syriac, and Coptic, not to mention the modern languages of scholarship (for example, German and French). And that is just for starters. Expertise requires years of patiently examining ancient texts and a thorough grounding in the history and culture of Greek and

Roman antiquity, the religions of the ancient Mediterranean world, both pagan and Jewish, knowledge of the history of the Christian church and the development of its social life and theology, and, well, lots of other things. It is striking that virtually everyone who has spent all the years needed to attain these qualifications is convinced that Jesus of Nazareth was a real historical figure. Again, this is not a piece of evidence, but if nothing else, it should give one pause. In the field of biology, evolution may be "just" a theory (as some politicians painfully point out), but it is the theory subscribed to, for good reason, by every real scientist in every established university in the Western world.

Still, as is clear from the avalanche of sometimes outraged postings on all the relevant Internet sites, there is simply no way to convince conspiracy theorists that the evidence for their position is too thin to be convincing and that the evidence for a traditional view is thoroughly persuasive. Anyone who chooses to believe something contrary to evidence that an overwhelming majority of people find overwhelmingly convincing—whether it involves the fact of the Holocaust, the landing on the moon, the assassination of presidents, or even a presidential place of birth—will not be convinced. Simply *will* not be convinced.

And so, with this book, I do not expect to convince anyone in that boat. What I do hope is to convince genuine seekers who really want to know how we know that Jesus did exist, as virtually every scholar of antiquity, of biblical studies, of classics, and of Christian origins in this country and, in fact, in the Western world agrees. Many of these scholars have no vested interest in the matter. As it turns out, I myself do not either. I am not a Christian, and I have no interest in promoting a Christian cause or a Christian agenda. I am an agnostic with atheist leanings, and my life and views of the world would be approximately the same whether or not Jesus existed. My beliefs would vary little. The answer to the question of Jesus's historical existence will not make me more or less happy, content, hopeful, likable, rich, famous, or immortal.

But as a historian I think evidence matters. And the past matters. And for anyone to whom both evidence and the past matter, a dispassionate consideration of the case makes it quite plain: Jesus did exist. He may not have been the Jesus that your mother believes in or the Jesus of the stained-glass window or the Jesus of your least favorite televangelist or the Jesus proclaimed by the Vatican, the Southern Baptist Convention, the local megachurch, or the California Gnostic. But he did exist, and we can say a few things, with relative certainty, about him.

In any event, I need to admit that I write this book with some fear and trepidation. I know that some readers who support agnostic, atheist, or humanist causes and who typically appreciate my other writings will be vocal and vociferous in rejecting my historical claims. At the same time certain readers who have found some of my other writings dangerous or threatening will be surprised, possibly even pleased, to see that here I make common cause with them. Possibly many readers will wonder why a book is even necessary explaining that Jesus must have existed. To them I would say that *every* historical person, event, or phenomenon needs to be established. The historian can take nothing for granted. And there are several loud voices out there, whether you tune in to them or not, who are declaring that Jesus is a myth. This mythicist position is interesting historically and phenomenologically, as part of a wider skepticism that has infiltrated parts of the thinking world and that deserves a clearheaded sociological analysis in its own right. I do not have the skills or expertise to provide that wider analysis, although I will make some brief remarks about the broad mythicist phenomenon in my conclusion. In the meantime, as a historian I can show why at least one set of skeptical claims about the past history of our civilization is almost certainly wrong, even though these claims are seeping into the popular consciousness at an alarming rate. Jesus existed, and those vocal persons who deny it do so not because they have considered the evidence with the dispassionate eye of the historian, but because they have some other agenda that this denial serves. From a dispassionate point of view, there was a Jesus of Nazareth.

PART I

Evidence for the Historical Jesus

CHAPTER ONE

An Introduction to the Mythical
View of Jesus

MODERN SCHOLARS OF THE New Testament are famous—or infamous—for making claims about Jesus that contradict what most people, especially Christians, believe about him. Some scholars have maintained that Jesus was a political revolutionary who wanted to incite the masses in Israel to a violent uprising against their Roman overlords. Others have claimed that he was like an ancient Cynic philosopher who had no real interest in Israel as the people of God or even in the Hebrew Bible (the Jewish scriptures) but was concerned to teach people how to live simply apart from the material trappings of this life. Others have insisted that Jesus was principally interested in the economic plight of his oppressed people and urged socioeconomic reform, as a kind of proto-Marxist. Yet others have asserted that he was chiefly concerned about the oppression of women and was a proto-feminist. Some have said that he was mainly interested in religious issues but that he was a Pharisee, others that he was a

member of the Dead Sea Scrolls community, an Essene. Some have
said that he taught a completely bourgeois ethic and that he was
married with children. Yet others have suggested that he was gay.
And these are only some of the more serious proposals.

Despite this enormous range of opinion, there are several points
on which virtually all scholars of antiquity agree. Jesus was a Jewish
man, known to be a preacher and teacher, who was crucified (a
Roman form of execution) in Jerusalem during the reign of the
Roman emperor Tiberius, when Pontius Pilate was the governor of
Judea. Even though this is the view of nearly every trained scholar
on the planet, it is not the view of a group of writers who are usually
labeled, and often label themselves, mythicists.

In a recent exhaustive elaboration of the position, one of the
leading proponents of Jesus mythicism, Earl Doherty, defines the
view as follows: it is "the theory that no historical Jesus worthy of
the name existed, that Christianity began with a belief in a spiritual,
mythical figure, that the Gospels are essentially allegory and fiction,
and that no single identifiable person lay at the root of the Galilean
preaching tradition."[1] In simpler terms, the historical Jesus did not
exist. Or if he did, he had virtually nothing to do with the founding
of Christianity.

To lend some scholarly cachet to their view, mythicists sometimes quote a passage from one of the greatest works devoted to the
study of the historical Jesus in modern times, the justly famous *Quest
of the Historical Jesus,* written by New Testament scholar, theologian,
philosopher, concert organist, physician, humanitarian, and Nobel
Peace Prize–winning Albert Schweitzer:

> There is nothing more negative than the result of the critical
> study of the life of Jesus. The Jesus of Nazareth who came
> forward publicly as the Messiah, who preached the ethic of the
> Kingdom of God, who founded the Kingdom of heaven upon
> earth, and died to give his work its final consecration, never

had any existence. This image has not been destroyed from without, it has fallen to pieces, cleft and disintegrated by the concrete historical problems which come to the surface one after the other.[2]

Taken out of context, these words may seem to indicate that the great Schweitzer himself did not subscribe to the existence of the historical Jesus. But nothing could be further from the truth. The myth for Schweitzer was the liberal view of Jesus so prominent in his own day, as represented in the sundry books that he incisively summarized and wittily discredited in *The Quest*. Schweitzer himself knew full well that Jesus actually existed; in his second edition he wrote a devastating critique of the mythicists of his own time, and toward the end of his book he showed who Jesus really was, in his own considered judgment. For Schweitzer, Jesus was an apocalyptic prophet who anticipated the imminent end of history as we know it. Jesus thought that he himself would play a key role in the future act of God, in which the forces of evil in control of this world would be overthrown and a new kingdom would appear. For Schweitzer, Jesus was very much mistaken in this understanding of himself and the future course of events. The end, after all, never did come, and Jesus was crucified for his efforts. But he was very much a real person, a Jewish preacher about whom a good deal could be known through a careful examination of the Gospels.

The problem with the historical Jesus for Schweitzer was that he was in fact all *too* historical. That is, Jesus was so firmly rooted in his own time and place as a first-century Palestinian Jew—with an ancient Jewish understanding of the world, God, and human existence—that he does not translate easily into a modern idiom. The Jesus proclaimed by preachers and theologians today had no existence. That particular Jesus is (or those particular Jesuses are) a myth. But there was a historical Jesus, who was very much a man of his time. And we can know what he was like.

Schweitzer's view of the historical Jesus happens to be mine as well, at least in rough outline. I agree with Schweitzer and virtually all scholars in the field since his day that Jesus existed, that he was ineluctably Jewish, that there is historical information about him in the Gospels, and that we can therefore know some things about what he said and did. Moreover, I agree with Schweitzer's overarching view, that Jesus is best understood as a Jewish prophet who anticipated a cataclysmic break in history in the very near future, when God would destroy the forces of evil to bring in his own kingdom here on earth. I will explain at the end of this book why so many scholars who have devoted their lives to exploring our ancient sources for the historical Jesus have found this understanding so persuasive. For now I want to stress the most foundational point of all: even though some views of Jesus could loosely be labeled myths (in the sense that mythicists use the term: these views are not history but imaginative creation), Jesus himself was not a myth. He really existed.

Before giving evidence for this scholarly consensus, I will set the stage by tracing, very briefly, a history of those who take the alternative view, that there never was a historical Jesus.

A Brief History of Mythicism

THERE IS NO NEED for me to give a comprehensive history of the claim that Jesus never existed. I will simply say a few words about some of the most important representatives of the view up to Schweitzer's time in the early twentieth century and then comment on some of the more influential contemporary representatives who have revitalized the view in recent years.

The first author to deny the existence of Jesus appears to have been the eighteenth-century Frenchman Constantin François Volney, a member of the Constituent Assembly during the French

Revolution.³ In 1791 Volney published an essay (in French) called "Ruins of Empire." In it he argued that all religions at heart are the same—a view still wildly popular among English-speaking people who are not religion scholars, especially as articulated in the second half of the twentieth century by Joseph Campbell. Christianity too, for Volney, was simply a variant on the one universal religion. This particular variation on the theme was invented by early Christians who created the savior Jesus as a kind of sun-god. They derived Jesus's most common epithet, "Christ," from the similar-sounding name of the Indian god Krishna.

Several years later a much more substantial and influential book was published by another Frenchman, Charles-François Dupuis, who was secretary of the revolutionary National Convention. *The Origin of All Religions* (1795) was an enormous work, 2,017 pages in length. Dupuis's ultimate objective was to uncover the nature of the "original deity" who lies behind all religions. In one long section of the study Dupuis paid particular attention to the so-called mystery religions of antiquity. These various religions are called mysteries because the exact teachings and rituals were to be kept secret by their devotees. What we do know is that these various secret religions were popular throughout the Roman Empire, in regions both east and west. Dupuis subjected the fragmentary information that survived to his day to careful scrutiny, as he argued that such gods as Osiris, Adonis (or Tammuz), Bacchus, Attis, and Mithra were all manifestations of the solar deity. Dupuis agreed with his compatriot Volney: Jesus too was originally invented as another embodiment of the sun-god.

The first bona fide scholar of the Bible to claim that Jesus never existed was a German theologian named Bruno Bauer, generally regarded among New Testament scholars as both very smart and highly idiosyncratic.⁴ He had virtually no followers in the scholarly world. Over the course of nearly four decades Bauer produced several books, including *Criticism of the Gospel History of John* (1840);

Criticism of the Gospels (2 vols., 1850–1852); and *The Origin of Christianity from Graeco-Roman Civilization* (1877). When he started out as a scholar, Bauer concurred with everyone else in the field that there was historically reliable material in the first three Gospels of the New Testament, known as the "Synoptic Gospels" (Matthew, Mark, and Luke; they are called "synoptic" because they are so much alike in the stories they tell that you can place them in parallel columns next to each other so that they can be "seen together," unlike the Gospel of John, which for the most part tells a different set of stories). As he progressed in his research, however, and subjected the Gospel accounts to a careful, detailed, and hypercritical evaluation, Bauer began to think that Jesus was a literary invention of the Gospel writers. Christianity, he concluded, was an amalgamation of Judaism with the Roman philosophy of Stoicism. This was obviously an extreme and radical view for a professor of theology to take at the state-supported German University of Bonn. It ended up costing him his job.

The mythicist view was taken up some decades later in English-speaking circles by J. M. Robertson, sometimes considered the premier British rationalist of the beginning of the twentieth century. His major book appeared in 1900, titled *Christianity and Mythology.*[5] Robertson argued that there were striking similarities between what the Gospels claim about Jesus and what earlier peoples believed about pagan gods of fertility, who, like Jesus, were said to have died and been raised from the dead. These fertility gods, Robertson and many others believed, were based on the cycles of nature: just as the crops die at the beginning of winter but then reappear in the spring, so too do the gods with which they are identified. They die and rise again. Jesus's death and resurrection was based, then, on this primitive belief, transposed into Jewish terms. More specifically, while there once may have been a man named Jesus, he was nothing like the Christ worshipped by Christians, who was a mythical figure based on an ancient cult of Joshua, a dying-rising vegetative god who was ritually sacrificed and eaten. Only later was this divine Joshua transposed by his devotees into a historical figure, the alleged founder of Christianity.

Many of these views came to be popularized by a German scholar of the early twentieth century named Arthur Drews, whose work, *The Christ Myth* (1909), was arguably the most influential mythicist book ever produced because it made a huge impact on one reader in particular.[6] It convinced Vladimir Ilyich Lenin that Jesus was not a real historical figure. This, in large measure, led to the popularity of the myth theory in the emerging Soviet Union.

After a relative hiatus, the mythicist view has resurfaced in recent years. In chapters 6 and 7 I review the major arguments for this position, but here I want to say something about the authors themselves, a doughty and colorful ensemble. I have already mentioned Earl Doherty, seen by many as the leading representative of the view in the modern period. By his own admission, Doherty does not have any advanced degrees in biblical studies or any related field. But he does have an undergraduate degree in classics, and his books show that he has read widely and has a good deal of knowledge at his disposal, quite admirable for someone who is, in his own view, an amateur in the field. His now-classic statement is *The Jesus Puzzle: Did Christianity Begin with a Mythical Christ?* This has recently been expanded in a second edition, published not as a revision (which it is) but rather as its own book, *Jesus: Neither God nor Man: The Case for a Mythical Christ.* The overarching theses are for the most part the same between the two books.

By contrast, Robert Price is highly trained in the relevant fields of scholarship. Price started out as a hard-core conservative evangelical Christian, with a master's degree from the conservative evangelical Gordon-Conwell Theological Seminary. He went on to do a Ph.D. in systematic theology at Drew University and then a second Ph.D. in New Testament studies, also at Drew. He is the one trained and certified scholar of New Testament that I know of who holds to a mythicist position. As with other conservative evangelicals who have fallen from the faith, Price fell hard. His first significant book, *The Incredible Shrinking Son of Man: How Reliable Is the Gospel Tradition?*, answers the question of the subtitle with no shade of ambiguity. The Gospel tradition about Jesus is not at all reliable. Price makes his case through a detailed exploration of all the Gospel traditions, arguing forcefully and intelligently. Price has written other works, the most significant for my present purposes being *The Christ-Myth Theory and Its Problems*, which is due to be published (as I write) within a few weeks. I am grateful to Robert and the publisher of Atheist Press for making it available to me.[7]

That publisher is Frank Zindler, another outspoken representative of the mythicist view. Zindler is also an academic, but he does not have credentials in biblical studies or in any field of antiquity. He is a scientist, trained in biology and geology. He taught in the community college system of the State University of New York for twenty years before—by his own account—being driven out for supporting Madalyn Murray O'Hair and her attempt to remove "In God We Trust" from American currency. Extremely prolific, Zindler writes in a number of fields. Many of his publications have been brought together in a massive four-volume work called *Through Atheist Eyes: Scenes from a World That Won't Reason*. The first volume of this magnum opus is called *Religions and Scriptures* and contains a number of essays both directly and tangentially related to mythicist views of Jesus, written at a popular level.[8]

A different sort of support for a mythicist position comes in the work of Thomas L. Thompson, *The Messiah Myth: The Near Eastern Roots of Jesus and David*. Thompson is trained in biblical studies, but he does not have degrees in New Testament or early Christianity. He is, instead, a Hebrew Bible scholar who teaches at the University of Copenhagen in Denmark. In his own field of expertise he is convinced that figures from the Hebrew Bible such as Abraham, Moses, and David never existed. He transfers these views to the New Testament and argues that Jesus too did not exist but was invented by Christians who wanted to create a savior figure out of stories found in the Jewish scriptures.[9]

Some of the other mythicists I will mention throughout the study include Richard Carrier, who along with Price is the only mythicist to my knowledge with graduate training in a relevant field (Ph.D. in classics from Columbia University); Tom Harpur, a well-known religious journalist in Canada, who did teach New Testament studies at Toronto before moving into journalism and trade-book publishing; and a slew of sensationalist popularizers who are not, and who do not bill themselves as, scholars in any recognizable sense of the word.

Other writers who are often placed in the mythicist camp present a slightly different view, namely, that there was indeed a historical Jesus but that he was not the founder of Christianity, a religion rooted in the mythical Christ-figure invented by its original adherents. This view was represented in midcentury by Archibald Robinson, who thought that even though there was a Jesus, "we know next to nothing about this Jesus."[10]

The best-known mythicist of modern times—at least among the New Testament scholars who know of any mythicists at all—is George A. Wells, who takes a similar position. Wells is a professor emeritus of German at the University of London and an expert on modern German intellectual history. Over the years he has written many books and articles advocating a mythicist position, none more incisive than his 1975 book, *Did Jesus Exist?*[11] Wells is certainly one who does the hard legwork necessary to make his case: although an outsider to New Testament studies, he speaks the lingo of the field and has read deeply in its scholarship. Although most New Testament scholars will not (or do not) consider his work either convincing or particularly well argued, it was by far the best mythicist work available before the studies of Price.

On Taking Mythicists Seriously

IT IS FAIR TO say that mythicists as a group, and as individuals, are not taken seriously by the vast majority of scholars in the fields of New Testament, early Christianity, ancient history, and theology. This is widely recognized, to their chagrin, by mythicists themselves. Archibald Robertson, in one of the classic works in the field, says with good reason, "The mythicist . . . does not get fair play from professional theologians. They either meet him with a conspiracy of silence or, if that is impossible, treat him as an amateur whose lack of academic status . . . robs his opinion of any value. Such treatment naturally makes the mythicist bellicose."[12]

Not much has changed in the sixty-five years since Robertson's brief volume appeared. Established scholars continue to be dismissive, and mythicists as a rule are vocal in their objections. As mentioned, the one mythicist within the vision of many New Testament scholars is G. A. Wells. In the massive and justly acclaimed four-volume study of the historical Jesus by one of the leading scholars in the field, John Meier, Wells and his views are peremptorily dismissed in a single sentence: "Wells's book, which builds its arguments on these and similar unsubstantiated claims, may be allowed to stand as a representative of the whole type of popular Jesus book that I do not bother to consider in detail."[13]

Even books that one might expect to take up the issue of Jesus's existence simply leave it alone. A case in point is the volume *I Believe in the Historical Jesus* by British New Testament specialist I. Howard Marshall. The title gives one a glimmer of hope that at least some attention will be paid to whether there actually was a historical Jesus, but the book presents only Marshall's theologically conservative views of the historical Jesus. Marshall mentions only one mythicist, Wells, disposing of him in a single paragraph with the statement that no scholar in the field finds his views persuasive

since the abundant Gospel sources, based on a variety of oral traditions, show that Jesus must have existed.[14]

As I will indicate more fully later, I think Wells—and Price, and
several other mythicists—do deserve to be taken seriously, even if
their claims are in the end dismissed.[15] A number of other mythicists,
however, do not offer anything resembling scholarship in support
of their view and instead present the unsuspecting reading public
with sensationalist claims that are so extravagant, so wrongheaded,
and so poorly substantiated that it is no wonder that scholars do not
take them seriously. These sensationalist books may have a reading
public. They are, after all, written to be read. But if scholars take
note of them at all, it is simply out of amazement that such inaccurate and poorly researched publications could ever see the published
light of day. Here I can give two examples.

The Christ Conspiracy

IN 1999, UNDER THE nom de plume Acharya S, D. M. Murdock
published the breathless conspirator's dream: *The Christ Conspiracy:
The Greatest Story Ever Sold*.[16] This book was meant to set the record
straight by showing that Christianity is rooted in a myth about the
sun-god Jesus, who was invented by a group of Jews in the second
century CE.

Mythicists of this ilk should not be surprised that their views are
not taken seriously by real scholars, that their books are not reviewed
in scholarly journals, mentioned by experts in the field, or even read
by them. The book is filled with so many factual errors and out-
landish assertions that it is hard to believe that the author is serious.
If she is serious, it is hard to believe that she has ever encountered
anything resembling historical scholarship. Her "research" appears
to have involved reading a number of nonscholarly books that say
the same thing she is about to say and then quoting them. One

looks in vain for the citation of a primary ancient source, and quotations from real experts (Elaine Pagels, chiefly) are ripped from their context and misconstrued. Still, in opposition to scholars who take alternative positions, such as that Jesus existed (she calls them "historicizers"), Acharya states, "If we assume that the historicizers' disregard of these scholars [that is, the mythicists] is deliberate, we can only conclude that it is because the mythicists' arguments have been too intelligent and knifelike to do away with."[17] One cannot help wondering if this is all a spoof done in good humor.

The basic argument of the book is that Jesus is the sun-god: "Thus the son of God is the sun of God" (get it—son, sun?). Stories about Jesus are "in actuality based on the movements of the sun through the heavens. In other words, Jesus Christ and the others upon whom he is predicated are personifications of the sun, and the gospel fable is merely a repeat of mythological formula revolving around the movements of the sun through the heavens."[18]

Christianity, in Acharya's view, started out as an astrotheological religion in which this sun-god Jesus was transformed into a historical Jew by a group of Jewish Syro-Samaritan Gnostic sons of Zadok, who were also Gnostics and Therapeutae (a sectarian group of Jews) in Alexandria, Egypt, after the failed revolt of the Jews against Rome in 135 CE. The Jews had failed to establish themselves as an independent state in the Promised Land and so naturally were deeply disappointed. They invented this Jesus in order to bring salvation to those who were shattered by the collapse of their nationalistic dreams. The Bible itself is an astrotheological text with hidden meanings that need to be unpacked by understanding their astrological symbolism.

Later we will see that all of Acharya's major points are in fact wrong. Jesus was not invented in Alexandria, Egypt, in the middle of the second Christian century. He was known already in the 30s of the first century, in Jewish circles of Palestine. He was not originally a sun-god (as if that equals Son-God!); in fact, in the earliest traditions we have about him, he was not known as a divine being at all. He was understood to be a Jewish prophet and messiah. There are no astrological phenomena associated with Jesus in any of our earliest traditions. These traditions are attested in multiple sources that originated at least a century before Acharya's alleged astrological creation at the hands of people who lived in a different part of the world from the historical Jesus and who did not even speak his language.

Just to give a sense of the level of scholarship in this sensationalist tome, I list a few of the howlers one encounters en route, in the order in which I found them. Acharya claims that:

- The second-century church father Justin never quotes or mentions any of the Gospels (25). [This simply isn't true: he mentions the Gospels on numerous occasions; typically he calls them "Memoirs of the Apostles" and quotes from them, especially from Matthew, Mark, and Luke.]
- The Gospels were forged hundreds of years after the events they narrate (26). [In fact, the Gospels were written at the end of the first century, about thirty-five to sixty-five years after Jesus's death, and we have physical proof: one fragment of a Gospel manuscript dates to the early second century. How could it have been forged centuries after that?]
- We have no manuscript of the New Testament that dates prior to the fourth century (26). [This is just plain wrong: we have numerous fragmentary manuscripts that date from the second and third centuries.]
- The autographs "were destroyed after the Council of Nicaea" (26). [In point of fact, we have no knowledge of what happened to the original copies of the New Testament; they were probably simply used so much they wore out. There is not a scintilla of evidence to suggest that they survived until Nicaea or that they were destroyed afterward; plenty of counterevidence indicates they did not survive until Nicaea.]

- "It took well over a thousand years to canonize the New Testament," and "many councils" were needed to differentiate the inspired from the spurious books (31). [Actually, the first author to list our canon of the New Testament was the church father Athanasius in the year 367; the comment about "many councils" is simply made up.]

- Paul never quotes a saying of Jesus (33). [Acharya has evidently never read the writings of Paul. As we will see, he does quote sayings of Jesus.]

- The Acts of Pilate, a legendary account of Jesus's trial and execution, was once considered canonical (44). [None of our sparse references to the Acts of Pilate indicates, or even suggests, any such thing.]

- The "true meaning of the word gospel is 'God's Spell,' as in magic, hypnosis and delusion" (45). [No, the word *gospel* comes to us from the Old English term *god spel,* which means "good news"—a fairly precise translation of the Greek word *euaggelion.* It has nothing to do with magic.]

- The church father "Irenaeus was a Gnostic" (60). [In fact, he was one of the most virulent opponents of Gnostics in the early church.]

- Augustine was "originally a Mandaean, i.e., a Gnostic, until after the Council of Nicaea" (60). [Augustine was not even born until nineteen years *after* the Council of Nicaea, and he certainly was no Gnostic.]

- "'Peter' is not only 'the rock' but also 'the cock,' or penis, as the word is used as slang to this day." Here Acharya shows (her own?) hand drawing of a man with a rooster head but with a large erect penis instead of a nose, with this description: "Bronze sculpture hidden in the Vatican treasure of the Cock, symbol of St. Peter" (295). [There is no penis-nosed statue of Peter the cock in the Vatican or anywhere else except in books like this, which love to make things up.]

In short, if there is any conspiracy here, it is not on the part of the ancient Christians who made up Jesus but on the part of modern authors who make up stories about the ancient Christians and what they believed about Jesus.

The Jesus Mysteries

ALSO APPEARING IN 1999 was the (intended) blockbuster work by Timothy Freke and Peter Gandy, *The Jesus Mysteries: Was the "Original Jesus" a Pagan God?* Freke and Gandy have collaborated on a number of books in recent years, most of them uncovering the conspiratorial secrets of our shared past. Like Acharya S, remarkably, they argue that Jesus was invented by a group of Jews who resembled the Therapeutae in Alexandria, Egypt, leading to the invention of a new mystery religion (the Jesus Mysteries), which flourished at the beginning of the third century. In their view, however, Jesus was not a sun-god. He was a creation based on the widespread mythologies of dying and rising gods known throughout the pagan world. And so their main thesis: "The story of Jesus is not the biography of a historical Messiah, but a myth based on perennial Pagan stories. Christianity was not a new and unique revelation but actually a Jewish adaptation of the ancient Pagan Mystery religion."[19]

At the heart of all the various pagan mysteries, Freke and Gandy aver, was a myth of a godman who died and rose from the dead. This divine figure was called by various names in the pagan mysteries: Osiris, Dionysus, Attis, Adonis, Baccus, Mithras. But "fundamentally all these godmen are the same mythical being" (4). The reason that Freke and Gandy think so is that supposedly all these figures share the same mythology: their father was God; their mother was a mortal virgin; each was born in a cave on December 25 before three shepherds and wise men; among their miracles they turned water to wine; they all rode into town on a donkey; they all were crucified

at Eastertime as a sacrifice for the sins of the world; they descended
to hell; and on the third day they rose again. Since these same things
are said of Jesus as well, it is obvious that the stories believed by the
Christians are all simply imitations of the pagan religions.

Real historians of antiquity are scandalized by such assertions—
or they would be if they bothered to read Freke and Gandy's book.
The authors provide no evidence for their claims concerning the
standard mythology of the godmen. They cite no sources from the
ancient world that can be checked. It is not that they have provided
an alternative interpretation of the available evidence. They have
not even cited the available evidence. And for good reason. No such
evidence exists.

What, for example, is the proof that Osiris was born on December 25 before three shepherds? Or that he was crucified? And that his
death brought atonement for sin? Or that he returned to life on earth
by being raised from the dead? In fact, no ancient source says any such
thing about Osiris (or about the other gods). But Freke and Gandy
claim that this is common knowledge. And they "prove" it by quoting other writers from the nineteenth and twentieth centuries who
said so. But these writers too do not cite any historical evidence. This
is all based on assertion, believed by Freke and Gandy simply because
they read it somewhere. This is not serious historical scholarship. It is
sensationalist writing driven by a desire to sell books.

In any event, as Freke and Gandy work out their scheme, the
original "Christ" was a godman like all the other pagan godmen.
Only at a second stage was he taken over by Jews and turned into a
Jewish messiah who was imagined as a historical figure, thereby creating the Jesus of history. The apostle Paul, on this reconstruction,
knew nothing about this historical Jesus, and neither did anyone
else in the early church. They worshipped the pagan Christ who
had been Judaized before anyone thought to make him into a real
person who actually lived and died in Judea. The Gospel by Mark
was instrumental in making this actual person come to life; it was

he who historicized the myth for the sake of Jews who needed not a divinity but a real historical figure to save them. Freke and Gandy contend that many Christians in the eastern part of the Roman Empire—who, like Paul, were Gnostics—understood that the historicized version of the myth was not a literal truth but a kind of extension of the myth. Only Christians in the western empire failed to realize this. Their center of activity was Rome. And so there emerged the Roman Catholic Church, which took the historicized view of a savior figure literally and came to suppress the original mythological views of the Gnostics. This led to traditional Christianity, with a historical figure of Jesus at its beginning. But he did not really exist. He was an invention modeled on the gods of the pagan mystery religions.

The problems with this thesis are rife, as will become clear in later chapters. For now it is enough to say that what we know about Jesus—the historical Jesus—does not come from Egypt toward the end of the first century, in circles heavily influenced by pagan mystery religions, but from Palestine, among Jews committed to their decidedly antipagan Jewish religion, from the 30s.

Quite apart from the enormous problems with the book's major contentions, it is hard to take it seriously. In both its detail and its overarching thesis, the book often reads like an undergraduate thesis, filled with patently false information and inconsistencies. When the authors do quote "scholarly" sources, it is almost always extremely dated scholarship, from 1925, 1899, and so on. It is easy to see why. The views they assert may have been believable more than a century ago, but no scholars hold to them today. As an example of inconsistency, consider these two statements made within two pages of one another. First:

Jerusalem Christians had always been Gnostics, because in the first century the Christian community was made up entirely of different types of Gnosticism! (174)

And then, a page later:

> The more we looked at the evidence we had uncovered,
> the more it seemed that to apply the terms "Gnostic" and
> "Literalist" to the Christianity of the first century was actually
> meaningless. (175)

So which is it? Were the Jerusalem Christians of the first century Gnostic? Or is the term *Gnostic* meaningless with respect to the
first century? It is hard to have it both ways.

Moreover, as with Acharya, here too the factual errors abound
at an embarrassing rate. As some examples, in the order one finds
them (this is by no means an exhaustive list):

- Constantine made Christianity the state religion of the empire
  (11). [No, he did not. He made it a legal religion. It was not
  made the state religion until the end of the fourth century under Theodosius.]
- Eleusinian mysteries focused on the godman Dionysus (18, 22).
  [Not true. These mysteries were not about Dionysus but about
  the goddess Demeter.]
- "Descriptions by Christian authors of Christian baptism are in-
  distinguishable from pagan descriptions of Mystery baptism"
  (36). [How could we possibly know this? We don't have a single
  description in any source of any kind of baptism in the mystery
  religions.]
- The "Gospel writers" "deliberately constructed" the Greek
  name Jesus out of "an artificial and forced transliteration of
  the Hebrew name Joshua" so as "to make sure that it expresses"
  the "symbolically significant number" of 888 (116). [Actually, the
  Gospel writers did not "construct" the Greek name Jesus at all.
  It is the Greek name for the Aramaic Yeshua, Hebrew Joshua. It
  is found in the Greek Old Testament, for example, long before

the Gospel writers lived and is a common name in the writings of the Jewish historian Josephus.]

- The Romans were "renowned for keeping careful records of all their activities, especially their legal proceedings," making it surprising that "there is no record of Jesus being tried by Pontius Pilate or executed" (133). [If Romans were careful record keepers, it is passing strange that we have no records, not only of Jesus but of nearly *anyone* who lived in the first century. We simply don't have birth notices, trial records, death certificates—or other standard kinds of records that one has today. Freke and Gandy, of course, do not cite a single example of anyone else's death warrant from the first century.]

- Many early Christians rejected Mark's Gospel as noncanonical (146). [Actually, Mark was everywhere accepted as canonical; in fact, every surviving Christian document that refers to it accepts its canonicity.]

- Paul never mentions Jesus in his ethical teachings (152). [As we will see, this is simply wrong; see 1 Corinthians 7:10–11; 9:14; 11:22–24.]

- The original version of Mark "did not include the resurrection at all" (156). [Not true. The original version of Mark does not have an episode in which Jesus appears to his disciples after the resurrection, but the text is completely unambiguous that Jesus has been raised from the dead. See, for example, Mark 16:6, which was an original part of the Gospel.]

- Ancient Christians "of all persuasions," including even the famous church historian Eusebius, did not accept the letters of 1 and 2 Timothy and Titus as part of their canon of scripture (161). [In point of fact, virtually everyone who mentions these letters accepts them as canonical, including Eusebius, who quotes them repeatedly in his writings.]

- The word for spiritual gifts, *charismata,* is taken from "the Mystery term *makarismos,* referring to the blessed nature of one who has seen the Mysteries" (162). [They just made that up. The two words are etymologically unrelated. *Charismata* comes from the Greek word *charisma,* which means "gift." It is not connected with the mystery religions.]

- The Romans "completely destroyed the state of Judea in 112 CE" (178). [This is a bizarre claim. There was not even a war between Rome and Judea in 112 CE; there were wars in 66–70 and 132–35 CE.]

While it is useful to provide a taste of the sensationalist claims that one can find in this literature, I do not think that the serious authors who have pursued a mythicist agenda (for example, G. A. Wells, Robert Price, and now Richard Carrier) can be tarnished with the same brush or be condemned with guilt by association. Their work has to stand or fall on its own, independent of the foibles and shortcomings of the sensationalists. Those who have done research do indeed make a case that Jesus did not exist. Although they use some of the same arguments, they do not use the total package as those I've just mentioned. I will be dealing with these arguments at greater length later. First, however, I want to show the positive evidence that convinces everyone except the mythicists that Jesus existed. But to make sense of that evidence, I need at the very least to give a rough idea about why some of the smarter and better informed writers have said he did not exist.

The Basic Mythicist Position

THE CASE THAT MOST mythicists have made against the historical existence of Jesus involves both negative and positive arguments, with far more of the former.[20]

On the negative side, mythicists typically stress that there are no reliable references to the existence of Jesus in any non-Christian sources of the first century. Jesus allegedly lived until about the year 30 CE. But no Greek or Roman author (or any other non-Christian author, for that matter) mentions him for over eighty years after that. If Jesus was such an important figure—or even if he wasn't so important—wouldn't there be a reference to him in some of our many surviving sources from the first century? We have the writings of historians, politicians, philosophers, religion scholars, poets, and scientists; we have inscriptions placed on buildings and personal letters written by average people. In none of these non-Christian writings of the first century is Jesus ever mentioned, not even once.

It is typically argued by those who hold to Jesus's historical existence that he is, in fact, mentioned by one author: the Jewish historian Josephus, who wrote a number of surviving books near the end of the first century. Mythicists, however, claim that the two references to Jesus in Josephus's book *Jewish Antiquities* (these are the only two mentions of Jesus in all of Josephus's abundant writings) were not written originally by Josephus but were inserted into his writings by later Christian scribes. If they are right, this would mean that we don't have a single reference to Jesus in non-Christian texts before the writings of Pliny, a Roman governor of a province in what is now Turkey, in 112 CE and in the writings of the Roman historians Tacitus and Suetonius a few years later. Some mythicists claim that these references too were inserted into these writings, that they are not original. We will be looking at all of these references soon; for now it is enough to note that mythicists argue that it is hard to believe that Jesus would not be talked about, argued with, commented on, or even mentioned by writers of his own day or in the decades afterward if he really existed.

In addition, they typically claim that the historical Jesus does not appear prominently even in early Christian writings apart from the New Testament Gospels. In particular, they maintain that the apostle Paul says hardly anything about the historical Jesus or that he says nothing at all. This may come as a shock to most readers of the New Testament, but a careful reading of Paul's letters shows the problems. Paul has a lot to say about Jesus's death and resurrection—especially the resurrection—and he clearly worships him as his Lord. But he says very little indeed about anything that Jesus said and did while he was alive. Why would that be, if Jesus was in fact a historical person? Why doesn't Paul quote the words of Jesus, such as the Sermon on the Mount? Why does he never refer to any of Jesus's parables? Why doesn't he indicate what Jesus did? Why not mention any of his miracles? His exorcisms? His controversies? His trip to Jerusalem? His trial before Pontius Pilate? And on and on.

Here again defenders of Jesus's historicity point out that Paul on several occasions does appear to quote Jesus (for example, 1 Corinthians 11:22–24). Some mythicists argue that these quotations, like those of Josephus, were not originally in the writings of Paul but were inserted by later scribes. Other mythicists argue that Paul is not quoting the words of the historical Jesus but is quoting the words the heavenly "Jesus" has spoken through Christian prophets in Paul's communities. For both kinds of mythicist, Paul did not know or think about a historical person Jesus. For him Christ was a heavenly being of mythical proportions. How, you might wonder, could a nonhistorical person die? Mythicists have an explanation for that too, as we will see. For now it is enough to know that they generally insist that Paul did not refer to the historical Jesus, and they point out that this would be very strange if in fact he knew that he existed. The same can be said of the other writings of the New Testament, outside the Gospels.

This means that Matthew, Mark, Luke, and John are our only real sources for knowing about the historical Jesus, and mythicists find these four sources highly problematic as historical documents. For one thing, they were written near the end of the first century at best, four or five decades or more after Jesus allegedly lived. If he really did live, wouldn't we have some earlier sources? And how can we rely on such hearsay from so many years later?

Moreover, mythicists typically point out that the Gospels cannot be trusted in what they do say. Their many accounts of what Jesus said and did are chock-full of contradictions and discrepancies and so are completely unreliable. The Gospels are thoroughly biased toward their subject matter and so do not present anything like disinterested history "as it really was." They can be shown to have modified the stories they relate, and in some places they obviously have made up stories about Jesus. In fact, virtually all—or even all—of the stories may have been invented. This is especially the case with the so-called miracles of Jesus, narrated by the Gospel writers to convince others to believe in him but incredible to the point that, well, they are literally incredible—not to be believed.

Furthermore, many mythicists insist that the four Gospels ultimately all go back to just one of the Gospels, Mark, on which the other three were based. This means that of all the many writers—pagan, Jewish, and Christian—that we have from the first century (assuming Mark was written as early as the first century), we have only one that describes or even mentions the life of the historical Jesus. How plausible is that, if Jesus actually lived?

Given all these problems, some mythicists insist that the burden of proof rests on anyone who wants to claim that Jesus did in fact exist. Added to these negative arguments is one very important positive one, that the stories about Jesus—many of them incredible, all of them based on late and unreliable witnesses—are paralleled time and again in the myths about pagan gods and other divine men discussed in the ancient world. And so mythicists typically appeal to accounts of other gods or demigods, such as Heracles, Osiris, Mithras, Attis, Adonis, and Dionysus, who were said to have been born on December 25 to a virgin mother, to have done miraculous deeds for the sake of others, to have died (often for the sake of others), and to have been raised from the dead and later departed to live in the divine realm.

I have already said a few words about such claims, and we will examine them in greater detail at a later point. For now it is enough to stress that mythicists make a two-pronged argument: given the negative argument, that we have no reliable witness that even mentions a historical Jesus, and the positive one, that his story appears to have been modeled on the accounts told of other divinities, it is simplest to believe that he never existed but was invented as another supernatural being. In this reading of the evidence, Christianity is founded on a myth.

Before countering the claims of the mythicists, I will set out the evidence that has persuaded everyone else, amateur and professional scholar alike, that Jesus really did exist. That will be the subject of the next several chapters.

CHAPTER TWO

Non-Christian Sources for the Life of Jesus

I AM EXPECTING TO GET a very different reaction from this book than from others I have written over the years. Typically, but to my honest surprise, I get accused—or thanked, depending on who is writing me—of being anti-Christian because of the things I say in my books. I find this surprising because I don't consider myself anti-Christian. When I tell people this, I often get a disbelieving response: of *course* you're anti-Christian. Look at all the ways you attack Christianity!

But I have never seen it this way. In my view, the only thing I attack in my writings (and not even directly) is a fundamentalist and conservative evangelical understanding of Christianity. But to say for that reason that I attack Christianity is like saying that if you don't like raspberry sherbet you don't like any kind of ice cream. You can make the case (and you would be right) that sherbet isn't ice cream at all, so not liking it has nothing to do with ice cream. But even if you think sherbet is close enough to ice cream that you may as well call it ice cream, by saying you don't like raspberry sherbet you're simply saying that there is one flavor of it you would rather not eat, given the choice.

I certainly do not mean to say that I consider myself either a Christian or an apologist for Christian causes. I am neither. But in my writings I have never attacked Christianity itself. I have attacked a particular flavor of it. It is true that in my part of the world, the American South, the flavor I have attacked happens to be the flavor preferred by the majority of practicing Christians. But in a historical and worldwide perspective, highly conservative Protestant Christianity, whether fundamentalism or hard-core evangelicalism, is a minority voice. It is the voice that says that the Bible is the inerrant Word of God, with no contradictions, discrepancies, or mistakes of any kind. I simply don't think this is true. And neither have most Christians over the course of history.

I do happen to think that the Bible is a great book or set of books. With this I may be disagreeing with many of my atheist, agnostic, and humanist friends who have been cheering me on from the sidelines. But I personally love the Bible. I read it all the time, in the original Greek and Hebrew; I study it; I teach it. I have done so for over thirty-five years. And I don't plan to stop any time soon. But I don't think the Bible is perfect. Far from it. The Bible is filled with a multitude of voices, and these voices are often at odds with one another, contradicting one another in minute details and in major issues involving such basic views as what God is like, who the people of God are, who Jesus is, how one can be in a right relationship with God, why there is suffering in the world, how we are to behave, and on and on. And I heartily disagree with the views of most of the biblical authors on one point or another.

Still, in my judgment all of these voices are valuable and they should all be listened to. Some of the writers of the Bible were religious geniuses, and just as we listen to other geniuses of our tradition—Mozart and Beethoven, Shakespeare and Dickens—so we ought to listen to the authors of the Bible. But they were not inspired by God, in my opinion, any more than any other genius is. And they contradict each other all over the map.

Even though there are innumerable historical problems in the New Testament, they are not of the scope or character to call seriously into doubt the existence of Jesus. He certainly lived, and in my view he too was a kind of religious genius, even more than the later authors who wrote about him. At the same time, he probably was not well educated. He may have been only semiliterate. But he certainly lived, and his teachings have impacted the world ever since. Surely that is one gauge of genius.

Since that is the view I am sketching in this book, I can imagine readers who think me anti-Christian taking umbrage at my refusal to toe their line. And Christian readers may well be pleased to see that even someone like me agrees with them on key points (although they certainly won't like other things I have to say in the book). My goal, however, is neither to please nor to offend. It is to pursue a historical question with all the rigor that it deserves and requires and in doing so to show that there really was a historical Jesus and that we can say certain things about him.

Preliminary Remarks

BEFORE I SHOW THE evidence for the existence of Jesus, I need to make a few preliminary remarks about historians and how they go about establishing what probably happened in the past. The first thing to stress is that this is, in fact, what historians do. We have no direct access to the past. Once something happens, it is over and done with. There is no way to repeat a past event all over again. This makes historical evidence different from the kinds of evidence used in the hard sciences. In science you can repeat an experiment.

In fact, you have to repeat the experiment. Once an experiment is repeated sufficiently and with the same results, a kind of predictive probability is established that the same results will obtain if the experiment is conducted one more time. An example that I use with my first-year undergraduates: if I want to prove that a bar of iron sinks in lukewarm water but that a bar of Ivory soap floats, all I need are a hundred tubs of water and a hundred bars of each kind. When I start tossing them in the water, the iron will sink every time and the soap will float. This proves what will no doubt happen if I decide to repeat the experiment yet another time.

With history, though, we don't have the luxury of being able to repeat an event once it happens, and so we look for other kinds of evidence. How do we know if we've proved something historically? Technically, we cannot prove a single thing historically. All we can do is give enough evidence (of kinds I will mention in a moment) to convince enough people (hopefully nearly everyone) about a certain historical claim, for example, that Abraham Lincoln really did deliver the Gettysburg Address or that Julius Caesar really did cross the Rubicon. If you want to demonstrate that either historical event actually occurred, you need to marshal some convincing evidence. In neither of these particular cases, of course, is there really much doubt.

What about the historical existence of Jesus? It has become somewhat common among mythicists to think that the default position on the question of Jesus's existence should be that he did not exist unless someone can demonstrate that he did. This is the position expressed cogently by Robert Price: "The burden of proof would seem to belong with those who believe there was a historical man named Jesus."[1] I myself do not think that is true. On one hand, since every relevant ancient source (as we will see) assumes that there was such a man, and since no scholar who has ever written on it, except the handful of mythicists, has ever had any serious doubts, surely the burden of proof does not fall on those who take the almost universally accepted position. On the other hand, and to be a bit more generous to Price and his fellow mythicists, perhaps the matter should be put more neutrally. As my former colleague, E. P. Sanders, an eminent professor of New Testament studies at nearby Duke University, used to say, "The burden of proof belongs with whoever is making a claim." That is, if Price wants to argue that Jesus did not exist, then he bears the burden of proof for his argument. If I want to argue that he did exist, then I do. Fair enough.

Price enunciates another historical principle that I do agree with, however, one that ties in closely with what I just said, that historians cannot repeat the past and so have to base their judgments on evidence that establishes most probably what happened. In Price's clearly expressed judgment, "The historian does not claim clairvoyant knowledge of the past. . . . The historian, so to speak 'postdicts' based on traceable factors and analogy. *But it is all a matter of probabilities.*"[2] Unlike scientists, who can with almost certain reliability "predict" what will happen based on their knowledge of what *does* happen, historians "postdict," that is, they indicate what probably did happen based on their knowledge of the evidence.

But what kind of evidence is there? This is a basic methodological question: How can we establish with reasonable probability that anyone from the past actually existed, whether our aforementioned Abraham Lincoln and Julius Caesar, or anyone else: Harry Truman, Charlemagne, Hypatia, Jerome, Socrates, Anne Frank, or Bilbo Baggins?

The Kinds of Sources Historians Want

HISTORIANS CAN APPEAL TO many different kinds of evidence to establish the past existence of a person. First, there is a real preference for hard, physical evidence, for example, photographs. It is rather hard to deny that Abraham Lincoln lived since we have all seen photos. Of course, the photos could have all been doctored in some insidious plot to rewrite American history. And that is what the conspiracy theorists among us claim (not just about Lincoln but about even better documented events, such as the Holocaust). But for most of us, a stack of good photographs from different sources will usually be convincing enough.

In addition to physical evidence, we look for surviving products that can be traced with relative certainty back to the person. This might include pieces of construction in some cases: the houses and buildings of Frank Lloyd Wright, for example. But in even more cases it would include literary remains, writings. Julius Caesar left us an account of the Gallic Wars. Anne Frank left us a diary. And we have lots of writings that can be traced with some assurance back to a man (also photographed) named Charles Dickens. They all almost certainly existed.

Finally, historians look to other kinds of evidence not *from* the person but *about* the person—that is, reference to, quotations of, or discussions about the person by others. These are of course our most abundant kinds of historical sources, the kinds that we have for the vast majority of persons from the past, especially before the invention of photography. What do we look for in evidence of this kind, especially when dealing with someone like Jesus, a person who lived, if he lived, some two thousand years ago? What kinds of sources do historians need to be convinced of his existence?

Historians prefer to have lots of written sources, not just one or two. The more, obviously, the better. If there were only one or two sources, you might suspect that the stories were made up (although you would probably want to have some reasons for thinking so; it is not good enough to doubt a source simply because you have a mean, negative, or pessimistic streak and choose to do so). But if there are lots of sources—just as when there are lots of eyewitnesses to a car accident—then it is hard to claim that any one of them just happened to make it all up.

Historians also prefer to have sources that are relatively near the date of the person or event that they are describing. As time goes on, things do indeed get made up, and so it is much better to have near-contemporary accounts. If our first reports about Moses come from six hundred years after he allegedly lived, those reports are not nearly as trustworthy as reports that can plausibly be dated to six years after he lived. The closer in temporal proximity, the better.

Historians also like these numerous and early sources to be extensive in scope. If all you have is the mere mention of a person's name in a source, that is not nearly as good as having long and extensive stories told (in lots of ancient sources). Moreover, it is obviously best if these extensive stories are reported in sources that are disinterested. That is to say, if someone is biased toward the subject matter, the bias has to be taken into account. The problem, of course, is that most sources are biased: if they didn't have any feelings about the subject matter, they wouldn't be talking about it. But if we find stories that clearly do not serve the purposes of the persons telling the story, we have a good indicator that the stories are (reasonably) disinterested.

Moreover, in an ideal situation, the various sources that discuss a figure or an event should corroborate what each of the others has to say, at least in major points if not in all the details. If one ancient source says that Octavian was a Roman general who became the emperor but another source says that he was a North African peasant who never traveled outside his native village, you know that you have a problem, either with Octavian himself or, as in this case, with the source. But if you have multiple sources from near the time that tell many stories about the Roman emperor Octavian—that is, that corroborate one another's stories—then you have good historical evidence.

At the same time, it is important to know that the various sources are independent of one another and do not rely on each other for all of their information. If four ancient authors mention Marcus Billius as a Roman aristocrat in Ephesus, but it turns out that three of these authors derived their information from the fourth, then you no longer have multiple sources but only one. Their agreements do not represent corroboration but collaboration, and that is much less useful.

In short, if a historian were drawing up a wish list of sources for an ancient person, she would want a large number of sources that derive from near the time of the person they discuss; that are extensive in what they have to say about that person; that are disinterested, to some extent, in what they say; and that corroborate one another's accounts without having collaborated.

With that wish list in mind, what can we say about the evidence for the existence of Jesus?

The Sources for Jesus: What We Do Not Have

IT MAY BE USEFUL to start by considering what we do *not* have by way of historical records for Jesus, to set the stage for a more detailed consideration in the next chapter of what we *do* have.

Physical Evidence?

To begin with, there is no hard, physical evidence for Jesus (eighteen hundred years before photography was invented), including no archaeological evidence of any kind. This is not much of an argument against his existence, however, since there is no archaeological evidence for anyone else living in Palestine in Jesus's day except for the very upper-crust elite aristocrats, who are occasionally mentioned in inscriptions (we have no other archaeological evidence even for any of these). In fact, we don't have archaeological remains for any nonaristocratic Jew of the 20s CE, when Jesus would have been an adult. And absolutely no one thinks that Jesus was an upper-class aristocrat. So why would we have archaeological evidence of his existence?

We also do not have any writings from Jesus. To many people this may seem odd, but in fact it is not odd at all. The vast majority of people in the ancient world could not write, as we will see in greater detail. There are debates about Jesus's literacy, if of course he lived. But even if he could read, there are no indications from our early sources that he could write, and there is no reference to any of his writings in any of our Gospels.[3] So there is nothing strange about having nothing in writing from him. I should point out that we have nothing in writing from over 99.99 percent of people who lived in antiquity. That doesn't mean, of course, that they didn't live. It means that if we want to show that any one of them lived, we have to look for other kinds of evidence.

Non-Christian Sources of the First Century?

It is also true, as the mythicists have been quick to point out, that no Greek or Roman author from the first century mentions Jesus. It would be very convenient for us if they did, but alas, they do not. At the same time, the fact is again a bit irrelevant since these same sources do not mention many millions of people who actually did live. Jesus stands here with the vast majority of living, breathing human beings of earlier ages.

Moreover, it is an error to argue, as is sometimes done by one mythicist or another, that anyone as spectacular as Jesus allegedly was, who did so many miracles and fantastic deeds, would certainly have been discussed or at least mentioned in pagan sources if he really did exist.[4] Surely anyone who could heal the sick, cast out demons, walk on water, feed the multitudes with only a few loaves, and raise the dead would be talked about! The reason this line of reasoning is in error is that we are not asking whether Jesus really did miracles and, if so, why they (and he) are not mentioned by pagan sources. We are asking whether Jesus of Nazareth actually existed. Only after establishing that he did exist can we go on to ask if he did miracles. If we decide that he did, only then can we revisit the question of why no one, in that case, mentions him. But we may also decide that the historical Jesus was not a miraculous being but a purely human being. In that case it is no surprise that Roman sources never mention him, just as it is no surprise that these same sources never mention any of his uncles, aunts, cousins, nieces, or nephews—or in fact nearly any other Jew of his day.

In that connection, I should reiterate that it is a complete "myth" (in the mythicist sense) that Romans kept detailed records of everything and that as a result we are inordinately well informed about the world of Roman Palestine and should expect then to hear about Jesus if he really lived. If Romans kept such records, where are they? We certainly don't have any. Think of everything we do not know about the reign of Pontius Pilate as governor of Judea. We know from the Jewish historian Josephus that Pilate ruled for ten years, between 26 and 36 CE. It would be easy to argue that he was the single most important figure for Roman Palestine for the entire length of his rule. And what records from that decade do we have from his reign—what Roman records of his major accomplishments, his daily itinerary, the decrees he passed, the laws he issued, the prisoners he put on trial, the death warrants he signed, his scandals, his interviews, his judicial proceedings? We have none. Nothing at all.

I might press the issue further. What archaeological evidence do we have about Pilate's rule in Palestine? We have some coins that were issued during his reign (one would not expect coins about Jesus since he didn't issue any), and one—only one—fragmentary inscription discovered in Caesarea Maritima in 1961 that indicates that he was the Roman prefect. Nothing else. And what writings do we have from him? Not a single word. Does that mean he didn't exist? No, he is mentioned in several passages in Josephus and in the writings of the Alexandrian Jewish philosopher Philo and in the Gospels. He certainly existed even though, like Jesus, we have no records from his day or writings from his hand. And what is striking is that we have far more information about Pilate than about any other governor of Judea in Roman times.[5] And so it is a modern "myth" to say that we have extensive Roman records from antiquity that surely would have mentioned someone like Jesus had he existed.

It is also worth pointing out that Pilate is mentioned only in passing in the writing of the one Roman historian, Tacitus, who does name him. Moreover, that happens to be in a passage that also refers to Jesus (*Annals* 15). If an important Roman aristocratic ruler of a major province is not mentioned any more than that in the Greek and Roman writings, what are the chances that a lower-class Jewish teacher (which Jesus must have been, as everyone who thinks he lived agrees) would be mentioned in them? Almost none.

I might add that our principal source of knowledge about Jewish Palestine in the days of Jesus comes from the historian Josephus, a prominent aristocratic Jew who was extremely influential in the social and political affairs of his day. And how often is Josephus mentioned in Greek and Roman sources of his own day, the first century CE? Never.

Think of an analogy. If a historian sixty years from now were to write up a history of the American South in, say, the twentieth and twenty-first centuries, is he likely to mention Zlatko Plese? (Zlatko is my brilliant colleague who teaches courses in ancient philosophy, Gnosticism, varieties of early Christianity, and other subjects.) Almost certainly not. What does that prove? Technically speaking, it proves nothing. But it does suggest either that Zlatko never existed or that he did not make a huge impact on the political, social, or cultural life of the South. As it turns out, Zlatko does exist (I bought him dinner last night). So if he is not mentioned in a future history of the South, it will no doubt be because he did not make a big impact on the South. To show he existed, one would have to look at other evidence, for example, copies of the two books he has written. (Unlike Jesus, Zlatko can write. And unlike the first century, we have the mass production and distribution of books plus libraries to house them in.) So too with Jesus. If he is rarely mentioned, it is barely relevant to the question of his existence. It is possible that he simply made too little impact, just like the overwhelming mass of people who lived in the Roman Empire of the first century. Many Christians do not want to hear that Jesus did not make an enormous splash on the world of his day, but it appears to be true. Does that mean he did not exist? No, it means that to establish his existence, we need to look to other kinds of evidence.

Eyewitness Accounts?

Still, to press yet further on the issue of evidence we do not have, I need to stress that we do not have a single reference to Jesus by anyone—pagan, Jew, or Christian—who was a contemporary eyewitness, who recorded things he said and did. But what about the Gospels of the New Testament? Aren't they eyewitness reports? Even though that was once widely believed about two of our Gospels, Matthew and John, it is not the view of the vast majority of critical historians today, and for good reason.

The early church tradition held that the four Gospels of the New Testament were written by Matthew, Mark, Luke, and John. Even in that tradition, Mark and Luke were not themselves eyewitnesses to the life of Jesus. Mark was allegedly the (later) companion of Peter, who heard him preach about Jesus and reorganized his teachings into a narrative that became the Gospel that goes under his name; even if we accept the tradition that Mark was indeed the one who wrote the Gospel, his information came secondhand. Luke was yet further removed: he was said to be a companion of the apostle Paul, who was himself not one of Jesus's earthly followers. Luke was allegedly a Gentile physician who researched the life of Jesus and then wrote up his account. If the tradition about Luke is true, we are dealing with an author who was a disciple of someone who was not a disciple. Matthew, by contrast, was widely claimed to be one of the twelve disciples, the tax collector Jesus called to be one of his followers (see Matthew 9: 9–13). And John was thought to be the mysterious "Beloved Disciple" of the Fourth Gospel (see, for example, John 19:26–27), identified as one of Jesus's closest followers, John the son of Zebedee.

Scholars today, outside the ranks of fundamentalists and conservative evangelicals, are virtually unified in thinking that none of these ascriptions of authorship is probably correct. One important point to notice is that none of the Gospel writers ever identifies himself by name or narrates any of his stories about Jesus in the first person. The Gospels are all written anonymously, and the authors describe the disciples, including the disciples Matthew and John, in the third person, talking about what "they" did (not what "I" or "we" did). Even more important, the immediate followers of Jesus were, like him, lower-class Aramaic-speaking peasants from rural Galilee. Could they have written Gospels?

Several significant studies of literacy have appeared in recent years showing just how low literacy rates were in antiquity. The most frequently cited study is by Columbia professor William Harris in a book titled *Ancient Literacy*.[6] By thoroughly examining all the surviving evidence, Harris draws the compelling though surprising conclusion that in the very best of times in the ancient world, only about 10 percent of the population could read at all and possibly copy out writing on a page. Far fewer than this, of course, could compose a sentence, let alone a story, let alone an entire book. And who were the people in this 10 percent? They were the upper-class elite who had the time, money, and leisure to afford an education. This is not an apt description of Jesus's disciples. They were not upper-crust aristocrats.

In Roman Palestine the situation was even bleaker. The most thorough examination of literacy in Palestine is by a professor of Jewish studies at the University of London, Catherine Hezser, who shows that in the days of Jesus probably only 3 percent of Jews in Palestine were literate.[7] Once again, these would be the people who could read and maybe write their names and copy words. Far fewer could compose sentences, paragraphs, chapters, and books. And once again, these would have been the urban elites.

The issue becomes even sharper when one other consideration is thrown into the mix. The native tongue of Jesus, his disciples, and most people in Palestine was Aramaic. But the Gospels were written not in Aramaic but in Greek. And in very good Greek. Highly proficient Greek. The authors of the Gospels were unusually well-educated speakers and writers of Greek. They must have been from the relatively higher classes, and they almost certainly were from urban areas outside Palestine. Scholars typically date these Greek compositions to the end of the first century, with Mark probably being the first Gospel, written around 70 CE or so; Matthew and Luke being a bit later, possibly 80–85 CE; and John being last, around 90–95 CE. The authors of these books were not the original followers of Jesus or probably even followers of the twelve earthly disciples of Jesus. They were later Christians who had heard stories about Jesus as they circulated by word of mouth year after year and decade after decade and finally decided to write them down.

It is true that the Gospel writers may have had written sources in front of them as well as oral traditions they had heard, as we will see at greater length in the next chapter. Luke explicitly states that he knows of earlier written accounts of Jesus's life (1:1–4), and there are very good reasons for thinking that both he and Matthew had access to a version of Mark's Gospel, from which they derived many of their stories. They probably also both had access to a document that scholars have labeled Q (from the German word for "source," Quelle). This is a document that no longer survives, but it appears

to have once existed, in Greek, and consisted of a number of sayings and a few of the deeds of Jesus. Along with these two documents, Matthew and Luke may have had yet other sources for their
accounts; we do not know what sources Mark had for his. John is
a different case altogether, as the stories he narrates about Jesus are
so different from those found in the synoptic Gospels of Matthew,
Mark, and Luke.[8]

My point in this discussion, in any event, is that the Gospels of the
New Testament are not eyewitness accounts of the life of Jesus. Neither are the Gospels outside the New Testament, of which we have
over forty, either in whole or in fragments.[9] In fact, we do not have
any eyewitness report of any kind about Jesus, written in his own day.

This fact too, however, should not be overblown when considering the question of whether or not Jesus lived. The absence of
eyewitness accounts would be relevant if, and only if, we had reason
to suspect that we *should* have eyewitness reports if Jesus really lived.
That, however, is far from the case. Think again of our earlier point
of comparison, Pontius Pilate. Here is a figure who was immensely
significant in every way to the life and history of Palestine during
the adult life of Jesus (assuming Jesus lived), politically, economi-
cally, culturally, socially. As I have indicated, there was arguably no
one more important. And how many eyewitness reports of Pilate do
we have from his day? None. Not a single one. The same is true of
Josephus. And these are figures who were of the highest prominence
in their own day.

In no small measure this relates, again, to the problem of literacy
in that time and place. Hardly anyone could write, and most of the
people who could write did not produce writings that have survived
from antiquity. As it turns out—this is as astounding as it is true—
from Roman Palestine of the entire first century we have precisely
one, only one, author of literary texts whose works have survived
(by literary texts I mean literary books of any kind: fictional, historical, philosophical, scientific, poetic, political, you name it). That

one author is Josephus. We have no others. What is equally striking, in all of our historical records we know the name of only one other author of such writings, a man named Justin of Tiberius; his books, obviously, have not survived.[10]

So would we expect eyewitness accounts about Jesus if he had lived? How could we possibly expect them? The one and only Palestinian author of books of any kind that we have was an author (Josephus) who was born several years after Jesus died.

Non-Christian References to Jesus

Now THAT WE HAVE considered at some length the sources we do *not* have for establishing whether Jesus lived, we can begin to look at the sources we *do* have. I start with a brief survey of sources that are typically appealed to as non-Christian references to Jesus. I will restrict myself to sources that were produced within about a hundred years of when Jesus is traditionally thought to have died since writings after that time almost certainly cannot be considered independent and reliable witnesses to his life but were undoubtedly based simply on what the authors had heard about Jesus, probably from his followers. The same may be true with even the non-Christian references I discuss here, as we will see. For the sake of convenience I will categorize these non-Christian references as Roman, on the one hand, and Jewish, on the other.

Roman References

Within a century of the traditional date of Jesus's death, he is referred to on three occasions by Roman authors. None of them wrote, as we have seen, during Jesus's lifetime or even in the first Christian century. They were all writing about eighty to eighty-five years after the traditional date of his death.

Pliny the Younger

The first surviving reference to Jesus by a non-Christian, non-Jewish source of any kind appears in the writings of Pliny the Younger, the governor of the Roman province of Bithynia-Pontus in Asia Minor (now Turkey). Pliny is called "the Younger" in order to differentiate him from his even more famous uncle, Pliny "the Elder," who is best known to history not as a Roman administrator but as a natural scientist who wrote many scientific tomes that still survive. Pliny the Elder was inverately curious, as scientists tend to be, and when he learned that Mount Vesuvius was erupting in 79 CE, he decided to get as close as he could in order to investigate. Unfortunately, his ship got too close, and he perished in the fumes. His nephew, Pliny the Younger, also observed the eruption, but from a considerable distance, and wrote about it in one of his surviving works.

Among scholars of early Christianity, the younger Pliny is best known for a series of letters that he wrote later in life to the Roman emperor, Trajan, seeking advice for governing his province. In particular, letter number 10 from the year 112 CE is important, as it is the one place in which Pliny appears to mention the existence of Jesus. The letter is not about Jesus himself; it is dealing with a political problem. In Pliny's province a law had been passed making it illegal for people to gather together in social groups. This may seem like an odd law, but it had a very practical function. The Roman authorities were afraid that people in that locale might band together for political reasons and that this might lead to armed uprisings. But by forbidding groups from coming together for any purpose whatsoever, the Romans had created a problem, though not one you might expect. The law applied to every social group, including fire brigades. As a result, there were no effective measures in Pliny's province to deal with the outbreak of fires, and so villages were burning.

In his letter 10 to the emperor Pliny discusses the fire problem, and in that context he mentions another group that was illegally gathering together. As it turns out, it was the local community of Christians.[11]

Pliny learned from reliable sources that the Christians (illegally) gathered together in the early morning. He provides us with some important information about the group: they included people from a variety of socioeconomic levels, and they ate meals together of common food. Pliny may tell the emperor this because of rumors, which we hear from other later sources, that Christians committed cannibalism. (They did, after all, eat the flesh of the Son of God and drink his blood.) Moreover, Pliny informs the emperor, the Christians "sing hymns to Christ as to a god."

That is all he says about Jesus: the Christians worshipped him by singing to him. He does not, as you can see, even call him Jesus but instead uses his most common epithet, Christ. Whether Pliny knew the man's actual name is anyone's guess. One might be tempted to ask as well whether he knew that Christ was (at one time?) a man, but the fact that he indicates that the songs were offered to Christ "as to a god" suggests that Christ was, of course, something else.

This reference is obviously not much to go on. But it does tell us that there were Christians worshipping someone named Christ in the early second century in the region of Asia Minor. We already knew this, of course, from other (Christian) sources, as we will see in a later chapter. In any event, whatever Pliny knows about Christ he appears to have learned from the Christians who informed him, and so he does not provide us with completely independent testimony that Jesus actually existed, only the testimony of Christians living some eighty years after Jesus would have died. These Christians might have read some of the Gospels, and they certainly heard stories about Jesus. So at the least we can say that the idea of Jesus having existed was current by the early second century, but the reference of Pliny does not provide us with much more than that.

Suetonius

Even less helpful is a reference found in the writings of the Roman biographer Suetonius, often also cited in discussions of the existence of Jesus. Suetonius is most famous for having produced twelve biographies of Roman emperors. His *Lives of the Caesar,* written in 115 CE, still makes for interesting reading today. It was, in fact, the basis for Robert Graves's historical novel, *I Claudius* (1934), on which the even better-known BBC miniseries of the same name was based. It is in Suetonius's biography of Claudius, emperor of Rome from 41 to 54 CE, that a second reference to Jesus is sometimes thought to occur. Suetonius indicates that at one point in his reign Claudius deported all the Jews from Rome because of riots that had occurred "at the instigation of Chrestus."

He says nothing more about the man. But a large number of scholars over the years have thought that the situation in Rome is relevant for understanding early Christian history. In this theory, it was Roman Jews who believed that Jesus was the messiah, or Christ (Chrestus), who had stirred up the passions of Jews who did not believe. This led to violent reactions that got out of hand: the riots mentioned by Suetonius. And so Claudius expelled the whole lot of them.

The reading of the situation may receive some support from the New Testament book of Acts, which also refers to the incident (18:2). One problem with this reconstruction of events is that if Suetonius did have some such situation in mind, he misspelled Jesus's epithet, since *Christ* in Latin would be *Christus,* not *Chrestus* (although this kind of spelling mistake was common). Moreover, since *Chrestus* itself could be a name, it may well be that there simply was a Jew named Chrestus who caused a disturbance that led to riots in the Jewish community.

In any event, even if Suetonius is referring to Jesus by a misspelled epithet, he does not help us much in our quest for non-

Christian references to Jesus. Jesus himself would have been dead for some twenty years when these riots in Rome took place, so at best Suetonius would be providing evidence, if he can count for evidence, that there were Christians in Rome during the reign of Claudius. But this could have been the case whether Jesus lived or not, since mythicists would argue that the "myth" of Christ had already been invented by then, as had the supposed life of the made-up figure of Jesus.

Whereas these first two sparse references are of limited use, a third by the Roman historian Tacitus seems more promising.

Tacitus

Tacitus wrote his famous *Annals of Imperial Rome* in 115 CE as a history of the empire from 14 to 68 CE. Probably the best-known single passage of this sixteen-volume work is the one in which he discusses the fire that consumed a good portion of Rome during the reign of the emperor Nero, in 64 CE. According to Tacitus, it was the emperor himself who had arranged for arsonists to set fire to the city because he wanted to implement his own architectural plans and could not very well do so while the older parts of the city were still standing. But the plan backfired, as many citizens—including those, no doubt, who had been burned out of house and home—suspected that the emperor himself was responsible. Nero needed to shift the blame onto someone else, and so, according to Tacitus, he claimed that the Christians had done it. The populace at large was willing to believe the charge, Tacitus tells us, because the Christians were widely maligned for their "hatred of the human race."

And so Nero had the Christians rounded up and executed in very public, painful, and humiliating ways. Some of them, Tacitus indicates, were rolled in pitch and set aflame while still alive to light Nero's gardens; others were wrapped in fresh animal skins and had wild dogs set on them, tearing them to shreds. It was not a pretty sight.

In the context of this gory account, Tacitus explains that "Nero falsely accused those whom . . . the populace called Christians. The author of this name, Christ, was put to death by the procurator, Pontius Pilate, while Tiberius was emperor; but the dangerous superstition, though suppressed for the moment, broke out again not only in Judea, the origin of this evil, but even in the city [of Rome]."

Once again, Jesus is not actually named here, but it is obvious in this instance that he is the one being referred to and that Tacitus knows some very basic information about him. He was called Christ, he was executed at the order of Pontius Pilate, and this was during the reign of Tiberius. Moreover, this happened in Judea, presumably, since that was where Pilate was the governor and since that was where Jesus's followers originated. All of this confirms information otherwise available from Christian sources, as we will see.

Some mythicists argue that this reference in Tacitus was not actually written by him—they claim the same thing for Pliny and Suetonius, where the references are less important—but were inserted into his writings (interpolated) by Christians who copied them, producing the manuscripts of Tacitus we have today. (We have no originals, only later copies.)[12] I don't know of any trained classicists or scholars of ancient Rome who think this, and it seems highly unlikely. The mythicists certainly have a reason for arguing this: they do not want to think there are *any* references to Jesus in our early sources outside the New Testament, and so when they find any such reference, they claim the reference was not original but was inserted by Christians. But surely the best way to deal with evidence is not simply to dismiss it when it happens to be inconvenient. Tacitus evidently did know some things about Jesus.

At the same time, the information is not particularly helpful in establishing that there really lived a man named Jesus. How would Tacitus know what he knew? It is pretty obvious that he had heard of Jesus, but he was writing some eighty-five years after Jesus would have died, and by that time Christians were certainly telling stories of Jesus (the Gospels had been written already, for example), whether the mythicists are wrong or right. It should be clear in any event that Tacitus is basing his comment about Jesus on hearsay rather than, say, detailed historical research. Had he done serious research, one might have expected him to say more, if even just a bit. But even more to the point, brief though his comment is, Tacitus is precisely wrong in one thing he says. He calls Pilate the "procurator" of Judea. We now know from the inscription discovered in 1961 at Caesarea that as governor, Pilate had the title and rank, not of procurator (one who dealt principally with revenue collection), but of prefect (one who also had military forces at his command). This must show that Tacitus did not look up any official record of what happened to Jesus, written at the time of his execution (if in fact such a record ever existed, which is highly doubtful). He therefore had heard the information. Whether he heard it from Christians or someone else is anyone's guess.

These three references are the only ones that survive from pagan sources within a hundred years of the traditional date of Jesus's death (around the year 30 CE). At the end of the day, I think we can discount Suetonius as too ambiguous to be of much use. Pliny is slightly more useful in showing us that Christians by the early second century knew of Christ and worshipped him as divine. Tacitus is most useful of all, for his reference shows that high-ranking Roman officials of the early second century knew that Jesus had lived and had been executed by the governor of Judea. That, at least, is a start.

Jewish Sources

As I have already indicated, we do not have nearly as many Jewish sources from within a hundred years of Jesus's life as we have pagan sources (Greek and Roman). The Dead Sea Scrolls, which do not mention or allude to Jesus, despite what you might read in sensationalist books, were probably written in the first century BCE. We do have the writings of the important Jewish philosopher Philo from the early to mid-first century. He never mentions Jesus, but we would not expect him to do so, as Christianity had probably not reached his native Alexandria by the time of his death in 50 CE, whatever one thinks of the mythicist view of Jesus. From within Palestine, the only surviving author of the time is Josephus, as we have seen. The matter is hotly disputed by mythicists, but it appears, at least from the remains that survive, that Josephus does refer to Jesus twice.

Josephus

Flavius Josephus is one of the truly important figures from ancient Judaism. His abundant historical writings are our primary source of information about the life and history of Palestine in the first century. He himself was personally involved with some of the most important events that he narrates, especially in his eight-volume work, *The Jewish Wars*.[13]

Josephus was born to an aristocratic family in Palestine some six or seven years after the traditional date of Jesus's death. Before he was an author he became actively involved in the political and military affairs of Jews in Palestine. In 66 CE there was a major uprising in which the Judeans sought to throw off the yoke of their Roman overlords. Josephus was appointed to be the general of the Jewish troops in the northern part of Palestine, Galilee. The Romans responded to the uprising by sending in the legions from Syria. To get to the heart of the rebellion they had to pass through Galilee, and they did so with relative ease, as Josephus's forces were no match for the Roman armies. As Josephus himself later tells us in his autobiography, he and his remaining troops were surrounded and chose to make a suicide pact rather than surrender to the enemy. The men each drew a numbered lot; the first man was to be killed by the second, who was to be killed by the third, and so on until only two remained, and these two were then to take their own lives. The troops did as they were told, and by luck or design, Josephus drew one of the final two lots. When all the other soldiers were dead, he then convinced his partner not to commit suicide but to turn themselves in to the Romans.

As an aristocrat and military leader, Josephus was brought before the Roman general in charge of the assault, a man named Vespasian. With his wits about him, Josephus did a very smart thing. He informed Vespasian that he had learned in a revelation from God that he, Vespasian, was destined to become the future emperor of Rome. As it turned out, Josephus's prophecy came true. After the emperor Nero committed suicide in 68 CE, there was a series of very brief reigns by three other emperors, after which Vespasian's troops declared him emperor. He returned to Rome to assume the position, leaving his son Titus in charge of the assault on Jerusalem.

Josephus himself was used as an interpreter during the three-year siege of the city. After it fell, the Jewish opposition was slaughtered and the holy Temple as well as much of the city was destroyed. Josephus was taken to Rome and given a prestigious place in the court of Vespasian, and with imperial support he then wrote his various historical works. The first was his account of all that had happened during the war in which he himself had played such an important part. About twenty years later (around 93 CE) he completed his magnum opus, a twenty-volume account of the history of the Jewish people from the time of Adam (the very beginning!) down to his own day, called *The Antiquities of the Jews*.

In his various writings Josephus mentions a large number of Jews, especially as they were important for the social, political, and historical situation in Palestine. As it turns out, he discusses several persons named Jesus, and he deals briefly also with John the Baptist. And on two occasions, at least in the writings as they have come down to us today, he mentions Jesus of Nazareth.

It is somewhat simpler to deal with these two references in reverse order. The second of them is very brief and occurs in Book 20 of the *Antiquities*. Here Josephus is referring to an incident that happened in 62 CE, before the Jewish uprising, when the local civic and religious leader in Jerusalem, the high priest Ananus, misused his power. The Roman governor had been withdrawn, and in his absence, we are told, Ananus unlawfully put to death a man named James, whom Josephus identifies as "the brother of Jesus, who is called the messiah" (*Antiquities* 20.9.1). Here, unlike the pagan references we examined earlier, Jesus is actually called by name. And we learn two things about him: he had a brother named James, and some people thought that he was the messiah. Both points are abundantly attested as well, of course, in our Christian sources, but it is interesting to see that Josephus is aware of them.

Mythicists typically argue that this passage was not originally in Josephus but was inserted by later Christian scribes. Before dealing with that claim I should consider the second passage, the one over which there is the most debate. This passage is known to scholars as the *Testimonium Flavianum,* that is, the testimony given by Flavius Josephus to the life of Jesus.[14] It is the longest reference to Jesus that we have considered so far, and it is by far the most important. In the best manuscripts of Josephus it reads as follows:

> At this time there appeared Jesus, a wise man, if indeed one should call him a man. For he was a doer of startling deeds, a teacher of people who receive the truth with pleasure. And he gained a following both among many Jews and among many of Greek origin. He was the messiah. And when Pilate, because of an accusation made by the leading men among us, condemned him to the cross, those who had loved him previously did not cease to do so. For he appeared to them on the third day, living again, just as the divine prophets had spoken of these and countless other wonderous things about him. And up until this

very day the tribe of Christians, named after him, has not died out. (*Antiquities* 18.3.3)

The problems with this passage should be obvious to anyone with even a casual knowledge of Josephus. We know a good deal about him, both from the autobiography that he produced and from other self-references in his writings. He was thoroughly and ineluctably Jewish and certainly never converted to be a follower of Jesus. But this passage contains comments that only a Christian would make: that Jesus was more than a man, that he was the messiah, and that he arose from the dead in fulfillment of the scriptures. In the judgment of most scholars, there is simply no way Josephus the Jew would or could have written such things. So how did these comments get into his writings?

It needs to be remembered that Josephus, by his own admission, was something of a turncoat in the war with Rome. This is how most Jews throughout history have remembered him. Among his own people he was not a beloved author read through the ages. In fact, his writings were transmitted in the Middle Ages not by Jews but by Christians. This shows how we can explain the extraordinary Christian claims about Jesus in this passage. When Christian scribes copied the text, they added a few words here and there to make sure that the reader would get the point. This is *that* Jesus, the super-human messiah raised from the dead as the scriptures predicted.

The big question is whether a Christian scribe (or scribes) simply added a few choice Christian additions to the passage or whether the entire thing was produced by a Christian and inserted in an appropriate place in Josephus's *Antiquities.*

The majority of scholars of early Judaism, and experts on Josephus, think that it was the former—that one or more Christian scribes "touched up" the passage a bit. If one takes out the obviously Christian comments, the passage may have been rather innocuous, reading something like this:[15]

At this time there appeared Jesus, a wise man. He was a doer of startling deeds, a teacher of people who receive the truth with pleasure. And he gained a following both among many Jews and among many of Greek origin. When Pilate, because of an accusation made by the leading men among us, condemned him to the cross, those who had loved him previously did not cease to do so. And up until this very day the tribe of Christians, named after him, has not died out.

If this is the original form of the passage, then Josephus had some solid historical information about Jesus's life: Jesus was known for his wisdom and teaching; he was thought to have done remarkable deeds; he had numerous followers; he was condemned to be crucified by Pontius Pilate because of Jewish accusations brought against him; and he continued to have followers among the Christians after his death.

Mythicists have argued, however, that the entire passage was made up by a Christian author and inserted into the writings of Josephus. If that is the case, then possibly the later reference to James as "the brother of Jesus, who is called the messiah" was also interpolated, in order to reinforce the point of the earlier insertion. One of the fullest arguments for this position is offered by Earl Doherty, both in his original work, *The Jesus Puzzle,* and in an amplified form in his more recent *Jesus: Neither God nor Man.* In his view, "a good case can be made for saying that Josephus wrote nothing about Jesus and was probably unaware of any such figure."[16] Doherty mounts argument after argument against the view that Josephus made any reference at all to Jesus, often repeating the arguments of others, sometimes coming up with his own. Here I will consider his most important points.

First, some (such as G. A. Wells) have maintained that if one removes the entire *Testimonium* from its larger context, the preceding paragraph and the one that follows flow together quite nicely. This one seems, then, intrusive.[17] As Doherty rightly notes, however, it was not at all uncommon for ancient writers (who never used footnotes) to digress from their main points, and in fact other digressions can be found in the surrounding context of the passage. So this argument really does not amount to much.

More striking for Doherty is the fact that no Christian authors appear to be aware of this passage until the church father Eusebius, writing in the early fourth century. In the second and third centuries there were many Christian writers (Justin, Tertullian, Origen, and so on) who were intent on defending both Christianity and Jesus himself against charges leveled against him by their opponents. And yet they never, in defense of Jesus, mention this passage of Josephus. Is that really plausible? Wouldn't Christian apologists want to appeal to a neutral witness in support of their claims about Jesus in the face of pagan opposition?

This too does not strike me as a strong argument. The pared-down version of Josephus—the one that others have thought was original, without the Christian additions—contains very little that could have been used by the early Christian writers to defend Jesus and his followers from attacks by pagan intellectuals. It is a very neutral statement. The fact that Jesus is said to have been wise or to have done great deeds would not go far in the repertoire of the Christian apologists. We have no way of knowing if they were familiar with this passage from Josephus, but if they were, I don't see that it would have seemed so striking to them that they would have used it to defend Jesus against pagan accusations. These accusations typically included such claims as that he was born out of wedlock to a peasant Jewish woman who was seduced by a Roman soldier; that he was an unskilled carpenter; that he could not control his temper; and that he died a shameful death on the cross.[18] Nothing in the possibly original statement of Josephus seems relevant to any of these charges.

Doherty goes on to claim that the passage does not ring true to Josephus otherwise, in part because "in the case of every other would-be messiah or popular leader opposed to or executed by the Romans, he has nothing but evil to say."[19] This is the case with all messianic pretenders of Josephus's day: he was completely opposed to anyone who might foment an uprising against Rome (remember: he was writing as a privileged guest in the court of the Roman emperor). But it needs to be stressed that in the possibly original form of the *Testimonium* there is not a word about Jesus being a messiah figure or even a political leader. He is simply a teacher with followers, accused on unknown grounds by (specifically) Jewish leaders and then executed. Moreover, if one reads the passage without the rose-tinted lenses of the Christian tradition, its view of Jesus can be seen as basically negative. The fact that he was opposed by the leaders of the Jewish people would no doubt have shown that he was not an upright Jew. And the fact that he was condemned to crucifixion, the most horrific execution imaginable to a Roman audience, speaks for itself. Even though Jesus may have been a good teacher, he was a threat to the state, or at least a nuisance, and so the state dealt with him fairly and strongly, by condemning him.

Doherty also objects to the idea that Josephus could call Jesus "wise" and one who appears to have taught the "truth." If Josephus knew the teachings of Jesus—with which he surely would have vehemently disagreed—then he never could say any such things. To this it can easily be objected on one hand that there is no reason for thinking that Josephus knew any of the things that Jesus taught, and on the other that many of the things Jesus taught were in fact what many other famous teachers of Judaism taught: for example, that followers of God should love God above all else; that they should love their neighbors as themselves; that they should do good unto others; that they should feed the hungry and care for the poor and oppressed; and, well, lots of other things that have seemed through the ages to Christian believer and unbeliever alike as both wise and true.

Doherty makes many other points, but most of them, frankly, are even weaker than these and do not need to be given serious attention here. In the revised edition of his book, however, he does devote an extended discussion to summarizing the views of Ken Olson, a graduate student at Duke University, who argues that the language of the *Testimonium* does not appear to be stylistically consistent with the language Josephus uses throughout his other works. Olson has been a student of mine (taking some of my graduate seminars at UNC) and is a very sharp fellow. For what it is worth, he is not a mythicist. Olson's Ph.D. dissertation is devoted to the *Testimonium,* and many of his key arguments are summarized in an article that he published in the academic journal *Catholic Biblical Quarterly* in 1999.[20] In this article Olson argues that the first author to mention the *Testimonium,* the Christian church father Eusebius (who was writing before any of our manuscripts of Josephus was produced), was in fact the one who forged it and so was ultimately responsible for its being inserted into Josephus's writings. The basis for the argument is a very careful analysis of the words and phrases used in the *Testimonium.* Olson argues in case after case that the wording and phrasing of the passage has numerous parallels with Eusebius's writings but not with those of Josephus. In other words, the vocabulary and style of the passage suggest that it was written by Eusebius.

Olson has made an intriguing case in his article, but I am afraid— as impressed by him as I am—that it has not held up under critical scrutiny. The responses to it by such scholars of Josephus and of early Christianity as J. Carleton Paget and Alice Whealey have been compelling.[21] There is in fact little in the *Testimonium* that is more like Eusebius than Josephus, and a good deal of the passage does indeed read like it was written by Josephus. It is far more likely that the core of the passage actually does go back to Josephus himself.[22]

An additional reason for thinking so is this: if a scribe (or Eusebius or anyone else) wanted to insert a strong testimony about the virtues of Jesus into the writings of Josephus (so that the *Testimonium* is a later interpolation), he surely would have done so in a much more glowing and obvious way. Those who wrote apocryphal stories about Jesus are flamboyant both in what they relate (recounting lots of Jesus's miracles, for example) and in how they say it (stressing his divine nature, not simply that he was the messiah). The *Testimonium* is so restrained, with only a couple of fairly reserved sentences here and there, that it does not read like a Christian apocryphal account of Jesus written for the occasion. It reads much more like what you get elsewhere throughout the manuscript tradition of ancient writings: a touch-up job that a scribe could easily do.

The payoff is that most scholars continue to be convinced that Josephus did indeed write about Jesus, probably in something like the pared-down version that I quote above.

But that is not the main point I want to make about the *Testimonium*. My main point is that whether the *Testimonium* is authentically from Josephus (in its pared-down form) or not probably does not ultimately matter for the question I am pursuing here. Whether or not Jesus lived has to be decided on other kinds of evidence from this. And here is why. Suppose Josephus really did write the *Testimonium*. That would show that by 93 CE—some sixty or more years after the traditional date of Jesus's death—a Jewish historian of Palestine had some information about him. And where would Josephus have derived this information? He would have heard stories about Jesus that were in circulation. There is nothing to suggest that Josephus had actually read the Gospels (he almost certainly had not) or that he did any kind of primary research into the life of Jesus by examining Roman records of some kind (there weren't any). But as we will see later, we already know for lots of other reasons and on lots of other grounds that there were stories about Jesus floating around in Palestine by the end of the first century and much earlier. So even if the *Testimonium,* in the pared-down form, was written by Josephus, it does not give us much more evidence than we already have on the question of whether there really was a man Jesus.

If, by contrast, the *Testimonium* was not written by Josephus,

we again are neither helped nor hurt in our quest to know whether
Jesus lived. There is certainly no reason to think if Jesus lived that
Josephus must have mentioned him. He doesn't mention most Jews
of the first century. Recent estimates suggest that there were possibly up to a million Jews living in Palestine at any one time in the
early first century. (If you add up the different persons living in any
given year, as new people are born and others die, the total numbers
of Jews living throughout the period are obviously much higher.)[23]
Josephus does not mention 99 percent of them—or rather, more
than 99 percent. So why would he mention Jesus? You cannot say
that he would have mentioned Jesus because anyone who did all
those amazing miraculous deeds would surely be mentioned. As
I pointed out earlier, the question of what Jesus actually *did* has to
come after we establish that he lived, not before. As a result, even
though both the mythicists and their opponents like to fight long
and hard over the *Testimonium* of Josephus, in fact it is only marginally relevant to the question of whether Jesus existed.

Rabbinic Sources

In order to complete my tally of early references to Jesus, I need
to say a few words about the Jewish Talmud. This is not because it
is relevant but because when talking about historical references to
Jesus, many people *assume* it is relevant.[24] The Talmud is a collection
of disparate materials from early Judaism: legal disputes, anecdotes,
folklore, customs, and sayings. Most of the material relates directly to
teachings of and stories about the early rabbis, that is, Jewish teachers.
The collection was put together long after the days of Jesus.

The core of the Talmud is the Mishnah, a collection of rabbinic teachings about the Jewish law, based on oral traditions that
had long been in circulation, and written in the early third century, some two hundred years after Jesus would have died. Most of
the Talmud, however, consists of a series of commentaries by later

rabbis on the Mishnah, called the Gemara. There are two different sets of these commentaries, one produced in the fourth century by Jewish scholars who lived in Palestine, the other produced in the fifth century by scholars of Babylon. The latter is considered the more authoritative.

For a long time scholars treated the Talmud as if it presented historically accurate information about Jewish life, law, and custom from a much earlier period, all the way back to the first century. Few critical scholars take that view today. In both its iterations, it is a product of its own time, even though it is based on earlier oral reports.

Jesus is never mentioned in the oldest part of the Talmud, the Mishnah, but appears only in the later commentaries of the Gemara. One of the problems even with these very late references is that Jesus is not actually called by name even though it is reasonably clear that he is the one being referred to. There are some passages, for example, that refer to a person named "Ben [son of] Panthera." Panthera was the name traditionally given to the Roman soldier who was said to have seduced Mary, who in these passages is called a hairdresser. Her child, then, was born out of wedlock. Scholars have long recognized that this tradition appears to represent a subtle attack on the Christian view of Jesus birth as the "son of a virgin." In Greek, the word for virgin is *parthenos,* close in spelling to *Panthera.*

In other references in the Talmud we learn that Jesus was a sorcerer who acquired his black magic in Egypt. Recall the Gospel accounts of how Jesus fled with his family to Egypt soon after his birth and his abilities later in life to perform miracles. He is said in the Talmud to have gathered five disciples and to have been hanged on the eve of the Passover, after a herald proclaimed the charges of sorcery against him for forty days. Here again we may have a biased version of the Gospel accounts, where Jesus is killed during the Passover but with injudicious speed after a very quick trial, his execution occurring some twelve hours after his arrest.

These Talmudic references to Jesus were written hundreds of years after he would have lived and so are really of very little use for us in our quest. By the time they were set down, Christianity was a major force in the Roman Empire, and every single Christian telling stories about Jesus naturally assumed that he had really existed as a historical person. If we want evidence to support the claim that he did in fact once exist, we therefore have to turn to other sources.

CHAPTER THREE

The Gospels as Historical Sources

At the beginning of the last chapter I mentioned one criticism I have received over the years that has surprised me. And here is another. Sometimes in a review or an e-mail a reader will provide a short but hard-hitting laundry list of complaints about one or another book I've written, and two items on the list are (a) that I'm needlessly attacking the Bible (I objected to this complaint in chapter 2) and (b) that I am saying nothing new but am merely rehearsing what scholars have known for a long time. I find this two-pronged critique a bit odd for lots of reasons but in particular because the two prongs seem to be at odds with each other. How am I attacking *anything* if I am simply saying what scholars have long known? I don't see how a critic can have it both ways.

At the same time, I do understand the critique. Very conservative evangelical and fundamentalist Christians do not agree with what other scholars have long said about the Bible. And what the critics are objecting to is my decision to make this information public. Fair enough. But in my view, the public has the right to know what scholars have discovered after spending countless hours, days, months, and years grappling with the hard issues. And to discount it all as "saying nothing new" is simply an ad hominem attack. My popular books (as opposed to my scholarly books, which are written for the six people in the world who care) are meant for laypeople and so are designed to show a wider audience, in nontechnical language, the findings of true and intriguing importance that scholars have made. How can anyone complain about making the public more knowledgeable?

The same complaint can well be made about the present chapter. In it I do not advance scholarship or come up with some new theory. What I discuss here is common knowledge among scholars in the field. In fact, most of it is standard information that even my conservative critics will by and large agree with, either to their pleasant surprise or to their dismay. It deals with why our Gospel sources are important for the question of whether Jesus existed, and my claim is that once one understands more fully what the Gospels are and where they came from, they provide powerful evidence indeed that there really was a historical Jesus who lived in Roman Palestine and who was crucified under Pontius Pilate. We will see in the chapters that follow that this is not the only kind of evidence we have for the existence of Jesus. Quite the contrary, there are other compelling data to consider. But the Gospels are the obvious place to start.

A Preliminary Comment on the Gospels as Historical Sources

As I WILL TRY to show momentarily, the Gospels, their sources, and the oral traditions that lie behind them combine to make a convincing case that Jesus really existed. It is not that one can simply accept everything found in the Gospels as historically accurate. Far from it. The Gospels are filled with nonhistorical material, accounts of events that could not have happened. This is shown, for example, by the many discrepancies they contain in matters both great and small. If you have two contradictory accounts of the same event, both accounts cannot be accurate. And once you read the Gospels carefully, with keen attention to minute details, you will find such contradictions all over the map. Eventually these small details add up to big pictures, which also are sometimes at odds with one another.

At the same time, there is historical information in the Gospels. This historical material needs to be teased out by careful, critical analysis. Before doing so, I need to make a preliminary remark about the Gospels as historical sources. Sometimes the Gospels of the New Testament are separated from all other pieces of historical evidence and given a different kind of treatment because they happen to be found in the Bible, the collection of books that Christians gathered together and declared sacred scripture. The Gospels are treated in this way by two fundamentally opposed camps of readers, and my contention is that both of them are completely wrong. However else the Gospels are used—for example, in communities of faith—they can and must be considered historical sources of information.

At one end of the spectrum, fundamentalist and conservative evangelical Christians often treat the Gospels as literature unlike anything else that has ever been produced because, in their theological opinion, these books were inspired by God. In this view, inspired literature is not amenable to the same kind of historical and critical investigation as other kinds of literature.

I think this is wrong, and not simply because I am an agnostic who does not believe the Bible is the inspired word of God. I thought this approach was wrong even when I was a committed, believing Christian. It is wrong because whatever else you might think about the books of the Bible—whether you believe in them or not, whether you consider them inspired or not—they are still *books*.

That is, they were written by people in historical circumstances and contexts and precisely in light of those circumstances and contexts. There is no God-given way of interpreting God-given literature, even if such literature exists. It is still literature. And it has to be interpreted as literature is interpreted. There is no special hermeneutic handed down from above to direct the reading of these books as opposed to all others. Their authors were human authors (whether or not they were inspired); they wrote in human languages and in human contexts; their books are recognizable as human books, written according to the rhetorical conventions of their historical period. They are human and historical, whatever else you may think about them, and to treat them differently is to mistreat them and to misunderstand them.

At the other end of the spectrum is another group insisting that the books of the Bible need to be given separate treatment. These are certain agnostics and atheists who claim that since, say, the Gospels are part of Christian sacred scripture, they have less value than other books for establishing historical information. As odd as it might seem, the nonbelievers who argue this are making common cause with the fundamentalists who also argue it. Both groups treat the Gospels as nonhistorical, the fundamentalists because the Gospels are inspired and the atheists (those who hold this view) because the Gospels are accepted by some people as sacred scripture and so are not historical.

The (sometime) atheist opinion of the Bible as nonhistorical is no better than the (typical) fundamentalist opinion. The reality is that the authors of the books that became the Bible did not know they were producing books that would later be considered scripture, and they probably had no intention of producing scripture. The Gospel writers—anonymous Greek-speaking Christians living thirty-five to sixty-five years after the traditional date of Jesus's death—were simply writing down episodes that they had heard from the life of Jesus. Some of these episodes may be historically accurate, others may not be. But the authors did not write thinking they were providing the sacred scriptures for the Christian tradition. They were simply writing books about Jesus.

These authors had nothing to do with later developments, such as that their books were considered inspired and were placed in a canon and called the New Testament. The authors were real, living, breathing, historical persons; they had heard reports about Jesus; they had probably read earlier accounts of his life; and they decided to write their own versions. "Luke" (whoever he really was and whatever name he had) tells us this himself, in the beginning of the third Gospel: "Whereas many have attempted to compile a narrative of the things that have been fulfilled among us, just as the eyewitnesses and ministers of the word delivered them over to us, it seemed good to me also, having followed all these things closely from the beginning, to write for you an orderly account" (1:1–3).

I should stress that I am not saying that Luke and the other Gospel writers were trying to present disinterested accounts of the life of Jesus. These authors were anything but disinterested, and their biases need to be front and center in the critics' minds when evaluating what they have to say. But at the same time, they were historical persons giving reports of things they had heard, using historically situated modes of rhetoric and presentation. The fact that their books later became documents of faith has no bearing on the question of whether the books can still be used for historical purposes. To dismiss the Gospels from the historical record is neither fair nor scholarly.

Some mythicists, though, do precisely that. As just one example, the Gospel of Luke indicates that Jesus's hometown was Nazareth. As we will see later in the book, many mythicists deny that Nazareth even existed in the days of Jesus, and they refuse to take Luke's and the other Gospels' word for it, not deeming them as reputable historical sources since they are part of the Bible. But the reality is that Luke inherited oral traditions about Jesus and his connection with

Nazareth, and he recorded what he had heard. What he heard may have been right or it may have been wrong, but the fact that later Christians long after he was dead placed his book into the canon of the New Testament has nothing to do with it. Luke's writings about Jesus carry no more or less weight than the writings of any other ancient biographer (Suetonius, for example, or Plutarch)—or, perhaps a more apt comparison, of any other biographer of a religious person, such as Philostratus and his account of Apollonius of Tyana.

Consider an analogy. We don't dismiss early American accounts of the Revolutionary War simply because they were written by Americans. We take their biases into consideration and sometimes take their descriptions of events with a pound of salt. But we do not refuse to use them as historical sources. Contemporary accounts of George Washington, even by his devoted followers, are still valuable as historical sources. To refuse to use them as sources is to sacrifice the most important avenues to the past we have, and on purely ideological, not historical, grounds.

So too the Gospels. Whatever one thinks of them as inspired scripture, they can be seen and used as significant historical sources. With this major comment in view, what can we say about the Gospels and their witness to the life of the historical Jesus?

The Gospels and Their Written Sources

ONCE IT IS CONCEDED that the Gospels can and should be treated as historical sources, no different from other historical sources infused with their authors' biases, it starts to become clear why historians have almost universally agreed that whatever else one might say about him, Jesus of Nazareth lived in first-century Palestine and was crucified by the prefect of Judea. It is not because "the Gospels say so" and that it therefore must be true (the view, of course, of fundamentalist Christians). It is for a host of other reasons familiar to scholars who work in the field. This opening section will not be convincing to naysayers, for reasons I will explain, but we need to start somewhere, and the place to start is with the surviving witnesses that we have in hand.

We have already seen that historians, who try to establish that a past event happened or that a past person lived, look for multiple sources that corroborate one another's stories without having collaborated. And this is what we get with the Gospels and their witness of Jesus. Our earliest Gospel account of Jesus's life is probably Mark's, usually dated—by conservative and liberal scholars of the New Testament alike—to around 70 CE (some conservatives date it earlier; very few liberals date it much later). Eventually we will consider the question of Mark's sources; for now we are interested in the brute fact that within forty years or so of Jesus's (alleged) life, we have a relatively full account of many of the things he said and did and of his death by crucifixion. (How much of it we can trust as historically accurate is another question, which we will deal with at a later stage.)

It is almost (but not quite) universally thought among New Testament scholars that both Matthew and Luke had access to the Gospel of Mark and used it for many of their stories of Jesus. This is almost certainly right, for reasons that don't need to concern us here but are readily available elsewhere in a wide range of publications on the New Testament.[1] Some mythicists—as we will see in chapter 7—have taken this critical conclusion to a faulty end to argue that all of our Gospel accounts (even John, which has very little to do with Mark) ultimately go back to Mark so that we have only one source, not multiple sources, for the life of Jesus. Nothing could be further from the truth. Matthew and Luke did indeed use Mark, but significant portions of both Gospels are not related in any way to Mark's accounts. And in these sections of their Gospels Matthew and Luke record extensive, independent traditions about Jesus's life, teachings, and death. So while in their shared material they do not provide corroboration without collaboration, in their unique material they do. These Gospels were probably written ten or fifteen years after Mark, and so by the year 80 or 85 we have at least three independent accounts of Jesus's life (since a number of the accounts of both Matthew and Luke are independent of Mark), all within a generation or so of Jesus himself, assuming he lived.

But that is not all. There are still other independent Gospels. The Gospel of John is sometimes described as the "maverick Gospel" because it is so unlike the synoptic accounts of Matthew, Mark, and Luke.[2] Prior to the narrative leading up to Jesus's death, most of the stories in John are found only in John, whereas John does not include most of the stories found in the other three Gospels. And when they do share the same stories, John tells them in such a different way that he does not appear to have received his accounts from any or all of them.[3] This is especially the case, of course, in those passages (the majority of them) in which John's stories do not overlap with those of the synoptics. It is equally true of John's account of Jesus's death. John is generally considered the latest of our canonical Gospels, dated 90–95 CE. So within the first century we have four independent accounts of Jesus's life and death (Matthew and Luke being independent in a good number of their corroborative stories; John possibly in all, and certainly in most, of his).

Gospels continued to be written after John, however, and some of these later accounts are also independent. Since the discovery in 1945 of the famous Gospel of Thomas, a collection of 114 sayings of Jesus, scholars have debated its date.[4] Even though some continue to place the Gospel in the first century, possibly prior to all or some of the canonical Gospels, more widely it is thought that in its current form Thomas comes to us from the early second century, say 110–20 CE. Moreover, while some scholars think that Thomas relies on Matthew, Mark, and Luke for some of its sayings—there are overlaps in about half of them—it is more commonly thought that Thomas is independent, that it got its information from other sources. In either event, a good portion of Thomas, if not all of it, does not derive from the canonical texts. To that extent it is a fifth independent witness to the life and teachings of Jesus.

The same can be said of the Gospel of Peter, discovered in 1886. This is a fragmentary account of Jesus's trial, death, and resurrection.[5] Once again, even though there is some similarity in portions of the account to what is found in the canonical Gospels, it is widely thought that Peter preserves an independent narrative, drawn from other, noncanonical, sources. There are protracted debates among scholars about how much material from the life of Jesus this account originally contained. The fragment that survives begins in the middle of a sentence during the scene in which Pilate washes his hands of Jesus's blood (a scene found as well in the Gospel of Matthew, but in Peter it is narrated differently and probably comes from some different source). Some scholars think that the Gospel recounted only Jesus's Passion, but others, somewhat more convincingly, maintain that in fact it was a complete Gospel with a narrative of Jesus's ministry as well.[6] In either event, since it is in part or in whole different from the other Gospels, in these passages—and probably in its entirety, though this judgment does not affect my argument—this would be a sixth independent Gospel account of Jesus's life and death.

Another independent account occurs in the highly fragmentary text called Papyrus Egerton 2.[7] Here again it is difficult to know how extensive the full Gospel contained in these partial remains originally was; what survives are four episodes from the life of Jesus, one of which has no parallel in the Gospels of the New Testament or in any other known Gospel.[8] Here then, at least in the nonparalleled story, but probably in all four, is a seventh independent account.

There are, of course, lots of other Gospels, some forty or so, down to the early Middle Ages, that are not found in the New Testament. These include narratives of Jesus as a newborn and as a young child, where he uses his miraculous powers sometimes for

mischief and sometimes for good; narratives of his public ministry; narratives of his death and resurrection. Almost all of these accounts, of course, are highly legendary, and with the passing of time
they become less and less valuable as independent, historical sources.
But if we restrict ourselves here, as we did earlier, to a hundred years
after the traditional date of Jesus's death, we have at least seven independent accounts, some of them quite extensive. (It is important to
recall: even if some of these sources are dependent on one another
in some passages—for example, Matthew and Luke on Mark—they
are completely independent in others, and to that extent they are
independent witnesses.) And so it is quite wrong to argue that Mark
is our only independent witness to Jesus as a historical person. The
other six accounts are either completely or partially independent
as well. For a historian these provide a wealth of materials to work
with, quite unusual for accounts of anyone, literally anyone, from
the ancient world.

And that is not nearly all. It may be easy to discount these seven
witnesses on the grounds that they are not close to the time of the
events they narrate (the earliest is four decades removed) and that
they are heavily biased toward their subject matter. I will deal with
the matter of bias soon. For now it is important to begin moving
behind these independent accounts to see from where they found
their information about Jesus.

Written Sources for the Surviving Witnesses

WHAT IS SOMETIMES UNDERAPPRECIATED by mythicists who want
to discount the value of the Gospels for establishing the historical
existence of Jesus is that our surviving accounts, which began to be
written some forty years after the traditional date of Jesus's death,
were based on earlier written sources that no longer survive. But
they obviously did exist at one time, and they just as obviously had

to predate the Gospels that we now have. The opening words of the Gospel of Luke bear repeating: "Whereas many have attempted to compile a narrative of the things that have been fulfilled among us, just as the eyewitnesses and ministers of the word delivered them over to us, it seemed good to me also, having followed all these things closely from the beginning, to write for you an orderly account" (1:1–3).

As we will see more fully in a later context, one needs to approach everything that the Gospel writers say gingerly, with a critical eye. But there is no reason to suspect that Luke is lying here. He knew of "many" earlier authors who had compiled narratives about the subject matter that he himself is about to narrate, the life of Jesus. Since the mid-nineteenth century there has been a wide consensus among scholars concerning what these earlier sources were and what to call them. Again, I do not mean to say that every scholar agrees on every detail. On the contrary, scholars vigorously debate many specific issues. But in broad outline, which is what matters for my purposes here, there is considerable agreement, based on very thorough investigation of all the relevant issues by scholars who have devoted their entire lives to studying the question.

Virtually everyone agrees that Luke had as one of his predecessors the Gospel of Mark. This in itself is a matter of interest since Luke seems to imply, by what he says about the "many" who "attempted to compile a narrative" before him, that he did not consider these earlier attempts successful, that in fact they needed some correcting. That is why he himself (in contrast to them?) wants to provide "an orderly account." If that is Luke's implication, we can infer that he did not have a very high view of Mark's Gospel or at least that he thought it was inadequate for his purposes. And so he produced his own. But he certainly liked a good deal of Mark, as he copied many of Mark's stories in constructing his own Gospel, sometimes verbatim. But he had other sources as well.

One of them I have already mentioned, the no-longer-surviving

Gospel account that scholars have called Q.[9] The reason for thinking that this source was written prior to the synoptic Gospels, and that it was available to them, has to do with the literary relationship of Matthew, Mark, and Luke to one another. There is obviously some kind of relationship since they tell many of the same stories, often in the same sequence and frequently even in the same words. Someone is copying. Even though Matthew and Luke used Mark as one of their sources, they share a number of passages that are not found in Mark, such as the Lord's Prayer and the Beatitudes. The two later Gospels obviously did not get these passages from Mark since he didn't include them. And there are solid reasons for thinking that one of them did not derive these materials from a copy of the other. The best solution to the question of where they got these passages, then, is that they derived them from some other shared source.[10] The German scholars who most fully developed this theory called this other source the "sayings *Quelle*," the sayings source. The word *Quelle* is shortened in common parlance to Q. Q, then, is the material that Matthew and Luke have in common that is not found in Mark. And it derived from a written Gospel that no longer survives.

Q appears to have been made up predominantly of the sayings of Jesus, much like the later Gospel of Thomas. In the judgment of most scholars, Q did not include an account of Jesus's death and resurrection since Matthew and Luke do not share any stories of the Passion not also found in Mark. In my opinion it is very hard to know whether or not Q lacked a passion narrative. It would have been possible, for example, for Matthew to copy some of the stories of the Passion from Q and for Luke not to include those stories. If so, we would have no way of knowing whether the stories found only in Matthew—including some of the passages in the passion narrative—were in fact Q stories that Luke simply decided not to reproduce for reasons of his own.

Whether or not Q included an account of Jesus's death and resurrection, it appears that the source must date to a period no later than Mark, and a good number of scholars have dated it earlier, say, to the 50s.

Luke used other sources as well, as he intimates. He doesn't tell us how many. A lot of stories are found only in Luke, however, such as Jesus's parables of the prodigal son and of the good Samaritan. Luke must have gotten these from somewhere else: scholars have long offered good reasons for thinking Luke didn't just make everything else all up. And so they call this other now-lost source *L,* for Luke's special source. L may have been one document; it may have been a large number of documents; or it may have included both written documents and oral traditions about Jesus (I will be talking about oral traditions soon).

Matthew as well is based on written sources. As pointed out, he used Mark, even more than Luke did, and Q. But he too includes many stories found only in his Gospel: the visit of the wise men to worship the infant Jesus, for example, and the parable of the sheep and the goats at the last judgment. These then must have come from Matthew's special source(s), which scholars have therefore labeled *M.* Like L, M may have been a single written document, a number of documents, or a combination of oral traditions and written sources.

When dealing only with Matthew, Mark, and Luke, the synoptic Gospels, then, we are talking not just about three books written late in the first century. We are talking about at least four sources: Mark, Q, M, and L, the latter two of which could easily have represented several, or even many, other written sources.

Many leading scholars of the Gospel of Mark think that it too was compiled not just of oral traditions that had been circulating down to the author's day but of various written sources. It is often thought that Mark used a passion narrative that had been written years earlier in which the episodes of Jesus's arrest, trials, death, and resurrection were already put into written form. The most recent and most authoritative two-volume commentary on Mark, by Joel

Marcus, contends that Mark used a source, or a number of sources, for his account of Jesus's words and deeds prior to the passion narrative.[11] If this is right, then not just our later synoptics but even our earliest surviving Gospel was based on multiple sources.

The Gospel of John too is widely thought to have been based on written sources that no longer survive. As I have indicated, the reason for thinking that John does not rely on the synoptics is that whenever they tell the same story, it is in radically different ways and never in the same words. But scholars have long suspected that John had at his disposal an earlier written account of Jesus's miracles (the so-called Signs Source), at least two accounts of Jesus's long speeches (the Discourse Sources), and possibly another passion source as well.[12]

I have been speaking so far only of the four canonical Gospels. It cannot be determined with absolute certainty whether any of the later Gospels—say the Gospel of Peter or the Gospel of Thomas—go back to written sources although in both of these cases some scholars have mounted strenuous arguments that they do. The most plausible case has been made for the Gospel of Thomas by April DeConick, who makes a strong argument, based on a careful literary study of the text, that the core of the surviving Gospel of Thomas goes back to a Gospel in circulation prior to 50 CE.[13]

All of these written sources I have mentioned are earlier than the surviving Gospels; they all corroborate many of the key things said of Jesus in the Gospels; and most important they are all independent of one another. Let me stress the latter point. We cannot think of the early Christian Gospels as going back to a solitary source that "invented" the idea that there was a man Jesus. The view that Jesus existed is found in multiple independent sources that must have been circulating throughout various regions of the Roman Empire in the decades before the Gospels that survive were produced. Where would the solitary source that "invented" Jesus be? Within a couple of decades of the traditional date of his death, we have numerous accounts of his life found in a broad geographical span. In addition to Mark, we have Q, M (which is possibly made of multiple sources), L (also possibly multiple sources), two or more passion narratives, a signs source, two discourse sources, the kernel (or original) Gospel behind the Gospel of Thomas, and possibly others. And these are just the ones we know about, that we can reasonably infer from the scant literary remains that survive from the early years of the Christian church. No one knows how many there actually were. Luke says there were "many" of them, and he may well have been right. And once again, this is not the end of the story.

The Oral Traditions About Jesus

THE FURTHER QUESTION THAT needs to be asked is where all these Gospel sources—Mark, Q, M, L, sayings source, passion narratives, proto-Thomas and so on—got their stories. This is a question that has occupied New Testament scholars for nearly a hundred years. In the early part of the twentieth century there was a group of scholars in Germany who developed a method of studying the Gospels to address this question. The method has traditionally been called, in English, "form criticism."

Form Criticism and Oral Traditions About Jesus

The original impetus for the form-critical approach to the Gospels came from a well-known New Testament scholar named Karl Ludwig Schmidt; the approach was developed, in different ways, by the even more famous Martin Dibelius and especially by the most famous of them all, Rudolf Bultmann, arguably the greatest and most influential scholar of the New Testament in the twentieth century.[14]

These form critics were principally interested in knowing what happened while the stories about Jesus were being transmitted orally.

Their assumption was that after Jesus's life, when Christian missionaries founded churches throughout the Mediterranean, stories about Jesus were told and retold in various kinds of situations that Christians found themselves in. These scholars were called "form" critics because they wanted to know how different kinds of stories came to assume the shape or form they have. Why is it that so many miracle stories seem to follow the same basic pattern? A person comes up to Jesus, his or her problem (or illness) is described, there is a brief interchange with Jesus, Jesus agrees to heal the person, he does so by a word or by a touch, and all the crowds marvel. Every miracle story seems to have the same elements.

Or take the controversy stories. Jesus or his disciples do something that offends the Jewish leaders; the leaders protest; Jesus has a conversation with them; and the story ends with Jesus delivering a withering one-liner that shows that he gets the better of them. Time after time, same form.

The form critics were invested in two issues: what was the "situation in life" (German: *Sitz im Leben*) in which different kinds of stories about Jesus were told? And how did the various kinds of stories assume their various forms (so that there is one kind of form for miracle stories, another for controversy stories, and so on)? These critics did not agree among themselves on the specifics of their views. But their overarching understanding of the oral traditions about Jesus was fairly consistent. The stories about Jesus came to be shaped in the process of telling and retelling, as they assumed their characteristic forms. This means that the stories were changed, sometimes radically, when they were retold, and thus formed over the years. And some stories were made up in the process, developed to speak to the needs the Christian communities and to address the situations they found themselves in. If a community, for example, was facing opposition from the Jews of the local synagogue because they did not observe the Sabbath laws strictly, they might come up with a story in which Jesus himself was confronted by his Jewish opponents over the same issue. And watch! Jesus outshines his opponents by delivering a devastating rejoinder to their objections.

So far as I know, there are no longer any form critics among us who agree with the precise formulations of Schmidt, Dibelius, and Bultmann, the pioneers in this field. But the most basic idea behind their approach is still widely shared, namely, that before the Gospels came to be written, and before the sources that lie behind the Gospels were themselves produced, oral traditions about Jesus circulated, and as the stories about Jesus were told and retold, they changed their form and some stories came to be made up. I have already intimated that this was the case when speaking about the sources M and L, when I conceded that these may not have simply been written documents but entirely or partly oral traditions. This appears to be true of all of our sources for the historical Jesus. They are all based on oral traditions, and this has significant implications for our quest to determine if Jesus actually lived.

The reality appears to be that there were stories being told about Jesus for a very long time not just before our surviving Gospels but even before their sources had been produced. If scholars are right that Q and the core of the Gospel of Thomas, to pick just two examples, do date from the 50s, and that they were based on oral traditions that had already been in circulation for a long time, how far back do these traditions go? Anyone who thinks that Jesus existed has no problem answering the question: they ultimately go back to things Jesus said and did while he was engaged in his public ministry, say, around the year 29 or 30. But even anyone who just wonders if Jesus existed has to assume that there were stories being told about him in the 30s and 40s. For one thing, as we will see in the next chapter, how else would someone like Paul have known to persecute the Christians, if Christians didn't exist? And how could they exist if they didn't know anything about Jesus?

Mythicists often reply that the Christians known to the persecutor Paul before he was himself a Christian—as well as the later Christians in the churches he founded after converting—did not know anything about a historical Jesus but worshipped the divine Christ, who was based on pagan myths about dying and rising gods. We will see the flaws in this argument later, and we will also note that Paul does in fact talk about Jesus as a human being who delivered important teachings and was crucified at the instigation of Jewish leaders in Palestine. But even if we leave Paul out of the equation, there is still more than ample reason for thinking that stories about Jesus circulated widely throughout the major urban areas of the Mediterranean from a very early time. Otherwise it is impossible to explain all the written sources that emerged in the middle and end of the first century. These sources are independent of one another. They were written in different places. They contain strikingly different accounts of what Jesus said and did. Yet many of them, independent though they be, agree on many of the basic aspects of Jesus's life and death: he was a Jewish teacher of Palestine who was crucified on order of Pontius Pilate, for example. Where did all these sources come from? They could not have been dreamed up independently of one another by Christians all over the map because they agree on too many of the fundamentals. Instead, they are based on oral traditions. These oral traditions had been in circulation for a very long time before they came to be written down. This is not pure speculation. Aspects of the surviving stories of Jesus found in the written Gospels, themselves based on earlier written accounts, show clearly both that they were based on oral traditions (as Luke himself indicates) and that these traditions had been around for a very long time—in fact, that they had been around since Christianity first emerged as a religion in Palestine itself.

The Aramaic Origins of (Some) Oral Traditions

Here is one piece of evidence. Even though the Gospels were written in Greek, as were their sources, some of the surviving traditions were originally spoken in Aramaic, the language of Palestine. These traditions date at least to the early years of the Christian movement, before it expanded into the Greek-speaking lands elsewhere in the Mediterranean.

The evidence, in part, is this. In several passages in the Gospels a key word or phrase has been left in the original Aramaic, and the author, writing in Greek, has had to translate it for his audience. This happens, for example, in the intriguing account of Mark 5, where Jesus raises a young girl from the dead. The story begins by describing how the girl's father, Jairus, comes to Jesus and begs him to heal his very sick daughter. Jesus agrees to come, but he gets interrupted on the way. Before he can get to the girl, the household slaves appear and tell Jairus that it is too late, the girl has died. Jesus is not to be deterred, however. He goes to the house, comes into the girl's room, takes her lifeless hand, and says to her, "Talitha cumi." That is not a Greek phrase. It is Aramaic. And so Mark translates it for his readers: "It means, 'Little girl, I say to you, arise.'" She does so, to much rejoicing.

This is a story that was originally told in Aramaic, but when it was translated into Greek, the translator left the key line in the original language so that it required translation for those who were not bilingual. This might seem odd to readers, but it is not. It happens a lot in multilingual societies even today. In graduate school I had a professor who had spent a good deal of time in Germany and was fluent in the language. We too were supposed to know German in order to do our research. But most of us had learned only to read German, not speak it. My professor didn't appreciate our shortcomings, however. He would often tell a joke (in English) about something that had happened to him in Germany, but when he got to the punch line, he would revert to German. It was much funnier in the original, and we were supposed to understand. We would laugh heartily on cue, having no idea what he had just said but not wanting him to know.

That sort of thing happens in the Gospels. The punch line is left in Aramaic. And so, for example, at the end of Mark's Gospel, when Jesus is in his final moments on the cross, he cries out to God in Aramaic, "Eloi, eloi, lama sabachthani" (Mark 15:34), and Mark then explains what it means in Greek: "which means, 'my God, my God, why have you forsaken me?'"

Mark is not the only Gospel where this occurs. The Gospel of John, independently of Mark or the others, includes a number of Aramaic words. In John 1:35–52 alone there are three instances. Two disciples have learned from John the Baptist that Jesus is the "Lamb of God who takes away the sins of the world," and they want to meet him for themselves. They approach him and say to him "Rabbi," an Aramaic word that the author translates, "which means, 'Teacher.'" When Andrew, one of the two, becomes convinced of who Jesus is, he runs off to his brother Simon and tells him, "We have found the messiah." *Messiah* is the Aramaic word; John translates it: "which means Christ." Jesus then speaks with Simon and tells him, "You will be called Cephas." Once again, it is an Aramaic word, which John translates, "which means Peter."

There is very little dispute that some of the Gospel stories originated in Aramaic and that therefore they go back to the earliest stages of the Christian movement in Palestine. This is clearly shown, as well, by a second kind of evidence. Some Gospel passages do not contain Aramaic words, but they make sense only when their Greek words and phrases are translated back into Aramaic. This means they originated as Aramaic traditions that only later came to be transmitted in Greek.

One of the clearest examples is in Mark 2:27–28, where Jesus delivers a withering two-liner to silence his critics. His disciples have been walking through the grain fields on the Sabbath, and since they were hungry they started eating some of the grain. The Pharisees see this (the Pharisees seem to be *everywhere* in Mark) and protest that the disciples are breaking the Sabbath. For Jesus, though, as Mark portrays him, human needs (in this case hunger) take priority over strict interpretations about the Sabbath. And so he informs his opponents, "Sabbath was made for man, not man for the Sabbath. Therefore the Son of Man is Lord of the Sabbath."

That last line doesn't really make sense in the context, for two reasons. For one thing, even if Jesus, who is the Son of Man in Mark's Gospel, is the Lord (master) of the Sabbath, what has that to do with his critics' objection? They are objecting not to what he has done but to what his disciples have done. Even more, the last line doesn't follow at all from the first line. I sometimes tell my students that when they see the word *therefore* in a passage, they should ask, what is the *therefore* there for? The *therefore* in this case doesn't make sense. Just because Sabbath was made for humans and not the other way around, what does that have to do with Jesus being the Lord of the Sabbath?

Both problems are solved once you translate the passage back into Aramaic. As it turns out, Aramaic uses the same word for *man* and for *son of man*. It is the word *barnash*. And so the two-liner originally said, "Sabbath was made for *barnash*, not *barnash* for the Sabbath. Therefore *barnash* is lord of the Sabbath." Now the *therefore* makes sense. The reason that humans (*barnash*) are the lords of the Sabbath is because of what he just said: Sabbath was made for humans, not the other way around. Moreover, now the last line makes sense in the context of the story. The disciples (the *barnash*) are masters of the Sabbath, which was created for their sake.

Originally, then, this story circulated in Aramaic. When it came to be translated into Greek, the translator decided to make it not just about the disciples but also about Jesus. And so he translated *barnash* in two different ways, twice to refer to "humans" in general ("man") and once to refer to Jesus in particular ("the Son of Man)," creating a problem in the Greek that was not there in the Aramaic. The story stems from an Aramaic-speaking community of Christians located in Palestine during the early years of the Jesus movement.

I might add that this business of translating the Greek of the Gospels back into Aramaic has other significant payoffs for those interested in knowing what Jesus really said and did, a matter I will address later in the book once I've established more fully that Jesus almost certainly existed. As it turns out, some sayings of Jesus cannot be translated into Aramaic. Jesus could not have said these things since he spoke Aramaic. Let me give one rather famous example.

In John 3 comes the well-known story of Jesus's conversation with the rabbi Nicodemus. Jesus is in Jerusalem, and Nicodemus comes up to him and tells him that he knows he is a teacher from God. Jesus tells him: "Unless you are born *anothen* you will not be able to enter into the kingdom of God." I have left the key word here in Greek. *Anothen* has two meanings. It can mean "a second time," and it can mean "from above." And so this is the passage in which Jesus instructs his follower that he has to be "born again." At least that's how Nicodemus understands the word because he is shocked and asks how he can possibly crawl back into his mother's womb and be born a second time. But in fact Jesus does not mean "a second time"; he means "from above." This is what the word *anothen* means in the other instances it is used in John's Gospel, and it is what Jesus means by it here, as he then corrects Nicodemus and launches into a lengthy explanation that a person needs to be born from the Spirit who comes from above (the upper realm) if he wants to enter into the kingdom of God.

This is a conversation, in other words, that is rooted in the double meaning of the key word *anothen,* which Nicodemus understands in one way but Jesus means in another. Without that double entendre, the conversation does not flow and does not quite make sense. But here's the key point. Even though the Greek word *anothen* has this double meaning, the double meaning cannot be replicated in Aramaic. The Aramaic word for "from above" does not mean "a second time," and the word for "a second time" does not mean "from above." In other words, this conversation could not have been carried out in Aramaic. But Aramaic was the language Jesus spoke—and the language he certainly would have been speaking in Jerusalem with a leading Jewish rabbi (even if he were able to speak another language, which is doubtful). In other words, the conversation could not have happened as it is reported.

But other traditions in the Gospels certainly do go back to Aramaic originals. This is highly significant. Aramaic Jews in Jesus's native land were telling stories about him well before Paul wrote his letters in the 50s of the Common Era, arguably from within a few years of the traditional date of his death. One reason this matters is that most mythicists want to argue that the since the epistles of the New Testament were written earlier than the Gospels, and since the epistles, especially those of Paul, say little or nothing (it is argued) about the historical Jesus but instead speak only of the mythical Christ who like the pagan gods (again, it is argued) died and rose from the dead, then the earliest records of Christianity do not support the idea that Jesus actually lived; he was only a mythical concept. I will argue that this perspective is wrong on all counts. One major question, as we will see, is whether there was a common mythology of dying and rising gods. Moreover, it stretches credulity to think that such a mythology, if it existed, played any role in the world of Jesus's earliest Jewish followers in Palestine. In addition, there is good reason for thinking that Paul knew full well that there was a historical Jesus, whom he spoke of and actually quoted. Paul did think that this historical person was exalted to the level of divinity, but to Paul he was not a dying-rising god like those discussed among the pagans, if in fact there was such a pagan view at all.

Conclusion

THE EVIDENCE I OFFER in this chapter is not all there is. It is simply one part of the evidence. But it is easy to see why even on its own it has proved to be so convincing to almost every scholar who ever thought about the issue. We are not dealing with just one Gospel that reports what Jesus said and did from sometime near the end of the first century. We have a number of surviving Gospels—I named seven—that are either completely independent of one another or independent in a large number of their traditions. These all attest to the existence of Jesus. Moreover, these independent witnesses corroborate many of the same basic sets of data—for example, that Jesus not only lived but that he was a Jewish teacher who was crucified by the Romans at the instigation of Jewish authorities in Jerusalem. Even more important, these independent witnesses are based on a relatively large number of written predecessors, Gospels that no longer survive but that almost certainly once existed. Some of these earlier written texts have been shown beyond reasonable doubt to date back at least to the 50s of the Common Era. They derive from locations around the Mediterranean and again are independent of one another. If historians prefer lots of witnesses that corroborate one another's claims without showing evidence of collaboration, we have that in relative abundance in the written sources that attest to the existence of the historical Jesus.

But most significant of all, each of these numerous Gospel texts is based on oral traditions that had been in circulation for years among communities of Christians in different parts of the world, all of them attesting to the existence of Jesus. And some of these traditions must have originated in Aramaic-speaking communities of Palestine, probably in the 30s CE, within several years at least of the traditional date of the death of Jesus. The vast network of these traditions, numerically significant, widely dispersed, and largely independent of one another, makes it almost certain that whatever one wants to say about Jesus, at the very least one must say that he existed. Moreover, as we will now see, there is yet more evidence.

CHAPTER FOUR

Evidence for Jesus from Outside the Gospels

LIKE MOST AUTHORS, I receive tons of e-mail. Every now and again I receive a query, normally from a Christian believer, that I find completely puzzling. What is puzzling is my correspondent's puzzlement. Many people simply can't understand why I would teach the Bible in a university setting if I don't believe in the Bible.

I find this puzzling because I am so accustomed to the life of the university, where professors teach all kinds of things they don't "believe in." In most major universities, professors of classics teach the works of Plato, but the professors are not themselves necessarily Platonists, and professors in political science teach the writings of Karl Marx, but they do not have to be Marxists. So too English professors teach great literature even though they themselves are not practicing novelists or poets, and criminologists teach the history of crime, but they aren't mass murderers.

Why should it be different with the Bible? I teach the Bible not because I am personally a believer in the Bible but because, like all these other topics, it is important. In fact, it is unusually important. One could easily argue that the Bible is the most important book in the history of Western civilization. What other book comes even close in terms of its historical, social, and cultural significance? Who wouldn't want to know more about a book that has transformed millions of lives and affected entire civilizations? It is important not only for believers. Far from it. It is important for all of us—at least for all of us interested in human history, society, and culture.

One could argue as well that Jesus is the most important person in the history of the West, looked at from a historical, social, or cultural perspective, quite apart from his religious significance. And so of course the earliest sources of information we have about him, the New Testament Gospels, are supremely important. And not just the Gospels, but all the books of the New Testament.

I have to admit that when I teach my Introduction to the New Testament course to undergraduates, I spend more time on Jesus and the Gospels than on the rest of the New Testament, including the writings of Paul. It is not that Paul is unimportant. Quite the contrary, he too is enormously significant in every way. But given the choice, I personally am more interested in and compelled by the Gospels and Jesus. That is not true of many of my friends who teach New Testament in the colleges, universities, seminaries, and divinity schools throughout North America. A lot of them are completely enamored with Paul and focus all of their research and a good deal of their teaching on Paul. Paul too had a tremendous impact on the West, and in many respects his writings are much more difficult to interpret than the Gospels. Some scholars devote their entire scholarly lives to trying to fathom the teachings of a single one of Paul's letters.

Paul, as we will see in this chapter, is highly relevant for establishing the historical existence of Jesus, as are many other sources outside the Gospels. This chapter will be devoted to this evidence.

We will begin our considerations with later sources and then move
to the testimony of our earliest surviving Christian author, Paul.

Later Sources from Outside the New Testament

AT THE OUTSET I should emphatically state the obvious. Every
single source that mentions Jesus up until the eighteenth century
assumed that he actually existed. That is true no matter what
period you choose to examine: the Reformation, the Renaissance,
the Middle Ages, Late Antiquity, and before. It is true of every
source from our earliest periods, the fourth century, the third century, the second century, and the first century. It is true of every
author of every kind, Christian, Jewish, or pagan. Most striking,
it is true not just of those who came to believe in Jesus but also
of nonbelievers in general and of the opponents of Christianity in
particular. Many scholars have found this significant. Not even
the Jewish and pagan antagonists who attacked Christianity and
Jesus himself entertained the thought that he never existed. This is
quite clear from reading the writings of the Christian apologists,
starting with such authors as the anonymous writer of the Letter
to Diognetus and the more famous writers Justin Martyr, Tertullian, and Origen (all from the second and early third centuries), all
of whom defend Jesus against a number of charges, many of them
scandalous. But they do not drop one hint that anyone claimed
he did not exist. The same is clear from the fragments of writings
that still survive from the opponents of the Christians, such as the
Jew Trypho, discussed by Justin, or the pagan philosopher Celsus,
cited extensively by Origen. The idea that Jesus did not exist is a
modern notion. It has no ancient precedents. It was made up in
the eighteenth century. One might well call it a modern myth, the
myth of the mythical Jesus.

We have already seen that at least seven Gospel accounts of Jesus, all of them entirely or partially independent of one another, survived from within a century of the traditional date of his death. These seven are based on numerous previously existent written sources and on an enormous number of oral traditions about him that can be dated back to Aramaic sources of Palestine, almost certainly from the 30s of the Common Era. If we stay within those same time restrictions, what can we say about sources attested from outside the Gospels?

Non-Christian Sources

We should first return to the writings of Josephus and Tacitus. Tacitus almost certainly had information at his disposal about Jesus, for example, that he was crucified in Judea during the governorship of Pontius Pilate. Josephus appears as well to have known about Jesus, both some major aspects of his life and his death under Pontius Pilate. What I did not stress earlier but need to point out now is that there is absolutely nothing to suggest that the pagan Tacitus or the Jewish Josephus acquired their information about Jesus by reading the Gospels. They heard information about him. That means the information they gave predated their writings. Their informants were no doubt Christians, or—even more likely—(non-Christian) people they knew who themselves had heard stories about Jesus from Christians. It is impossible to know whether these Christians had been influenced by the sources we have already discussed, but it is completely possible that they themselves had simply heard stories about Jesus. Indirectly, then, Tacitus and (possibly) Josephus provide independent attestation to Jesus's existence from outside the Gospels although, as I stated earlier, in doing so they do not give us information that is unavailable in our other sources.

Christian Sources

There are also important independent sources among Christian writers from about the same time as Tacitus, writers who convey information about the historical Jesus and certainly attest to his existence. They do so without deriving all, or even most, of their information from the Gospel sources. Three of these are especially significant.

Papias

Papias was a church father of the early second century whose writings survive for us only in fragments, as they are quoted by later Christian authors.[1] From these later sources we learn that Papias had written a five-volume work called *Expositions of the Sayings of the Lord;* this (very?) large book is normally thought to have been written around 120–130 CE. We do not know for certain why Christian scribes did not copy the book and so preserve it for posterity. But it appears that some of the views that Papias advanced were seen to be offensive or at least naive. The great church historian of the fourth century, Eusebius, dismissed Papias by saying that he was "a man of very small intelligence" (*Church History* 3.39).

   Intelligent or not, Papias is an important source for establishing the historical existence of Jesus. He had read some Gospels although there is no reason to think that he knew the ones that made it into the New Testament, as I will show in a moment. But more important, he had other access to the sayings of Jesus. He was personally acquainted with people who had known either the apostles themselves or their companions. The following quotation of his work, from Eusebius, makes the point emphatically:

   I also will not hesitate to draw up for you, along with these expositions, an orderly account of all the things I carefully

learned and have carefully recalled from the elders; for I have
certified their truth. . . . Whenever someone arrived who
had been a companion of one of the elders, I would carefully
inquire after their words, what Andrew or Peter had said, or
what Philip or what Thomas had said, or James or John or
Matthew or any of the other disciples of the Lord, and what
things Aristion and the elder John, disciples of the Lord, were
saying. For I did not suppose that what came out of books
would benefit me as much as that which came from a living
and abiding voice.[2]

Eusebius summarizes what Papias claimed about his sources of
knowledge about Jesus, a passage worth citing at length:

This Papias, whom we have just been discussing, acknowledges
that he received the words of the apostles from those who
had been their followers, and he indicates that he himself had
listened to Aristion and the elder John. And so he often recalls
them by name, and in his books he sets forth the traditions that
they passed along. These remarks should also be of some use to
us. . . .
    And he sets forth other matters that came to him from
the unwritten tradition, including some bizarre parables of
the Savior, his teachings, and several other more legendary
accounts. . . .
    And in his own book he passes along other accounts of
the sayings of the Lord from Aristion, whom we have already
mentioned, as well as traditions from the elder John. We
have referred knowledgeable readers to these and now feel
constrained to add to these reports already quoted from him
a tradition that he gives about Mark, who wrote the Gospel.
These are his words:
    And this is what the elder used to say,

"When Mark was the interpreter [or translator] of Peter, he wrote down accurately everything that he recalled of the Lord's words and deeds—but not in order. For he neither heard the Lord nor accompanied him; but later, as I indicated, he accompanied Peter, who used to adapt his teachings for the needs at hand, not arranging, as it were, an orderly composition of the Lord's sayings. And so Mark did nothing wrong by writing some of the matters as he remembered them. For he was intent on just one purpose: to leave out nothing that he heard or to include any falsehood among them."

So that is what Papias says about Mark. And this is what he says about Matthew:

"And so Matthew composed the sayings in the Hebrew tongue, and each one interpreted [or translated] them to the best of his ability."

And he set forth another account about a woman who was falsely accused of many sins before the Lord,[3] which is also found in the Gospel according to the Hebrews. . . . [Eusebius, *Church History* 3.39]

This is such a valuable report because Eusebius is quoting, and then commenting on, the actual words of Papias. Papias explicitly states that he had access to people who knew the apostles of Jesus or at least the companions of the apostles (the "elders": it is hard to know from his statement if he is calling the companions of the apostles the elders or if the elders were those who knew the companions. Eusebius thinks it is the first option). When these people would come to his city of Hierapolis in Asia Minor, Papias, as leader of the church, would interview them about what they knew about Jesus and his apostles. Many conservative Christian scholars use this statement to prove that what Papias says is historically accurate (especially about Mark and Matthew), but that is going beyond what the evidence gives us.[4] Still, on one point there can be no doubt.

Papias may pass on some legendary traditions about Jesus, but he is quite specific—and there is no reason to think he is telling a bald-faced lie—that he knows people who knew the apostles (or the apostles' companions). This is not eyewitness testimony to the life of Jesus, but it is getting very close to that.

Where conservative scholars go astray is in thinking that Papias gives us reliable information about the origins of our Gospels of Matthew and Mark. The problem is that even though he "knows" that there was an account of Jesus's life written by Mark and a collection of Jesus's sayings made by Matthew, there is no reason to think that he is referring to the books that *we* call Mark and Matthew. In fact, what he says about these books does not coincide with what we ourselves know about the canonical Gospels. He appears to be referring to other writings, and only later did Christians (wrongly) assume that he was referring to the two books that eventually came to be included in scripture.[5]

This then is testimony that is independent of the Gospels themselves. It is yet one more independent line of testimony among the many we have seen so far. And this time it is a testimony that explicitly and credibly traces its own lineage directly back to the disciples of Jesus themselves.

Ignatius of Antioch

Ignatius was one of the most significant authors of early Christianity from outside the New Testament. He was bishop of the large and important church of Antioch in Syria and was caught up in a persecution of Christians that happened there, probably in 110 CE. The persecution had some kind of official Roman sanction. Ignatius himself was arrested for Christian activities. We do not know the specific charges that were leveled against him, but he was sentenced to be sent to Rome and to be executed in the arena by being thrown to the wild beasts. While he was en route to his martyrdom, he wrote seven letters, which we still have today. Six of these letters are written to churches of Asia Minor that had sent representatives to meet him on his way and provide moral support. One other was written to the Christians of Rome urging them, surprisingly enough, not to interfere in the proceedings against him. Ignatius desperately wanted to die a gory, martyr's death, thinking that then he would be a true imitator of Jesus, who also had been convicted and condemned to a bloody death.

The letters of Ignatius are nothing if not interesting.[6] The ones he wrote to the various churches are filled with exhortations to strive for unity and to follow the leadership of the bishop. Moreover, they attack the views of Christians who in the opinion of Ignatius represent "false opinions," that is, heresies. Some of the letters oppose forms of Christianity that continued to insist on keeping Jewish laws and customs. The ones I am most interested in here, however, are those that oppose Christians who insisted that Jesus was not a real flesh-and-blood human. These opponents of Ignatius were not ancient equivalents of our modern-day mythicists. They certainly did not believe that Jesus had been made up or invented based on the dying and rising gods supposedly worshipped by pagans. For them, Jesus had a real, historical existence. He lived in this world and delivered inspired teachings. But he was God on earth, not made of the same flesh as the rest of us.

Ignatius finds this view repugnant and completely at odds with who Jesus really was, as he states in the most emphatic terms possible in the following passages, once again worth quoting in full. First, from a letter that Ignatius wrote to the Christians in the city of Smyrna:[7]

> For you are fully convinced about our Lord, that he was truly from the family of David according to the flesh, Son of God according to the will and power of God, truly born from a virgin, and baptized by John that all righteousness might be

fulfilled by him. In the time of Pontius Pilate and the tetrarch Herod, he was truly nailed for us in the flesh—we ourselves come from the fruit of his divinely blessed suffering—so that through his resurrection he might eternally lift up the standard for his holy and faithful ones, whether among Jews or Gentiles, in the one body of his church.

For he suffered all these things for our sake, that we might be saved; and he truly suffered, just as he also truly raised himself—not as some unbelievers say, that he suffered only in appearance. They are the ones who are only an appearance; and it will happen to them just as they think, since they are without bodies, like the daimons. For I know and believe that he was in the flesh even after the resurrection. (Ignatius to the Smyrneans 1–2)

From these quotations it is crystal clear what Ignatius thought of the real existence of Jesus. He was fully human; he was really born; he was really baptized; he was really crucified. Even though there are allusions to traditions that made it into the Gospels, there is no conclusive evidence to suggest that Ignatius is basing his views on the books that later became part of the New Testament. The same can be said of his plea to the Christians of the town of Tralles:

And so, be deaf when someone speaks to you apart from Jesus Christ, who was from the race of David and from Mary, who was truly born, both ate and drank, was truly persecuted at the time of Pontius Pilate, was truly crucified and died, while those in heaven and on earth and under the earth looked on. (Ignatius to the Trallians, 9)

Ignatius, then, provides us yet with another independent witness to the life of Jesus. Again, it should not be objected that he is writing too late to be of any value in our quest. He cannot be shown to have been relying on the Gospels. And he was bishop in Antioch, the city where both Peter and Paul spent considerable time in the preceding generation, as Paul himself tells us in Galatians 2. His views too can trace a lineage straight back to apostolic times.

1 Clement

The letter of 1 Clement was written by the Christians in Rome to the church of Corinth in order to straighten out what was to them an unsatisfactory turn of events. The leaders of the Corinthian church had been ousted from power and replaced by others, and the Roman Christians, at least those responsible for the letter, did not like the situation. The letter is meant to urge the church in Corinth to return their "elders" to their rightful place.

It is a long letter filled with warnings against jealousy and the thirst for power. It is attributed by tradition to the fourth bishop of Rome, Clement, even though the letter itself does not claim to be written by him. Clement is never even mentioned in the letter. Be that as it may, there are compelling reasons for thinking that the letter was written sometime during the 90s CE, that is, some twenty years before Ignatius and at about the time some of the later books that made it into the New Testament.[8] The letter quotes extensively from the Greek Old Testament, and its author explicitly refers to Paul's first letter to the Corinthians. But he does not mention the Gospels of the New Testament, and even though he quotes some of the sayings of Jesus, he does not indicate that they come from written texts. In fact, his quotations do not line up in their wording with any of the sayings of Jesus found in our surviving Gospels.

It is all the more impressive that the author of 1 Clement, like Ignatius and then Papias, not only assumes that Jesus lived but that much of his life was well known. Among the many things he says about the historical Jesus are the following:

- Christ spoke words to be heeded (1 Clement 2.1).
- His sufferings were "before your eyes" (2.1).
- The blood of Christ is precious to the Father, poured out for salvation (7.4).
- The blood of the Lord brought redemption (12.7).
- Jesus taught gentleness and patience; the author here quotes a series of Jesus's sayings similar to what can be found in Matthew and Luke (13.1–2).
- The Lord Jesus Christ came humbly, not with arrogance or haughtiness (16.2).
- Jesus came from Jacob "according to the flesh" (32.2).
- The Lord adorned himself with good works (33.7).
- Another quotation of "the words of our Lord Jesus" (46.8, comparable to Matthew 26:24 and Luke 17:2).
- Those who experience love in Christ should do what Christ commanded (49.1).
- Out of his love, the Lord Jesus Christ "gave his blood for us, his flesh for our flesh, his soul for our souls" (49.6).

Here again we have an independent witness not just to the life of Jesus as a historical figure but to some of his teachings and deeds. Like all sources that mention Jesus from outside the New Testament, the author of 1 Clement had no doubt about his real existence and no reason to defend it. Everyone knew he existed. That is true of the writings of the New Testament as well, outside the four Gospels that we have already considered.

Canonical Sources Outside the Gospels and Paul

IT IS A LARGE mistake to think that when it comes to the New Testament, only the Gospels attest to the historical existence of

Jesus. This is sometimes claimed, or at least implied, by mythicists intent on narrowing down our sources for Jesus to just a few—or even to just one, the Gospel of Mark. So far as we can tell, all the authors of the New Testament knew about the historical Jesus. One exception might be the writer of the letter of James, who mentions Jesus only twice in passing (1:1 and 2:1) without saying anything about his earthly life. But even in a letter as short as Jude, we find the apostles of Jesus mentioned (verse 17), which presupposes, of course, that Jesus lived and had followers. The one book that talks at length about these apostles is the book of Acts, which was written by the author of the Gospel of Luke but which preserves traditions about the life of Jesus that are both independent of anything said in the Gospel and, in the judgment of most critical historians, based on traditions in circulation before the production of the Gospel.

The Book of Acts

The Acts of the Apostles provides a narrative of the spread of Christianity throughout the Roman Empire in the years after Jesus's death. Whereas in the Gospel of Luke Jesus is the principal figure, in this, the author's second volume, it is Jesus's followers who take center stage. In particular, the author is interested in the missionary activities of Peter (mainly in chapters 1–12) and Paul (chapters 13–28). In his account he shows how the Christian movement went from being a small group of Jesus's followers immediately after his death to becoming a worldwide phenomenon, a religion that was open not only to Jews like Jesus himself and his disciples but also to Gentiles, as God (according to the narrative) used the apostles to spread the good news of Jesus "to the ends of the earth" (1:18).

Jesus Tradition in Acts

The first important point for our quest to establish the historicity of Jesus is that the author of Acts has access to traditions that are not based on his Gospel account so that we have yet another independent witness. For the writer of Acts, Jesus was very much a man who really lived and died in Judea, as can be seen in the accounts of Jesus's resurrection in chapter 1 and in the speeches that occur abundantly throughout the narrative. Chapter 1 portrays the disciples meeting with Jesus after the resurrection. They receive their final instructions from him in Jerusalem, where he has just been killed. Among the interesting traditions found in this chapter is a statement by the apostle Peter about the betrayer, Judas Iscariot, who is said to have purchased a field with the money he received for turning Jesus in to the authorities. Judas is said to have fallen headlong on the field and spilled his innards out. It is for that reason, Peter indicates, that the field came to be known as "Akeldama," an Aramaic word meaning "Field of Blood" (1:16–19).

One of the reasons this passage is interesting is that in his earlier Gospel account Luke says nothing about the death of Judas. Neither does Mark or John. The most famous account of Judas's death is in the Gospel of Matthew, where we are told that after he performed the foul deed, he repented of what he had done and tried to return the thirty pieces of silver to the chief priests. They refused to take the money, and so he flung it down in the Temple and went out and hanged himself. The priests were unable to put the money into the Temple treasury since it was "blood money" (used to betray innocent blood), and so they used it to buy a field to serve as a cemetery. For that reason the field came to be known as the "Field of Blood" (Matthew 27:3–10).

These two accounts of Judas's death cannot be reconciled. In one Judas buys the field, in the other the priests do; in one it is called the Field of Blood because Judas bled all over it, in the other because it was purchased with blood money; in one Judas dies by hanging himself, in the other he falls headfirst and bursts open in the midst. These differences show that Luke had an independent tradition of the death of Judas, which was at least as early as the one in Matthew. There are reasons for thinking that at the heart of both stories is a historical tradition: independently they confirm that a field in Jerusalem was connected in some way both with the money Judas was paid to betray Jesus and with Judas's death. Moreover, it was known as the Field of Blood. Matthew calls it a "potter's field." Is it possible that it was actually a field of red clay used by potters, and so—because of its color—called the Field of Blood, which in one way or another was connected with the death of Jesus's betrayer?

However one resolves this issue, two points are of particular importance. One is that Matthew and Acts give disparate accounts of the event so that Acts here is an independent tradition. The other is that the Acts account gives clear evidence of being very early and Palestinian in origin: as happens occasionally in the Gospels, here too a key word is left in Aramaic (*Akeldama* means "Field of Blood"), the original language of the story. This is a tradition that goes back to the earliest Christian community in Palestine. Luke is not simply recording traditions from his own day, in the 80s CE; he is recording traditions that—some of them, at least—stemmed from as much as half a century earlier.

Moreover, that Luke has access to sayings of the historical Jesus not recorded otherwise, even in his Gospel, is clear from a passage such as Acts 20:35, where the apostle Paul is recorded as saying, "I have shown you that it is necessary by hard work to help the weak, and to remember the words of the Lord Jesus, that he said 'it is more blessed to give than to receive.'" It is not necessary to think that the historical Paul—the man himself—really said this. What we have here is a narrative by a later author *claiming* that Paul said it. Whether Paul himself really knew this saying of Jesus can be argued. But what is clear is that Luke thinks he knew it and, more important for our considerations, that it is a tradition of a saying of Jesus that has no parallel in any of our Gospels. And so the book of Acts provides further evidence from outside the Gospels that Christians from earliest times believed that Jesus actually lived, as a Jew, that he was a moral teacher, and that he was killed in Jerusalem after being betrayed by one of his own followers, Judas.

The Speeches in Acts

Even more significant for our purposes are the speeches recorded in the book of Acts, placed on the lips of the apostles at key moments of the narrative. About a fourth of Acts is made up of speeches delivered by Peter in the first third of the book and Paul in the final two-thirds. Scholars have long been intrigued by these speeches. We know from ancient historians such as Thucydides that it was customary for historical writers to invent the speeches of their main characters. There really was no other way to present a speech in an ancient biography or ancient history: the authors were almost never there to hear what was actually said on the occasion, and almost never (if ever) did anyone take notes. And so, as Thucydides indicates, historians came up with speeches that seemed appropriate for the occasion.

But the speeches in Acts are particularly notable because they are, in many instances, based not on Luke's fertile imagination but on oral traditions. The reason for thinking so is that portions of these speeches represent theological views that do not mesh well with the views of Luke himself, as these can be ascertained through a careful reading of his two-volume work. In other words, some of the speeches in Acts contain what scholars call preliterary traditions: oral traditions that had been in circulation from much earlier times that are found, now, only in their written forms in Acts. This is important information because, here again, it shows that Acts is not simply a document from the 80s CE. It incorporates much older traditions. And these traditions are quite emphatic that Jesus was a Jewish man who lived, did spectacular deeds, taught, and was executed, as a human, in Jerusalem.

One of the most striking features of several of the speeches in Acts is that they present a view of Jesus that scholars have long thought was one of the oldest, if not the oldest, Christian understanding of what it meant to call Jesus the Son of God. Eventually, of course, Christians came to think that Jesus had always been the Son of God, from eternity past, and that he came into the world only to conduct his miraculous ministry and deliver his supernatural teachings for a short while before returning to heaven whence he came. This is the view that can be found in the last of our Gospels, the Gospel of John. But this was not the earliest view of Jesus. Before anyone thought Jesus preexisted as the divine being who created the world (see John 1:1–18, for example), there were Christians who thought Jesus came into existence when he was born of a virgin and that it was because she was a virgin—and the "father" was God himself—that he was the Son of God.

This view seems to be embodied in the Gospel of Luke itself. Not a single word in Luke mentions Jesus preexisting his life on earth. Instead, his mother conceives of the Holy Spirit, and that is how he comes into being. As the angel Gabriel tells Mary at the Annunciation, informing her of how she will bear a child: "The Holy Spirit will come upon you and the power of the Most High will overshadow you. For that reason the one who is born of you will be called holy, the Son of God" (Luke 1:35). Here Jesus is the Son of God because God made his mother pregnant.

At an even earlier stage of the tradition, before Christians had begun to talk about either Jesus's preexistence or his virginal conception, they (or some of them) believed that he had become the Son of God by being "adopted" by God to be his son. In this view Jesus was not metaphysically or physically the son of God. He was the son of God in a metaphorical sense, through adoption. At one point Christians thought this happened right before he entered into his public ministry. And so they told stories about what happened at the very outset, when he was baptized by John: the heavens opened up, the Spirit of God descended upon him (meaning he didn't have the Spirit before this), and the voice from heaven declared, "You are my son. Today I have begotten you." One should not underplay the significance of the word *today* in this quotation from Psalm 2. It was on the day of his baptism that Jesus became God's son.[9]

There were yet earlier traditions about Jesus that did not speak of him as the Son of God from eternity past or from his miraculous birth or from the time he began his ministry. In these, probably the oldest, Christian traditions, Jesus became the Son of God when God raised him from the dead. It was then that God showered special favor on the man Jesus, exalting him to heaven, and calling him his son, the messiah, the Lord. Even though this view is not precisely that of Paul, it is found in an ancient creed (that is, a preliterary tradition) that Paul quotes at the beginning of his letter to the Romans, where he speaks of Christ as God's "son, who was descended from David according to the flesh and designated Son of God in power according to the Spirit of holiness at his resurrection from the dead" (1:3–4). One reason for thinking that this is an ancient creed—not the formulation of Paul himself—is that Paul holds other ideas about Jesus as the Son of God and expresses them in his own words elsewhere. But he quotes this creed here, probably because he is writing this letter to get on the good side of a group of Christians, the church in Rome, who do not know Paul or what he stands for, and the creed provides a standard formulation found throughout the churches of his day. It is, in other words, a very ancient tradition that predates Paul's writings.

More striking still, a similar tradition can be found in some of the speeches of Acts, showing that these speeches incorporate materials from the traditions about Jesus that existed long before Luke put pen to papyrus. So, for example, in a speech attributed to Paul in

Acts 13 (but not really by Paul; Luke wrote the speech, incorporating earlier materials), Paul is reputed to have said to a group of Jews he was evangelizing, "We proclaim to you that the good news that came to the fathers, this he has brought to fulfillment for us their children by raising Jesus, as is written in the second Psalm, 'You are my son, today I have begotten you'" (Acts 13:32–33).

Note once again the word *today*. It was on the day of the resurrection, according to this primitive tradition that long predated Luke, that Jesus was made the Son of God. A comparable view is found in an earlier speech delivered by the apostle Peter: "Let the entire house of Israel know with certainty, that God has made him both Lord and Christ, this one whom you crucified" (Acts 2:36).

In both of these speeches we have, then, remnants of much older pre-Lukan traditions, older not just than the book of Acts but than any of the Gospels and older in fact than any surviving Christian writing. They embody a certain adoptionist Christology where Jesus is exalted by God and made his son at the resurrection. In both of them Jesus is understood to be purely human and to have been crucified at the instigation of the Jews in Jerusalem. Only then did God adopt him into sonship.

That the speeches of Acts contain very ancient material, much earlier than the Gospels, is significant as well because these speeches are completely unambiguous that Jesus was a mortal who lived on earth and was crucified under Pontius Pilate at Jewish insistence. Consider the following extracts from three of the significant speeches:

> Men of Israel, hear these Words. Jesus the Nazarene, a man
> attested to you by God through miracles and wonders and signs
> that God did through him in your midst, just as you know, this
> one was handed over through the hand of the lawless by the
> appointed will and foreknowledge of God, and you nailed him

up and killed him; but God raised him by loosing the birth
pangs of death. (2:22–24)

God . . . glorified his child Jesus, whom you handed over
and denied before Pilate, who had decided to release him. But
you denied the holy and righteous one and demanded a murderer
to be given over to you. But you killed the Author of life, whom
God raised from the dead, as we are witnesses. (3:13–15)

For those who live in Jerusalem and their leaders . . . when
they found no charge worthy of death, they asked Pilate to
execute him; and when they had fulfilled all the things that
were written about him, they took him down from the tree
and placed him in a tomb. But God raised him from the dead.
(13:27–29)

These primitive traditions from the speeches in Acts are unambiguous about their views of Jesus. They are at least as old as our
earliest surviving Gospel stories about Jesus, and equally important,
they are independent of them. As was the case in the preceding
chapter, here we see that the historical witnesses to Jesus's life simply
multiply the deeper we look into our surviving materials.

The Non-Pauline Epistles

The epistles of the New Testament are chock-full of references to
a human Jesus, who really lived and died by crucifixion. There is
no need to provide a detailed analysis here; I can simply cite some
of the outstanding passages in books that were written by a range of
authors, none of whom knew each other's works or the writings of
the Gospels.

Among the writings that circulated under the name of Paul are
a number that Paul did not actually write.[10] One of them is the letter
of 1 Timothy, which records the tradition known from so many of

our other sources: "I command you before the God who makes all things alive and Christ Jesus, the one who, bearing his testimony before Pontius Pilate made the good confession . . ." (6:13). We do not know who this author was; we only know that he was not Paul and that he shows no evidence of knowing our Gospels. But he confirms one of the central claims of these other works.

Paul was not the only author imitated by later writers. Peter too probably did not write either book that bears his name in the New Testament.[11] It is quite clear that both of these other authors maintained that Jesus was a real, living human being. I begin with several passages from the book known as 1 Peter, which again shows no familiarity with our Gospels:

> For you were called to this end, because Christ suffered for you, leaving an example for you that you might follow in his steps, who did not commit sin, nor was deceit found in his mouth, who when reviled did not revile in return, while suffering uttered no threat, but trusted the one who judges righteously, who bore our sins in his body on the tree, in order that dying to sin we might live to righteousness, for by his wounds we were healed. (2:21–24)
>
> For Christ died for sins once and for all, the righteous for the unrighteous, that he might bring you to God, having put to death in the flesh but made alive in the spirit. (3:18)
>
> Since Christ suffered in the flesh, you also be armed with the same thought. (4:1)
>
> And so I admonish the elders among you, I who am a fellow elder and witness of the sufferings of Christ. . . . (5:1)

The fact that these lines were not really written by Peter are immaterial for my purposes here. Once again we have independent testimony to the life (in the flesh) of Jesus and his very tangible death. More emphatic is 2 Peter, another writing forged in Peter's name, which does not show clear evidence of any familiarity with the Gospels but clearly knows the tradition recorded in them of the experience of Jesus on the Mount of Transfiguration:

> For not by following sophistic myths have we made known to you the power and presence of our Lord Jesus Christ, but we were eyewitnesses of the majesty of that one. For when we received honor and glory from God the Father and the voice was brought to him by the magnificent glory, "this is my beloved Son in whom I am well pleased," we heard this voice that was brought from heaven to him, for we were on the holy mountain. (1:16–18)

Somewhat earlier than 2 Peter, probably sometime near the end of the first century, comes the treatise of 1 John, wrongly attributed in the tradition to Jesus's disciple John the son of Zebedee. The anonymous author of this treatise did not write the Gospel of John, but there are good reasons for thinking that he knew of it and that he lived in the same community that produced the Gospel. In any event, this author too is quite emphatic that when Jesus appeared on earth he was a real human who could be felt, handled, heard, and seen:

> What was from the beginning, what we have heard, what we have seen with our eyes, what we beheld and our hands handled, concerning the world of life. And the life was made manifest, and we saw and we bear witness and proclaim to you the eternal live which was with the Father and has been manifest to us. What we saw and heard we proclaim also to you, that you also may have fellowship with us. And our fellowship is with the Father and with his Son Jesus Christ. (1:1–4)

Even the book of Revelation, with all its bizarre imagery and fantastic apocalyptic views, understands that Jesus was a real historical figure. For this author he was one who "lived" and who "died" (1:18). Like the Gospel of John, but not dependent on it, this book, written by a different author, portrays Jesus as the "lamb who was slain" for salvation (5:6). Quite apart from the theological spin he puts on Jesus's death, the fact that matters for us in this context is that he too provides independent witness to the Christian tradition of a real Jesus.

As my final example I can turn to the letter of the Hebrews, a book that was written anonymously but was eventually accepted into the canon of the New Testament by church fathers who thought, incorrectly, that it had been produced by Paul. The book is not dependent on the letters of Paul and shows no evidence of any familiarity with the Gospels. And yet it contains numerous references to the life of the historical Jesus. The following are simply some of the key passages to consider:

- Jesus appeared in "these last days" (1:2).
- God spoke through him (that is, in his proclamation; 1:2).
- He "made a purification for sins" (that is, he died a bloody death; 1:3).
- He was told by God, "You are my Son, today I have begotten you," and was called "son of God" by the Father (1:5).
- He was the first to proclaim salvation (2:3).
- God bore witness to him and/or his followers through signs, wonders, various miracles, and gifts of the spirit (2:4).
- He tasted death "apart from God" (that is, apart from any divine solace; 2:9).
- He was made perfect by suffering (2:10).
- He partook of flesh and blood (2:14).
- He was like his brothers (the Jews? all people?) in all respects (2:17).
- He was tempted (2:18) in every way but without sin (4:15).
- He was faithful to God (3:2).

- He offered up prayers and loud cries and tears to be saved from death (presumably before his crucifixion; 5:7).
- He learned obedience by suffering (5:8).
- He was crucified (6:5; 12:2).
- He was descended from the tribe of Judah (7:14).
- He taught, about God: "You have not desired or taken pleasure in sacrifices and offerings and burnt offerings and sin offerings" (10:8).
- He said, "I have come to do your will" (10:9).
- He suffered "outside the gate" (that is, outside Jerusalem; 13:12).
- He endured abuse (13:13).

In sum, according to this unknown author, based on oral traditions that he had heard, Jesus was a real man who lived in the past, a flesh-and-blood human being, a Jew from the line of Judah who was tempted like all other people, suffered in obedience to God, and was crucified, dying without any solace that God could have provided. Here again is an independent witness to the life and death of Jesus. Thus we have not only the seven independent Gospel witnesses for knowing that Jesus existed; we have also the speeches of Acts, some of which are rooted in early Palestinian traditions, the narrative of Acts, the epistles of the New Testament, and three church fathers—all of them evidently independent of one another.[12]

The Witness of Paul

THE APOSTLE PAUL IS our earliest surviving Christian author of any kind. Many readers of the Bible assume that the Gospels were the first books of the New Testament to be written since they appear first in the New Testament and discuss the life of Jesus, who obviously started it all. But Paul was writing some years before the Gospels. His first letter (1 Thessalonians) is usually dated to 49 CE; his last (Romans?) to some twelve or thirteen years after that. It is commonly said among mythicists that Paul does not speak about the historical man Jesus and has no understanding of the historical man Jesus. This simply is not true, as an examination of his writings shows full well. Apparently one reason mythicists want to make this claim is precisely that Paul is our earliest available witness, writing within twenty years of the traditional date of Jesus's death. If Paul knew nothing about the historical Jesus, then maybe he did not exist. A second reason for the claim is related: mythicists want to argue that Paul, rather than thinking of Jesus as a human who lived a few years earlier, believed in a kind of mythical Christ, who had no real historical existence but was a divine being pure and simple, like the dying and rising gods allegedly worshipped by pagans. I will be dealing with that view in chapter 7. For now I want to look at the evidence that Paul understood Jesus to be a historical figure, a Jew who lived, taught, and was crucified at the instigation of Jewish opposition.

One way that some mythicists have gotten around the problem that this, our earliest Christian source, refers to the historical Jesus in several places is by claiming that these references to Jesus were not *originally* in Paul's writings but were inserted by later Christian scribes who wanted Paul's readers to *think* that he referred to the historical Jesus. This approach to Paul can be thought of as historical reconstruction based on the principle of convenience. If historical evidence proves inconvenient to one's views, then simply claim that the evidence does not exist, and suddenly you're right.

The Life of Jesus in Paul

The reality is that, convenient or not, Paul speaks about Jesus, assumes that he really lived, that he was a Jewish teacher, and that he died by crucifixion. The following are the major things that Paul says about the life of Jesus.

First, Paul indicates unequivocally that Jesus really was born, as a human, and that in his human existence he was a Jew. This he states in Galatians 4:4: "But when the fullness of time came, God sent his son, born from a woman, born under the law, that he might redeem those who were under the law. . . ." This statement also indicates that Jesus's mission was to Jews, a point borne out in another letter of Paul's, in Romans 15:8: "For I say that Christ became a servant to the circumcised to show the truthfulness of God, in order to confirm the promises given to the patriarchs." This claim that Jesus's ministry was to and for Jews, to fulfill what was promised in the scriptures, hints at one of the most important points Paul makes about Jesus, that he was in fact the Jewish messiah. So firmly rooted in Paul is this belief in Jesus as the messiah that the phrase *Jesus Christ,* which means "Jesus the messiah" (since the Greek word *Christ* is a literal translation of the Hebrew word *messiah*), is exceedingly common in Paul, as is the reversed sequence *Christ Jesus,* and the simple term *Christ* is used as an appellative. In other words, Paul was so convinced that Jesus was the Jewish messiah that he used the term *Christ* (messiah) as one of Jesus's actual names.

That in part is why Paul insisted that Jesus was a physical descendant of David. It was widely thought that the "son of David" would be the future ruler of the Jews; for Paul, that was Jesus. We have already seen the key passage in Romans 1:3–4, where Paul refers to "the gospel concerning his Son, who was descended from David according to the flesh." Jesus, then, was a fleshly being, even if he was God's son, and he was one of David's physical descendants.

When Jesus was born, he naturally came into a family. We have seen that Paul obliquely mentions Jesus's mother when he indicates that he was "born of a woman." In another place he mentions the brothers of Jesus, who after Jesus's death became missionaries along with their wives. This Paul states in 1 Corinthians 9:5, where he is pointing out that he too should have the right to take along a spouse on his missionary journeys but chooses not to do so (because, as he indicated two chapters earlier, he was not married): "Do we not have the right to take along a believing wife as do the other apostles and the brothers of the Lord and Cephas?" It should not be thought here that Paul is referring to "brothers of the Lord" in some kind of spiritual sense, in that in Christ all men are brothers. If that were what he meant, then the rest of the statement would make no sense because it would mean that the apostles themselves and even Cephas (Peter) were not the "spiritual brothers" of the Lord since they are differentiated from those who *are* brothers. And so interpreters are virtually unified in thinking that Paul means Jesus's actual brothers.

We know the names of some of Jesus's brothers from our early Gospel traditions. The Gospel of Mark names them as James, Joses, Judas, and Simon (6:3). It also indicates that Jesus had sisters, though these are not named. As it turns out, in one place Paul also names one of the brothers of Jesus, and it is none other than James, also mentioned by Mark. This is in one of the most disputed passages discussed by mythicists, and I will reserve a full treatment for the next chapter. The comment comes in Galatians 1:18–19, one of those rare autobiographical statements of Paul in which he reflects back on his life and indicates what he did after his conversion: "Then after three years I went up to Jerusalem to consult with Cephas. And I remained with him for fifteen days. I did not see any of the other apostles except James, the brother of the Lord. What I am writing to you, I tell you before God, I am not lying!"

When Paul swears he is not lying, I generally believe him. During those fifteen days he saw Cephas and James and no one else. Here again James cannot simply be a "brother" of Jesus the way any other Christian was since his being a brother is what differentiates him from Cephas, as I will explain yet more fully in the next chapter. At this point it is enough to know that Paul knew that Jesus had brothers and that one of them was James, a personal acquaintance of his.

Paul also appears to know that Jesus had twelve disciples, or perhaps it is better to say that Paul knows of a close-knit group of disciples of Jesus who were called "the twelve." I phrase it this way because some scholars think that what mattered was not the actual number of this group but the symbolic number attached to them. That Paul knew of them is shown by his statement concerning the appearances of Jesus after his resurrection, where he indicates that after Jesus was raised on the third day, "he appeared to Cephas and then to the twelve" (1 Corinthians 15:5). It is not necessary to conclude that Cephas was not one of the twelve himself; Paul may simply be saying that first there was an appearance to Peter and then to the entire group. It is interesting that he calls them "the twelve" in this context since according to both Matthew and the book of Acts the disciple Judas Iscariot, one of this inner circle, had already defected and in fact died (by hanging in Matthew, by falling headlong and bursting in Acts). The fact that Paul speaks of "the twelve" as having seen Jesus at the resurrection means either that he does not know the stories about Judas (as was possibly true of Mark and John as well) or, as I have suggested, that the name "the twelve" was attached to this group as a group, even when one of them was no longer with them.

Paul knows that Jesus was a teacher because he quotes several of his sayings. I will deal with these in a moment. For now it is worth noting that two of the sayings of Jesus that Paul quotes were delivered, he tells us, at the Last Supper on the very night that Jesus was handed over to the authorities to face his fate.

> For I received from the Lord what I also delivered to you, that the Lord Jesus on the night in which he was handed over took bread, and after giving thanks he broke it and said, "This is my body that is given for you. Do this in remembrance of me." Likewise also the cup after supper, saying, "This cup is the new covenant in my blood. Do this, whenever you drink, in remembrance of me." (1 Corinthians 11:22–24)

When Paul says that he "received" this tradition "from the Lord," he appears to mean that somehow—in a revelation?—the truthfulness of the account was confirmed to him by God, or Jesus, himself. But the terminology of "received" and "delivered," as often noted by scholars, is the kind of language commonly used in Jewish circles to refer to traditions that are handed on from one teacher to the next. In this case, we have a tradition about Jesus's Last Supper, which Paul obviously knows about. The scene that he describes is very close to the description of the event in the Gospel of Luke (with some key differences); it is less similar to Matthew and Mark.

One point I will stress in a later chapter is that Paul emphasizes that this event happened "on the night in which he was handed over." Traditionally this phrase is translated as "on the night in which he was betrayed" and is taken to indicate that he is referring to the betrayal of Judas Iscariot. The problem with this translation is that the word Paul uses here does not mean "betray" but "hand over," and he uses it in other passages to refer to what God did when he "handed over" his son to his fate, as in Romans 8:31–32: "If God is for us, who is against us? The one who did not spare his own son, but handed him over for all of us, how will he not with him freely give us all things?" This is the same Greek word: *handed over.*

So Paul probably is not referring to the betrayal of Judas in the passage about the Last Supper in 1 Corinthians 11:22–24. But he is clearly referring to a historical event. It is important to note that he indicates this scene happened at night. This is not some vague mythological reference but a concrete historical one. Paul knows that Jesus had a Last Supper with his disciples in which he predicted his approaching death, the very night he was handed over to the authorities.

Moreover, Paul thinks that Jesus was killed at the instigation of "the Jews." This is indicated in a passage that is much disputed—in this instance, not just among mythicists. In 1 Thessalonians Paul narrates a number of wrongful doings of his Jewish opponents who live in Judea:

> Be imitators, brothers, of the churches of God that are in Judea
> in Christ Jesus, because you yourselves suffer the same things
> by your own fellow citizens as they do by the Jews (or the
> Judeans), who killed both the Lord Jesus and the prophets, and
> persecuted us, and are not pleasing to God and to all people,
> who forbade us from speaking to the Gentiles that they might
> be saved, in order to fill up the full measure of their sins
> always. But wrath has come upon them at last. (1 Thessalonians
> 2:14–16)

It is this last sentence that has caused interpreters problems. What could Paul mean that the wrath of God has finally come upon the Jews (or Judeans)? That would seem to make sense if Paul were writing in the years after the destruction of the city of Jerusalem at the hands of the Romans, that is, after 70 CE. But it seems to make less sense when this letter was actually written, around 49 CE. For that reason a number of scholars have argued that this entire passage has been inserted into 1 Thessalonians and that Paul therefore did not write it. In this view some Christian scribe, copying the letter after the destruction of Jerusalem, added it.

I myself do not agree with this interpretation, for a number of reasons. To begin with, if the only part of the passage that seems truly odd on the pen of Paul is the last sentence, then it would make better sense simply to say that it is this sentence that was added by the hypothetical Christian scribe. There is no reason to doubt the entire passage, just the last few words.

But I do not doubt even these. For one thing, what is the hard evidence that the words were not in the letter of 1 Thessalonians as Paul wrote it? There is none. We do not of course have the original of 1 Thessalonians; we have only later copies made by scribes. But in not a single one of these manuscripts is the line (let alone the paragraph) missing. Every surviving manuscript includes it. If the passage was added sometime after the fall of Jerusalem, say, near the end of the first Christian century or even in the second, when Christians started blaming the fall of Jerusalem on the fact that the Jews had killed Jesus, why is it that none of the manuscripts of 1 Thessalonians that were copied before the insertion was made left any trace on the manuscript record? Why were the older copies not copied *at all?* I think there needs to be better evidence of a scribal insertion before we are certain that it happened. And recall, we are not talking about the entire paragraph but only the last line.

The other point to stress is that Paul did think the wrath of God was already manifesting itself in this world. A key passage is Romans 1:18–32, where Paul states unequivocally, "For the wrath of God is being revealed from heaven on all human ungodliness and unrighteousness, among those who by their unrighteousness suppress the truth." When Paul says that God's wrath is "being revealed," he does not simply mean that it is there to be seen in some ethereal way. He means it is being manifested, powerfully made present. God's wrath is even now being directed against all godless and unrighteous behavior. In this passage in Romans Paul is talking about God's wrath now being directed against pagans who refuse to acknowledge him here at the end of time before Jesus returns from heaven. It would not be at all strange to think that he also thought that God's wrath was being manifest against those Jewish people who also acted in such ungodly and unrighteous ways. And he has a full list of offenses against which God has responded.

In short, I think that Paul originally wrote 1 Thessalonians 2:14–16. He certainly wrote everything up to verse 16. What this means, then, is that Paul believes that it was the Jews (or the Judeans) who were ultimately responsible for killing Jesus, a view shared by the writers of the Gospels as well, even though it does not sit well with those of us today who are outraged by the wicked use to which such views were put in the history of anti-Semitism.

Finally, Paul is quite emphatic throughout his writings that Jesus was crucified. He never mentions Pontius Pilate or the Romans, but he may have had no need to do so. His readers knew full well what he was talking about. Crucifixion was the form of punishment used by Romans and could be used on criminals sentenced by Roman authorities. Jesus's crucifixion is one of Paul's constant themes throughout his letters. One brief summary statement of his view can be found in 1 Corinthians 2:2: "I decided to know nothing among you except Jesus Christ, and him crucified." Or consider 1 Corinthians 15:3–4, a passage that stresses that this teaching about Christ's death was the very core of Paul's message: "For I delivered over to you as of first importance what I also received, that Christ died for our sins in accordance with the scriptures, and that he was buried." I will later stress this latter point. Jesus was not only crucified, he was buried. In other words, he died a human death, by execution, at the hands of the Romans, and he really was dead, as evidenced by his burial.

The Teachings of Jesus in Paul

In addition to these data about Jesus's life and death, Paul mentions on several occasions the teachings he delivered. We have seen two of the sayings of Jesus already from Paul's first letter to the Corinthians (11:22–24). Paul indicates that these words were spoken during Jesus's Last Supper. These sayings are closely paralleled to the words of Jesus recorded years later in Luke's account of the supper (Luke 22:19–20).

Two other sayings of Jesus in the book of 1 Corinthians also find parallels in the Gospel tradition. The first occurs in Paul's instructions about the legitimacy of divorce, where he paraphrases a saying of Jesus in urging believers to remain married; that this is a saying tradition going back to Jesus is shown by the fact that at this point Paul stresses that it is not he who is giving this instruction but that it was already given by the Lord himself: "But to those who are married I give this charge—not I, but the Lord—a woman is not to be separated from her husband (but if she is separated, let her remain unmarried or else be reconciled to her husband), and a man should not divorce his wife."

The statement in the parentheses is widely seen as Paul's own addition to this commandment from Jesus. Editors and translators normally set it off as a separate part of the sentence with parentheses or brackets. The rest is the command that Paul learned from the Lord himself. And as it turns out, there is a close parallel to the command on the lips of Jesus, for example, in the Gospel of Mark: "And [Jesus] said to them, 'Whoever divorces his wife and marries another commits adultery against her; and if she divorces her husband and marries another, she commits adultery'" (Mark 10:11–12).

It has sometimes been argued that Jesus could not have said such a thing since in Palestine in his days a woman was not permitted to divorce her husband, and therefore Paul cannot really be quoting a saying of Jesus (since he never said it). For example, G. A. Wells argues that what we have here in Paul is not a quotation of the historical Jesus but a prophecy from heaven that came to a Christian prophet, which Paul understood, then, as having come "from the Lord."[13] I will deal with that larger claim momentarily. But at this stage I want to emphasize a couple of points about this particular saying. The most important is that there is an enormous difference between saying that some authorities in Roman Palestine did not allow women to divorce and saying that women did not divorce. Recent studies have shown that Jewish women in fact did divorce their husbands in Palestine, whatever the authorities may have thought about it, so Jesus's saying does indeed make perfect sense in its context.[14] He thought the practice was not good, and he too did not want to permit it.

At the same time, whether or not Jesus really gave this teaching is not directly relevant to the question we are asking here, so Wells's objection is immaterial. Mark *thought* Jesus said some such thing, so Paul stays close to what Jesus is alleged to have said. Moreover, Paul indicates that his source for this teaching is not his own wisdom and insight into familial concord but the Lord himself. It looks exceedingly likely that Paul is basing his exhortation on a tradition about divorce that he knows—or thinks he knows—going back to the historical Jesus.

Something similar can be said of yet another instance in 1 Corinthians where Paul appears to refer to a teaching of Jesus. In chapter 9 he addresses the question of whether apostles have the right to be financially supported by others during their missionary efforts. He thinks they have that right even though he himself does not regularly take advantage of it, and he supports his view by appealing to a teaching of Jesus: "For thus the Lord commanded that those who proclaim the Gospel should get their living from the gospel" (1 Corinthians 9:14). It has long been recognized that this command from the Lord is still found in our Gospel traditions, in slightly different forms in Matthew and Luke (that is, it comes from Q). Luke's version is the most apt. Here Jesus is instructing his disciples what to do as they go about spreading the gospel: "Stay in the same house [that you first come to] and eat and drink whatever they provide. For the worker is worthy of his wages" (Luke 10:7).

In both these instances—as with the sayings Paul quotes from the Last Supper tradition—we have close parallels between what Paul says Jesus said (in a quotation or a paraphrase) and what Jesus is recorded elsewhere as having actually said. This makes it clear to most interpreters of Paul that he really does intend here to quote the teachings of Jesus.

There are no other obvious places where Paul quotes Jesus, although scholars have often found traces of Jesus's teachings in Paul.[15] The big question is why Paul does not quote Jesus more often. This is a thorny issue that will require more sustained reflection at the end of this chapter. For now I need simply to stress the most important point: Paul obviously thought Jesus existed, and he occasionally quoted his teachings.

In several other instances Paul indicates that he is echoing a "word" or "commandment of the Lord." This happens in his earliest letter, 1 Thessalonians, where he is discussing the future return of Jesus from heaven, when all the dead will be raised and all living believers will join them in a heavenly reunion with the Lord (1 Thessalonians 4:13–18). In this context Paul states, "For this we say to you by a word of the Lord, that we who are living who are left until the coming of the Lord will certainly not precede those who are asleep. For the Lord himself will descend from heaven with the voice of an archangel and with the trumpet of God; and the dead in Christ will rise first. . . ." For Paul, those who had already died would meet the Lord first, to be immediately followed by those who had not yet died. And he learned this from a "word of the Lord."

As indicated earlier, the mythicist G. A. Wells argues that the sayings of Jesus in Paul's writings were given to him not from the traditions about the teachings of the historical Jesus but from prophecies delivered in Paul's churches, direct revelations from the Lord of heaven. In some instances that may indeed have been the case, and this passage in 1 Thessalonians may be one example of it. The reason for thinking so is that we do not have any record of the historical Jesus saying any such thing about what would happen at his return (though see Matthew 24:3–44). So there are two choices here: either Paul knew of a tradition in which the historical Jesus allegedly did discuss this matter or he learned this teaching through a prophecy in one of his churches.

At the end of the day I think it is impossible to decide between these two options. Jesus no doubt said lots of things—hundreds of things, thousands of things—that are not recorded in the early Gospels. Later many, many other things were attributed to Jesus that he probably did not say (for example, many of the sayings in the Gospel of Thomas and later Gospels). Paul may well have heard of sayings of Jesus, such as the one in 1 Thessalonians, that no longer survive otherwise (whether they are sayings Jesus actually said or not). Or he may have learned this information about the second coming from a prophecy. But here we are in a different category from the other sayings of Jesus in Paul's letters that we considered earlier. When Paul claims that the Lord said something, and we have a record of Jesus saying almost exactly that, it is surely most reasonable to conclude that Paul is referring to something that he believed Jesus actually said.[16]

Provisional Summary: Paul and Jesus

In sum, Paul does indeed show that he knew Jesus existed, and he reveals that he had at least some information about his life. Mythicists as a rule do not accept any of this information as being relevant to the question of whether Paul actually knew or believed there was a historical Jesus. I will give several of their most common arguments in a moment. Before doing so I want to stress several points by way of summary of what we have seen so far about Paul's view of the historical Jesus.

Paul obviously did not write a Gospel about Jesus, and he did not include enormous numbers of traditions about Jesus in his writings. This strikes many readers of the New Testament as odd. Why doesn't Paul tell us more about Jesus? You would think it would matter to him. I will address this question at greater length later, as it is one of the points insisted on by many mythicists, who think that if Paul had known there was a historical Jesus, he would have told us a lot more about him. At this stage I want to emphasize two things. The first is that we have to remember that the writings we have from Paul were letters that he directed to his churches (and to the church of Rome, which he did not found). He is writing these letters to deal with problems that had arisen in them. His letters are not meant to spell out everything that he knew or thought about God, Christ, the Spirit, the church, the human condition, and so forth. He addressed problems that his churches were facing. I myself have written hundreds of letters dealing with religious issues over the past thirty-five years. It would be, oh, so easy to collect seven of these letters and not find a single saying of Jesus quoted or a single reference to anything he is thought to have done or experienced. Does that mean I don't know that Jesus existed?

My second point is that what Paul does tell us makes it very clear that he knew or at least believed that Jesus had lived as a historical person some years earlier. Paul mentions that Jesus was born; that he was a Jew, a direct descendant of King David; that he had brothers, one of them named James; that he had a ministry to Jews; that he had twelve disciples; that he was a teacher; that he anticipated his own death; that he had the Last Supper on the night he was handed over; that he was killed at the instigation of Jews in Judea; and that he died by crucifixion. He also refers on several occasions to Jesus's teachings. Paul certainly knew that Jesus existed, and he knew some things about him.

I should stress in addition that Paul indicates on several occasions that the traditions about Jesus are ones that he himself inherited from those who came before him. This is clearly implied when he says that he "handed over" what he had earlier "received," technical language in antiquity for passing on traditions and teachings among Jewish rabbis. Even where Paul does not state that he is handing on received tradition, there are places where it is clear he is doing so. I have mentioned, for example, Romans 1:3–4, an ancient adoptionistic creed about Jesus that indicates he "became" the son of God only when he was raised from the dead. This creed was not written by Paul: it uses words and phrases not otherwise found in Paul (for example, *spirit of holiness*) and contains concepts otherwise alien to Paul (that Jesus was made the Son of God at the resurrection). He is using, then, an earlier creed that was in circulation before his writing.

Where did Paul get all this received tradition, from whom, and most important, when? Paul himself gives us some hints. He indicates in Galatians 1 that originally, before his conversion, he had been a fierce persecutor of the church of Christ, but then on the basis of some kind of mysterious revelation he came to see that Jesus really was the Son of God, and he converted. After three years, he tells us, he made a trip to Jerusalem, and there he spent fifteen days with Cephas and James. Cephas was one of Jesus's twelve disciples, and James was his brother. I will stress the importance of this fact in the next chapter. For now I simply want to point out that this visit is one of the most likely places where Paul learned all the received traditions that he refers to and even the received traditions that we otherwise suspect are in his writings that he does not name as such. And when would this have been?

Since Paul sometimes provides a time frame ("three years later" or "after fifteen years"), it is possible to put together a rough chronology of Paul's life. To give us a rock-solid start, we can say that Paul must have been converted sometime after the death of Jesus around 30 CE and sometime before 40 CE. The latter date is based on the fact that in 2 Corinthians 11:32 Paul indicates that King Aretas of the Nabateans was determined to prosecute Paul for being a Christian. Aretas died around the year 40. So Paul converted sometime in the 30s CE. When scholars crunch all the numbers that Paul mentions, it appears that he must have converted early in the 30s, say, the year 32 or 33, just two or three years after the death of Jesus.

This means that if Paul went to Jerusalem to visit Cephas and James three years after his conversion, he would have seen them, and received the traditions that he later gives in his letters, around the middle of the decade, say the year 35 or 36. The traditions he inherited, of course, were older than that and so must date to just a couple of years or so after Jesus's death.

All this makes it as clear as day that Jesus was known to have lived and died almost immediately after the traditional date of his death. We do not have to wait for the Gospel of Mark around 70 CE to hear about the historical Jesus, as mythicists are fond of claiming. This evidence from Paul dovetails perfectly with what we found from the Gospel traditions, whose oral sources almost certainly also go all the way back into the 30s to Roman Palestine. Paul too shows that just a few years after Jesus's life his followers were talking about the things he said, did, and experienced as a Jewish teacher in Palestine who was crucified by the Romans at the instigation of the Jewish authorities. This is a powerful confluence of evidence: the sources of the Gospels and the accounts of our earliest Christian author. It is hard to explain this confluence apart from the view that Jesus certainly existed.

Mythicist Counterarguments

Some scholars, as I mentioned, have devoted their lives to studying the life and letters of Paul. I personally know scores of scholars who have spent twenty, thirty, forty, or more years of their lives working to understand Paul. Some of these are fundamentalists, some are theologically moderate Christians, some are extremely liberal Christians, and some are agnostics or atheists. Not one of them, to my knowledge, thinks that Paul did not believe there was a historical Jesus. The evidence is simply too obvious and straightforward. Many mythicists, however, claim that this scholarly consensus is wrong, and they have some interesting arguments to show it. Even though I don't buy them, I think these arguments need to be addressed seriously.

Interpolation Theories

One relatively easy way to get around the testimony of Paul to the historical Jesus is the one I mentioned already. It is to claim that everything Paul says about the man Jesus was not originally in Paul's writings but was inserted instead by later Christian scribes who wanted Paul to say more about the earthly life of their Lord.

As I suggested, this seems to be a "scholarship of convenience," where evidence inconvenient to one's views is discounted as not really existing (even though it does in fact exist). I should stress that the Pauline scholars who have devoted many years of their lives to studying Romans and Galatians and 1 Corinthians are not the ones who argue that Paul never mentioned the details of Jesus's life—that he was born of a woman, as a Jew, and a descendant of David; that he ministered to Jews, had a last meal at night, and delivered several important teachings. It is only the mythicists, who have a vested interest in claiming that Paul did not know of a historical Jesus, who insist that these passages were not originally in Paul's writings. One always needs to consider the source.

Apart from the mythicist desire not to find such passages in Paul, there is no textual evidence that these passages were not originally in Paul (they appear in every single manuscript of Paul that we have) and no solid literary grounds for thinking they were not in Paul. Paul almost certainly wrote them. Moreover, if scribes were so concerned to insert aspects of Jesus's life into Paul's writings, it is passing strange that they were not more thorough in doing so, for example, by inserting comments about Jesus's virgin birth in Bethlehem, his parables, his miracles, his trial before Pilate, and so forth. In the end, it is almost certain that whatever else one thinks about Paul's view of Jesus—and however one explains why Paul himself does not say more—it is safe to say that he knew that Jesus existed and that he knew some fundamentally important things about Jesus's life and death.

The Argument of G. A. Wells

In my judgment a much more interesting argument about Paul's knowledge of the historical Jesus is one that is hammered time and again by G. A. Wells. If Paul knew about the historical Jesus, asks

Wells, why was he silent about almost everything that we hear about Jesus in the surviving Gospels? We hear almost nothing about Jesus's teachings (just three references to them in Paul). Were Jesus's other teachings irrelevant to Paul? If they were relevant, why didn't he mention them? Furthermore, we hear almost nothing about the events of Jesus's life: no descriptions of miracles or exorcisms or raisings of the dead. Were these things unimportant to Paul? We hear almost nothing about the details of Jesus's death: the trip to Jerusalem, the betrayal, the trial before Pontius Pilate, and so on. Did none of this matter to Paul? In Wells's view all of these traditions about Jesus should have been massively important to Paul, and he would have written about them had he known about them. That suggests that Paul in fact did not know about them.

For Wells it is particularly significant that Paul does not quote the sayings of Jesus extensively or refer to his miracles. Surely Jesus's teachings should have mattered, especially when Paul talks about the same issues. For example, Wells points out, Paul indicates that "we do not even know how to pray as we ought" (Romans 8:26).[17] But Jesus actually taught his disciples how to pray when he taught them the Lord's Prayer. If Paul knew anything about Jesus, wouldn't he at least know this? Paul also taught that followers of Jesus ought to be celibate (1 Corinthians 7). Surely if he knew about Jesus, he would know that Jesus too praised those who renounced marriage for the kingdom of heaven (Matthew 19:12). Paul taught that Christ's followers should "bless those who persecute you" (Romans 12:14). Why would he not quote Jesus's Sermon on the Mount to bolster his argument, to show that the injunction is not based simply on his own personal view? With respect to miracles—since, in Wells's words, "The Jews certainly expected that miracles would characterize the Messianic age"—it is almost impossible to understand why Paul would not appeal to a single miracle of Jesus or even mention that he did any if he wanted to authorize his gospel message.

With respect to all the silences of Paul, Wells makes one particularly significant methodological point. It is not simply that Paul does not mention some things about Jesus's life. It is that he does not mention things that would have bolstered precisely the points he was trying to make to his readers. In Wells's words: "Of course silence does not always prove ignorance, and any writer knows a great many things he fails to mention. A writer's silence is significant only if it extends to matters obviously relevant to what he has chosen to discuss."[18] In the end, Wells finds it puzzling that if Paul really thought Jesus lived just a few years earlier, "there is no mention of a Galilean ministry; no mention of Bethlehem, Nazareth, or Galilee; no suggestion that Jesus spoke parables or performed miracles; and no indication that he died in Jerusalem." With respect to the crucifixion, "he might be expected at least to allude to when and where this important event occurred, if that was known to him."[19] The conclusion that Wells draws is that Paul did not know about a Jesus who had lived just a few years before, a Galilean Jewish teacher who was crucified by the Romans under Pontius Pilate.

The Counter to the Counterargument

Wells does seem to make a strong argument, when it is stated baldly. But when examined closely, it falls apart for some compelling reasons. For one thing, when Wells says that Paul would have cited the Lord's Prayer or the command to bless one's persecutors had he known them, he might be right or he might be wrong (as we'll explore more fully below). But even if Paul knew about the historical Jesus, and even if he knew a *lot* about him, there is no reason to think that he therefore must have known these particular sayings of Jesus. Many authors, even those living after Paul, who knew full well that Jesus existed, say nothing about the Lord's Prayer or the injunction to bless those who persecute you. It is striking, for example, that neither of these passages is found in the Gospel of Mark. Did Mark think Jesus existed? Of course he did. Why then did he not include these two important sayings? Either they did not serve his purposes or he had not heard of them, even though he too is interested in both prayer and persecution. (The sayings came to Matthew and Luke from Q.)

Some of the materials that Wells expects Paul to refer to were completely irrelevant to what Paul was writing about and to whom. Take, for example, the claim that Paul would have referred to Jesus's miracles to demonstrate that Jesus was the messiah. It may well be that if Paul were arguing with a group of Jews over whether Jesus was the messiah, he would have mentioned Jesus's miracles. But the seven of Paul's letters that we have were not written to Jews to persuade them to believe in Jesus. Quite the contrary. They were written to congregations of Christians who already believed in Jesus and needed no convincing (and, by the way, the congregations were principally made up of Gentiles, not Jews). Why would Paul have needed to appeal to Jesus's miracles to convince people who already were committed to the cause?

One of the real weaknesses of Wells's argument is that he assumes that we know what Paul *would* have done. Second-guessing someone is always a dangerous historical enterprise, especially second-guessing someone from two thousand years ago whom we don't really know and have limited access to. What real evidence do we have to suggest what Paul would have done?

It bears noting in this connection that Paul's silences are not restricted to the life and teachings of Jesus. He is silent as well about many, many things that we desperately wish he would have talked about since we would like to know a good deal more about all sorts of matters. Think of all the silences of Paul with respect to Paul himself. Where was he from? Who were his parents? What was his education? Who were his teachers? Who were his friends? Who were his enemies? Why doesn't he name any of them? What were his religious activities before converting? What was the "revelation" that made him convert? What did he do during his three years in

Arabia or Damascus before meeting with Cephas in Jerusalem? Or in the following fourteen years? Where did he travel? What was his occupation? Or his daily routine? How did he convert people? Where did he meet them? What did he tell them? What happened once they accepted the gospel? And on and on and on.

There are thousands of things about Paul we would like to know. Why doesn't he tell us any of them? Mainly because he had no occasion to do so. He was writing letters to his churches to deal with their problems, and for the most part he spent his time in these letters addressing the situations at hand. It is important to bear in mind that his audiences were made up entirely of Christian believers. We don't know how much these people already knew—about Paul or, more important, about Jesus. If they were already fully informed about Jesus, then there was no need for Paul to remind them that Jesus walked on water, raised Jairus's daughter from the dead, and was executed in Jerusalem.

Is it then unreasonable that Paul tells us relatively little about Jesus? Why not double-check with other authors? For we have writings produced years after Paul by Christians who certainly believed Jesus existed, and we can see whether in those writings we find references to the words and deeds of Jesus missing from Paul.

An obvious place to turn is to the other books of the New Testament. How many times do 1 Timothy, Hebrews, 1 Peter, and Revelation—all written by authors, as we have seen, who clearly indicate that Jesus existed—talk about Jesus's parables, his miracles, his exorcisms, and so on? Never. Does that mean they don't know about Jesus? No, it probably means that these traditions about Jesus's life were not important to their purposes.

Or consider two even clearer cases, authors who certainly knew of actual Gospels of Jesus that we still have today. As I earlier mentioned, the author of 1, 2, and 3 John was living in the same community out of which the Gospel of John was produced, and he shows clear evidence of actually knowing John's Gospel. And how many times does he quote it in his three letters? None at all. How often does he talk about Jesus's parables, his miracles, his exorcisms, his trip to Jerusalem, his trial before Pilate? Never. Does that mean he doesn't think Jesus lived?

So too with the book of Acts. In this case we are dealing with an author who actually wrote a Gospel, the first volume of his work, the Gospel of Luke. As I earlier indicated, about one-fourth of the book of Acts is dedicated to speeches allegedly delivered by the apostles. And in how many of those speeches do the apostles quote the words of the historical Jesus or at least the words of Jesus found in the Gospel of Luke? Almost never. The clearest quotation of Jesus is the one we considered before, "It is more blessed to give than to receive," a saying that in fact is not even found in the Gospel of Luke. I should stress that these speeches deal with matters that Jesus himself often talked about—persecution, for example, and false teachers—but Jesus's words on the subject are not quoted.

Or take later authors from outside the New Testament. The authors of both 1 Clement (from around 95 CE) and the Epistle of Barnabas (around 135 CE) show clear and compelling evidence that they know about Jesus and understand that he was a real historical figure. They say a number of things about him. But their silences are nearly as large as those of Paul. Just to consider some of the matters mentioned by Wells as "surprisingly" absent from Paul's writings, neither 1 Clement nor Barnabas indicates that Jesus was born in Bethlehem to a virgin, that he came from Nazareth, that he experienced his temptations in the wilderness, that he ever told a parable, that he healed the sick, that he cast out demons, that he underwent a transfiguration, that he got into controversies with Pharisees, that he made a final journey to Jerusalem during the Passover, that he entered into the city riding a donkey, that he cleansed the Temple, that he had the Last Supper, that he went to Gethsemane, that he was betrayed by Judas Iscariot, that he was put on trial first before the high priest Caiaphas and then by the Roman governor Pontius

Pilate, that the Jewish crowds convinced Pilate to release Barabbas instead of Jesus, and so on.

What do these silences show? They do not show that these authors did not know about the historical Jesus, because they clearly did. If anything, the silences simply show that these traditions about Jesus were not relevant to their purposes.

Why then does Paul not say more about the historical Jesus, if he knew more? One point I want to reemphasize. From what Paul does tell us, it is clear that he did indeed know about the historical Jesus. He gives us important information about Jesus's life and quotes his teachings on several occasions. Why then doesn't he quote him more often, and why doesn't he give us more information? This is indeed a perennial question asked by scholars of the New Testament, and several possibilities can be considered.

One, obviously, is that Paul didn't say more about the historical Jesus because he didn't know much more. This strikes many readers of Paul as implausible: if he worshipped Jesus as his Lord, surely he wanted to know more about him. Wouldn't he want to know absolutely everything about him? It may seem so. But it is important to remember that when Christians today think about their faith, they often think about the ultimate source of their faith in the New Testament, which begins with Gospels that describe the things Jesus said and did. And so for Christians today, it only makes sense that a Christian is informed about Jesus's life. But when Paul was writing there were no Gospels. They were written later. It is not clear how important the details of Jesus's life were to Paul.

In this connection it is important to remember what Paul told the Corinthians about what he taught them when he was with them: "For I decided to know nothing among you except Jesus Christ, and him crucified" (1 Corinthians 2:2). It was the death of Jesus and his subsequent resurrection that really mattered to Paul. That is why when Paul summarized the matters of "primary importance" in his preaching (1 Corinthians 15:3–5), it consisted of a very short list:

Christ died in accordance with the scriptures; he was buried; he was raised from the dead in accordance with the scriptures; and he appeared to his followers (then to Paul). Those are the things—not the Sermon on the Mount—that mattered most to Paul.

The deeper question of why Paul would want to focus more on the death and resurrection of Jesus than on his life is intriguing—it has gripped scholars for many years—but it is not germane to the point I am trying to make here. Paul may have known about the teachings of Jesus found in the Sermon on the Mount, or he may not have. We can't know. What we can know is that on occasion he found the teachings of Jesus that he did know about useful to his purposes, and so he cited them. Why he didn't cite them more frequently is a matter of guesswork. Maybe he didn't know many of them. Maybe he didn't think they were all that important. Maybe he assumed his readers knew them already. Maybe in his other letters (the many that have been lost) he quoted them all over the map. We will never know.

What we can know is that Paul certainly thought that Jesus existed. He had clear knowledge of important aspects of Jesus's life—a completely human life, in which he was born as a Jew to a Jewish woman and became a minister to the Jews before they rejected him, leading to his death. He knew some of Jesus's teachings. And he knew how Jesus died, by crucifixion. For whatever reason, that was the most important aspect of Jesus's life: his death. And Paul could scarcely have thought that Jesus died if he hadn't lived.

Conclusion

As a result of our investigations so far, it should be clear that historians do not need to rely on only one source (say, the Gospel of Mark) for knowing whether or not the historical Jesus existed. He is attested clearly by Paul, independently of the Gospels, and in many other sources as well: in the speeches in Acts, which contain material that predate Paul's letters, and later in Hebrews, 1 and 2 Peter, Jude, Revelation, Papias, Ignatius, and 1 Clement. These are ten witnesses that can be added to our seven independent Gospels (either entirely or partially independent), giving us a great variety of sources that broadly corroborate many of the reports about Jesus without evidence of collaboration. And this is not counting all of the oral traditions that were in circulation even before these surviving written accounts. Moreover, the information about Jesus known to Paul appears to go back to the early 30s of the Common Era, as arguably does some of the material in the book of Acts. The information about Jesus in these sources corroborates as well aspects of the Gospel traditions, some of which can also be dated back to the 30s, to Aramaic-speaking Palestine. Together all of these sources combine to make a powerful argument that Jesus was not simply invented but that he existed as a historical person in Palestine. But there is yet more evidence, which we will examine in the following chapter.

CHAPTER FIVE

Two Key Data for the Historicity of Jesus

I SOMETIMES GET ASKED, USUALLY by supporters, why I do not make a practice of responding to scholars and bloggers who criticize my work and attack me personally. It's a good question, and I have several answers. For one thing, there are only so many hours in the day. If I responded to all the crazy things people say, I would have no time for my other work, let alone my life. For another thing, I suppose at the end of the day I simply trust human intelligence. Anyone should be able to see whether a point of view is plausible or absurd, whether a historical claim has merit or is pure fantasy driven by an ideological or theological desire for a certain set of answers to be right.

This past year a group of well-funded conservative Christians (at least one of whom was a former student who did not much like what I taught) launched an impressive website, *The Ehrman Project*. On it

one can find short film clips of (very) conservative evangelical scholars responding to just about everything I have written about, thought
about writing about, or, well, thought. The students in my class that
semester were not sure what to make of the site. I told them that I
thought it was perfectly legitimate, at least in theory. They should
read what I had said in my New Testament textbook or in any of my
other books, listen to what the talking heads on the website had to
say, weigh the evidence for themselves, and then decide.

I believe that better arguments will win out, if people approach
the question without a bias in favor of one view or another. Maybe
I'm too trusting.

As I indicated earlier, once this book gets published I'm afraid
I'll be getting it from all sides. Mythicists who appreciate the fact
that I have made public the scholarly skepticism toward the historical
reliability of the Bible will be upset that I don't side with them when
it comes to the question of the historical Jesus, the one question they
are most invested in. Conservative Christian readers will be glad
that I have taken this particular stand but will still be incensed at
the other things I say about Jesus in this book. Consensus scholarship is like that; it offends people on both ends of the spectrum. But
scholarship needs to proceed on the basis of evidence and argument,
not on the basis of what one would *like* to think. I am always highly
suspicious—completely and powerfully suspicious—of "scholars,"
from one side or another, whose "historical" findings just by chance
happen to confirm what they already think. This occurs, again, on
both sides of the spectrum, from those who breathlessly announce,
"Jesus never existed!" to those who strenuously insist, "Jesus was
physically raised from the dead—and I can *prove* it."

What I think is that Jesus really existed but that the Jesus who
really existed was not the person most Christians today believe in.
I will get to that latter point toward the end of this book. For now
I want to continue to mount the case that whatever else you may

want to say about Jesus, you can say with a high degree of certainty that he was a historical figure. In this chapter I will wrap up my discussion of the historical evidence by stressing just two points in particular. These two points are not the whole case for the historical Jesus. A lot of other evidence that we have already considered leads in precisely the same direction. But these two points are especially key. I think each of them shows beyond a shadow of reasonable doubt that Jesus must have existed as a Palestinian Jew who was crucified by the Romans. The first point reverts to Paul, but now we look not at what Paul said about Jesus but at whom Paul knew. Paul was personally acquainted with Jesus's closest disciple, Peter, and Jesus's own brother, James.

Paul's Associations

IT IS IMPORTANT TO begin by recalling a couple of important events in the chronology of Paul's life. As I pointed out earlier, it appears that Paul converted to be a follower of Jesus sometime around 32 or 33 CE, assuming that Jesus died around the year 30. In one of his rare autobiographical passages, Paul indicates that just a few years after his conversion he went to Jerusalem and met face-to-face with two significant figures in the early Christian movement: "Then after three years I went up to Jerusalem to consult with Cephas. And I remained with him for fifteen days. I did not see any of the other apostles except James, the brother of the Lord. What I am writing to you, I tell you before God, I am not lying!" (Galatians 1:18–20)

Cephas was, of course, Simon Peter (see John 1:42), Jesus's closest disciple.[1] James, Paul tells us, was the Lord's brother. These are two good people to know if you want to know anything about the historical Jesus. I wish I knew them.

The Disciple Peter

Peter was not simply a member of the twelve—the disciples who, according to all our Gospel traditions, Jesus chose to be his closest companions (in the final chapters I will show why this tradition is almost certainly historically accurate). He was a member of an even closer inner circle made up of Peter, James, and John. In the Gospels these three spend more time with Jesus than anyone else does during his entire ministry. And of these three, it is Peter, again according to all our traditions, who was the closest. In nearly all our sources Peter was Jesus's most intimate companion and confidant for his entire public ministry after his baptism.

In about the year 36, Paul went to Jerusalem to confer with Peter (Galatians 1:18–20). Paul spent fifteen days there. He may not have gone only or even principally to get a rundown on what Jesus said and did during his public ministry. It is plausible, in fact, that Paul wanted to strategize with Peter, as the leader (or one of the leaders) among the Jerusalem Christians, about Paul's own missionary activities, not among the Jews (Peter's concern) but among the Gentiles (Paul's). This was the reason stated for Paul's second visit to see Peter and the others fourteen years later, according to Galatians 2:1–10. But it defies belief that Paul would have spent over two weeks with Jesus's closest companion and not learned something about him—for example, that he lived.

Even more telling is the much-noted fact that Paul claims that he met with, and therefore personally knew, Jesus's own brother James. It is true that Paul calls him the "brother of the Lord," not "the brother of Jesus." But that means very little since Paul typically calls Jesus the Lord and rarely uses the name Jesus (without adding "Christ" or other titles).[2] And so in the letter to the Galatians Paul states as clearly as possible that he knew Jesus's brother. Can we get any closer to an eyewitness report than this? The fact that Paul knew Jesus's closest disciple and his own brother throws a real monkey wrench into the mythicist view that Jesus never lived.

The Brothers of Jesus

I need to say something further about the brothers of Jesus. I pointed out in an earlier chapter that Paul knows that "the brothers of the Lord" were engaged in Christian missionary activities (1 Corinthians 9:5), and we saw there that Paul could not be using the term *brothers* in some kind of loose, spiritual sense (we're all brothers and sisters, or all believers are "brothers" in Christ). Paul does frequently use the term *brothers* in this metaphorical way when addressing the members of his congregations. But when he speaks of "the brothers of the Lord" in 1 Corinthians 9:5, he is differentiating them both from himself and from Cephas. That would make no sense if he meant the term loosely to mean "believers in Jesus" since he and Cephas too would be in that broader category. And so he means something specific, not something general, about these missionaries. They are Jesus's actual brothers, who along with Cephas and Paul were engaged in missionary activities.

The same logic applies to what Paul has to say in Galatians 1:18–19. When he says that along with Cephas, the only apostle he saw was "James, the brother of the Lord," he could not mean the term *brother* in a loose generic sense to mean "believer." Cephas was also a believer, and so were the other apostles. And so he must mean it in the specific sense. This is Jesus's actual brother.

As a side note I should point out that the Roman Catholic Church has insisted for many centuries that Jesus did not actually have brothers. That does not mean that the church denied that James and the other brothers of Jesus existed or that they were unusually closely related to Jesus. But in the Roman Catholic view, Jesus's brothers were not related to Jesus by blood because they were not the children of his mother, Mary. The reasons the Catholic Church claimed this, however, were not historical or based on a close examination of the New Testament texts. Instead, the reasoning involved a peculiar doctrine that had developed in the Catholic Church dating all the way back to the fourth Christian century. In traditional Catholic dogma Mary, the mother of Jesus, was a virgin not simply when Jesus was born but throughout the rest of her life as well. This is the doctrine of the perpetual virginity of Mary.

In no small measure this doctrine is rooted in the view that sexual relations necessarily involve sinful activities. Mary, however, according to Catholic doctrine, did not have a sinful nature. She could not have had; otherwise she would have passed it along to Jesus when he was born. She herself was conceived without the stain of original sin: the doctrine of the immaculate conception. And since she did not have a sinful nature, she was not involved in any sinful activities, including sex. That is why, at the end of her life, rather than dying, Mary was taken up into heaven. This is the doctrine of the assumption of the virgin.

Protestants have long claimed that none of these doctrines about Mary is actually rooted in scripture, and from a historian's point of view, I have to say that I think they are right. These are theological views driven by theological concerns that have nothing to do with the earliest traditions about Jesus and his family. But if, for Roman Catholics, Mary was a perpetual virgin and never had sex, who exactly were the so-called brothers of Jesus?

Catholic thinkers developed two views of the matter, one of which became standard. In the older of the two views, the "brothers" of Jesus were the sons of Joseph from a previous marriage. This made them, in effect, Jesus's stepbrothers. This view can be found in later apocryphal stories about Jesus's birth, where we are told that Joseph was a very old man when he became betrothed to Mary. Presumably that is one of the reasons they never had sex; Joseph was too old. This perspective continued to exert its influence on Catholic thinkers for centuries. You may have noticed that in all those medieval paintings of Jesus's nativity, Joseph is portrayed as quite elderly, as opposed to Mary, who is in the blossom of youth. This is why. I should stress that even if this view were historically right—there is not single piece of reliable evidence for it—James still would have been unusually closely related to Jesus.

Eventually this view came to be displaced, however, and in no small measure because of the powerful influence of the fourth-century church father Jerome. Jerome was an ascetic, among other things, denying himself the pleasures of sex. He thought that the superior form of Christian life for everyone involved asceticism. But surely he was no more ascetic than the close relatives of Jesus. For Jerome, this means that not only Jesus's mother but also his father (who was not really his father, except by adoption) were ascetics as well. Even Joseph never had sex. But that obviously means he could not have children from a previous marriage, and so the brothers of Jesus were not related to Joseph. They were Jesus's cousins.

The main problem with this view is that when the New Testament talks about Jesus's brothers, it uses the Greek word that literally refers to a male sibling. There is a different Greek word for cousin. This other word is not used of James and the others. A plain and straightforward reading of the texts in the Gospels and in Paul leads to an unambiguous result: these "brothers" of Jesus were his actual siblings. Since neither Mark (which first mentions Jesus having four brothers and several sisters; 6:3) nor Paul gives any indication at all of knowing anything about Jesus being born of a virgin, the most natural assumption is that they both thought that Jesus's parents were his real parents. They had sexual relations, and Jesus was born. And then (later?) came other children to the happy couple. And so Jesus's brothers were his actual brothers.

Paul knows one of these brothers personally. It is hard to get much closer to the historical Jesus than that. If Jesus never lived, you would think that his brother would know about it.

Mythicist Views of James

Mythicists have long realized that the fact that Paul knew Jesus's brother creates enormous problems for their view, that in fact the otherwise convincing (to them) case against Jesus's existence is more or less sunk by the fact that Paul was acquainted with his blood relations. And so they have tried, with some futility in my view, to explain away Paul's statements so that even though he called James the brother of the Lord, he didn't really mean it that way. The most recent attempt to resolve the problem is in mythicist Robert Price's comprehensive study, where he cites three possible explanations for how James may not actually be Jesus's brother. Price has the honesty to admit that if these explanations "end up sounding like text-twisting harmonizations, we must say so and reject them."[3] In the end he doesn't say so, and he doesn't reject them. But he doesn't embrace any of them either, which at least must leave his readers puzzled.

One explanation has been most forcefully argued by G. A. Wells, who revives a theory floated without much success by J. M. Robertson back in 1927.[4] According to Wells, there was a small fraternity of messianic Jews in Jerusalem who called themselves "the brothers of the Lord." James was a member of this missionary group. And that is why he can be called "the brother of the Lord." Wells likens it to the situation that Paul refers to in the city of Corinth, where he calls himself the "father" of the community (1 Corinthians 4:15) and where some of the members of the congregation claim that they are "of Christ" (1 Corinthians 1:11–13). As Wells concludes, "Now if there was a Corinthian group called 'those of the Christ,' there could also have been a Jerusalem one called 'the brethren of the Lord,' who would not necessarily have had any more personal experience of Jesus than Paul himself. And James, as 'the brother of the Lord' could have been the leader of the group."[5] Wells cites as well Matthew 28:9–10 and John 20:17, where Jesus speaks of his unrelated followers as his "brothers."

This view sounds reasonable enough until it is examined in greater detail. The first thing to point out is that the final two Gospel passages that Wells cites are irrelevant. They do not refer to a distinct group of people who are zealous missionaries; they refer to the twelve disciples of Jesus, pure and simple. But Wells does not think that James (or anyone else) was a member of that group because he does not think Jesus lived in the recent past and even had disciples. And so the Gospel references to the disciples as Jesus's brothers does not support Wells's claim that there was a select missionary group in Jerusalem that included James.

Neither does it work to claim that there was an analogous situation in the church in Corinth. Paul thinks of himself as the "father" of the entire church of Corinth, not of a specific group within it. Even more important, and contrary to what Wells asserts, we decidedly do not know of a group that called themselves "Those of the Christ." There were, to be sure, Christians who said their ultimate allegiance was to Christ (not to Paul or Cephas or Apollos). But we have no idea what they called themselves because Paul never tells us. They are not, then, a named group comparable to what Wells imagines as being in Jerusalem, headed by James.

And what evidence does Wells cite for such a group of zealous messianic Jews in Jerusalem that separated themselves off from all the other Jerusalem Christians? None. At all. What evidence could there be? No such group is mentioned in any surviving source of any kind whatsoever. Wells (or his predecessor, Robinson) made it up.

And there is a good reason for thinking that such a group did not in fact exist. Throughout our traditions Cephas and James are portrayed as being completely aligned with each other. They are both Jews, believers in the resurrection of Jesus, residing in Jerusalem, working for the same ends, participating in the same meetings, actively leading the home church together. Cephas, moreover, is a missionary sent out from this church. If there was a group called "the brothers of the Lord," made up of zealous Jewish missionaries in Jerusalem, Cephas himself would certainly be a member. Why is James, then, the one called "the brother of the Lord," precisely to differentiate him from Cephas?

Since there is no evidence to support the idea that such a group existed, this explanation seems to be grasping at straws. It is important to review what we know. We have several traditions that Jesus actually had brothers (it is independently affirmed in Mark, John, Paul, and Josephus). In multiple independent sources one of these brothers is named James. So too Paul speaks of James as his Lord's brother. Surely the most obvious, straightforward, and compelling interpretation is the one held by every scholar of Galatians that, so far as I know, walks the planet. Paul is referring to Jesus's own brother.

Price puts forward a different way to interpret Paul's words so as not to concede that the James that Paul knew was actually related to Jesus. In this second view (which, I need to add, stands at odds with the first), James is said to be the brother of the Lord because he reflected on earth so well the views of Jesus in heaven that he was his virtual twin. For evidence, Price appeals to several apocryphal books from outside the New Testament, including the famous Acts of Thomas. This is the second-century account of the missionary endeavors of the apostle Thomas after Jesus's resurrection, most famous for its stories of how Thomas was the first to bring the gospel to India. In this account Thomas is called the "twin" of Jesus. And why is he Jesus's twin? For Price it is because Thomas, better than any of the other disciples, has a true understanding of who Jesus is, as indicated in yet another apocryphal book, the Gospel of Thomas (Gospel of Thomas 13). In addition, Price notes several apocryphal works that deal with James of Jerusalem, which also call him Jesus's brother. Price argues that this is because of his particularly close ties to Jesus and his clear understanding of Jesus and his teaching.

This last piece of evidence shows where Price's argument unravels. The reason James is called Jesus's brother in these other apocryphal works is that it was widely believed in early Christianity that James was in fact his brother. These texts say nothing, not a thing, to counteract that view. They simply assume a sibling relationship.

So too with the Acts of Thomas. The whole point of the narrative of this intriguing book is precisely that Thomas really is Jesus's brother. In fact, he is his twin. Not only that: he is his identical twin. This is not because he uniquely agrees with Jesus or understands him particularly well. Quite the contrary, the very first episode of the book shows that Thomas does not agree with Jesus and does not see eye to eye with him in the least. After Jesus's resurrection, the other apostles instruct Thomas to go to India to convert the pagans, and he refuses to go. It is only when Jesus appears from heaven that he forces his twin brother to proceed against his wishes. It is only in a different book, the Gospel of Thomas, that Thomas is said to understand Jesus better than any of the others. But strikingly, the Gospel of Thomas decidedly does not say that, for that reason, Thomas was Jesus's brother, let alone his twin.

The reality is that there was a tradition in some parts of the early church that Thomas really was the twin of Jesus. The Aramaic word *Thomas,* itself, means "twin." That Jesus and Thomas were identical twins plays a key role in the Acts of Thomas, in one of its most amusing episodes. While Thomas is en route (reluctantly) to India, his ship stops in a major port city, where the king's daughter is about to celebrate her marriage to a local aristocrat. Thomas as an outside guest is invited to the wedding, and after the ceremony he speaks to the wedded couple but in a highly unusual way. As a good ascetic Christian, Thomas believes that sex is sinful and that to be fully right with God, people—even married people—need to abstain. And so he tries to convince the king's daughter and her new husband not to consummate their marriage that night.

But he is frustratingly unsuccessful in his pleas. He leaves the scene, and the newlyweds enter their bridal chamber. But to their great surprise, there is Thomas again, sitting on their bed. Or at least they think it's Thomas since he does, after all, look exactly like the man they were just talking with. But it is not Thomas. It is his identical twin, Jesus, come down from heaven to finish the task that his brother had unsuccessfully begun. Jesus, more powerfully persuasive of course than his twin, wins the hearts of the newlyweds, who spend the night in conversation instead of conjugal embrace.

This tale is predicated on the view that Thomas and Jesus really were twins in a physical, not symbolic or spiritual, sense.

One wonders how the Christians who told such stories could possibly imagine that Jesus had a twin brother. Wasn't his mother a virgin? Then where did the twin come from?

None of our sources indicates an answer to that question, but I think a solution can come from the mythologies that were popular in the period. We have several myths about divine men who were born of the union of a god and a mortal. In some of those stories the mortal woman is also impregnated by her husband, leading to the birth of twins (it is hard to know how they could be identical twins, but anatomy was not the strong suit of most ancient storytellers). This in fact is how the divine man Heracles is born. His mother, Alcmene, is ravished by the king of the gods, Zeus, and afterward she is also made pregnant by her husband, Amphitryon. And so she bears twins, the immortal Zeus and the mortal Iphicles.

Is it possible that the Christians who told stories of Jesus and his twin brother, Thomas, had a similar idea—that Jesus was conceived while Mary was a virgin, but then her husband also slept with her so that two sons were born? We will never know if they thought this, but it at least is a viable possibility. What does not seem viable, given what the stories about Thomas and Jesus actually say, is that they were unrelated. On the contrary, for these stories they were actual twin brothers.

Price claims that his view that a mortal could be a special "brother" of Jesus because he so well reflected his views is supported by a range of the Apocryphal Acts.[6] He does not cite any of the others, however, only texts that deal with Thomas and James, the two figures in the early church best known precisely for being Jesus's actual brothers. But as a clinching argument, Price appeals to the nineteenth-century revolutionary leader in China, the so-called Taiping messiah named Hong Xiuquan, who called himself "the Little Brother of Jesus." Price says this figure provides compelling evidence of his view. In his words, "I find the possible parallel to the case of Hong Xiuquan to be, almost by itself, proof that James' being the Lord's brother need not prove a recent historical Jesus." That is, since Hong Xiuquan was not really Jesus's brother, the same could be true of James.[7]

Now we are really grasping at straws. A nineteenth-century man from China is evidence of what someone living in the 30s CE in Palestine thought about himself? Hong Xiuquan lived eighteen hundred years later, in a different part of the world, in a different social and cultural context. He was the heir of eighteen centuries' worth of Christian tradition. He has nothing to do with the historical Jesus or the historical James. To use his case to clinch the argument is an enormous stretch, even by Price's standards.

Price suggests a third alternative to interpreting "James the brother of the Lord" so as not to require that he was Jesus's actual sibling. This final view is not worked out as clearly as the other two. Sometimes, Price points out, a person named in the Bible embodies the characteristics of a larger group. And so in the book of Genesis the patriarch Jacob is renamed Israel, and in fact he becomes the father of the tribes of Israel; Ishmael is the father of the Ishmaelites; Benjamin represents the southern tribe of Israel, called Benjamin, and so forth. For Price, these are all fictional characters, and he claims that it could be similar with James. He was the head of a group that came to identify with Jesus. This was a sect within Judaism that, Price suggests, was in fact the community that produced the Dead Sea Scrolls. In order to stress the importance of their group and the closeness of their ties to Jesus, they much later came to claim that James was in fact the brother of the Lord. In fact, for Price he was a high priest of the Dead Sea Scroll community.

This view of who James really was, Price contends, explains "the otherwise puzzling rivalry between partisans of the Twelve and those of the Pillars (led by James)."[8]

Now we are getting even more wildly speculative. There are compelling reasons for thinking that the Dead Sea Scroll community had no direct ties to later Christian groups and for thinking that the historical James had no connections with the Dead Sea Scroll community, let alone that he was a high priest.[9] What ancient sources ever say any such thing? None at all. The sources that mention the Christian James, such as Paul, the book of Acts, and the later Christian books known as the Pseudo-Clementine writings, are unified in portraying him as the head of the church in Jerusalem from its early days; most of them (along with Mark and Josephus) indicate that he was Jesus's actual brother. He is not at all like Israel, Ishmael, or Benjamin. These were understood to be the *fathers* of the tribes or groups that descended from them and to have been related to them by blood. No one thinks that James's group in Jerusalem was made up of his children and grandchildren. Price does not cite any analogies for what he understands to be the reasons for calling James the "brother of the Lord" as the head of a special group in Jerusalem. And he is certainly wrong to claim that this theory explains any rivalry between the "twelve" and the "pillars." This latter term is used by Paul in Galatians to indicate the leaders of the Jerusalem church, Peter, James, and John—two of the three were members of the twelve. It is hard to know how these groups were in such rivalry. Unless, of course, Peter and John were just internally conflicted.

Price again is honest in his conclusion in saying that "we must guard against . . . a hell-bent adherence to a hobbyhorse of a theory" in order to explain away Paul's references to James as the brother of the Lord. But that is precisely what he appears to be doing. Paul came to know James around 35–36 CE, just a few years after the traditional date of Jesus's death. He calls him the brother of the Lord. In other traditions that long predate our Gospels it is stated that Jesus had actual brothers and that one of them was named James. Josephus too names James as a brother of Christ. Jesus, then, appears to have had a brother named James. And Paul personally knew him, starting in the mid-30s CE. Once again we are driven back to a time very near when Jesus must have lived. Surely James, his own brother, would know if he lived.

The Crucified Messiah

As I INDICATED AT the outset, I am devoting this chapter to two pieces of evidence that argue with particular cogency that there must have been a historical figure of Jesus. There is a good deal of other evidence that has proved compelling to just about everyone who has ever considered it with a dispassionate eye, wanting simply to know what happened in the past, wherever the evidence leads. But these two points are especially compelling. And they are not dependent on one another but are completely separate. The first had to do with whom Paul knew: Jesus's closest disciple, Peter, and his blood brother James, sometime companions of Paul from the mid-30s CE in Palestine. The second has to do, by contrast, with what Paul knew even earlier. And not with just what Paul knew but with what everyone among the early followers of Jesus knew. These early Christians from day one believed that Jesus was the messiah. But they knew that he had been crucified.

For reasons that may not seem self-evident at first, claiming that Jesus was crucified is a powerful argument that Jesus actually lived. It is important to begin by recalling an element from the chronology of Paul's life. According to both the book of Acts and the narrative that Paul himself provides in his letters (Galatians 1), before Paul came

to believe in Jesus he had been a violent persecutor of Jesus's followers. Since he converted around 32 or 33 CE, his persecution activities
would have taken place earlier in the 30s.

As a zealous Jew persecuting Christians, Paul himself says that
he was intent on "destroying" the "church of God" (Galatians
1:13). Obviously the followers of Jesus were saying things, or at least
something, that Paul considered both colossally wrong and dangerous. Unfortunately, Paul never tells us what that something was, but
it is not hard to figure out once one knows Paul's later teachings and
the standard Jewish expectations of the messiah.

Before detailing these, let me stress that Paul necessarily had
close, personal contact with the people he was persecuting, on one
level or another, and what little he knew about Jesus at the outset of
his outrage (in say 31–32 CE or so) would have been augmented by
these contacts. These people themselves would have come to know
what they knew about Jesus before Paul persecuted them. And so
we can say with virtual certainty that there were Christians with
information about Jesus from within a year or two, at the very latest,
of the traditional date of his death and that Paul knew at least something about what these people were saying about Jesus.

As we will see in greater detail in a later chapter, these Christians were not calling Jesus a dying-rising God. They were calling
him the Jewish messiah. And they understood this messiah to be
completely human, a person chosen by God to mediate his will
on earth. That is the Jesus Paul first heard of. But there was nothing blasphemous about calling a Jewish teacher the messiah. That
happened on and off throughout the history of Judaism, and it still
happens in our day. In itself the claim that someone is the messiah is
not blasphemous or, necessarily, problematic (though it may strike
outsiders—and usually does—as a bit crazed). What Paul appears to
have found offensive was that Jesus in particular was being called the
messiah. The reason that was offensive is that Paul and everyone else

knew that Jesus had been condemned to death by crucifixion. Jesus could scarcely then have been the messiah of God, for reasons that Paul would have found altogether compelling before changing his mind and becoming a follower of Jesus.

First it is necessary to see that Paul himself hints at the problem in his letter to the Galatians, which he wrote much later in his life, long after his conversion and early missionary work. In a particularly poignant passage in Galatians, Paul quotes a passage of scripture that must have been important to him even in his pre-Christian days, Deuteronomy 21:23: "Everyone who hangs on a tree is cursed." In its original context in Deuteronomy, this is referring to the practice of hanging a human corpse on a tree as a public statement of shame and humiliation. Centuries later, when Romans were executing the most heinous criminals and lowlifes by crucifying them, this verse was taken to be equally applicable. Obviously anyone who was killed in this way stood under God's curse.

Jesus too was crucified, as everyone knew—or at least said. And that was probably what led Paul, in the early 30s, to decide to persecute the Christians. They were saying that Jesus was God's special chosen one, his beloved son, the messiah. But for the pre-Christian Paul it was quite clear: Jesus was not anything like God's chosen one, the one selected to do his will on earth. Jesus did not enjoy God's blessing. Just the opposite: he was under God's curse. Evidence? He was hung on a tree.

But why would that be a problem? Wasn't the messiah *supposed* to suffer horribly for the sins of others and be raised from the dead? Not according to ancient Jews. On the contrary, the messiah was not supposed to be killed at all. It is at this point that we need to consider what ancient Jews, including the pre-Christian Paul, thought about the messiah.

Ancient Views of the Messiah

The first thing to state, and to state emphatically, is that no Jew ever thought the messiah would be God. The only reason this point has to be raised is that today many Christians appear to think that this is what the messiah was supposed to be, God the savior come to earth. But this is not and never was a Jewish view. It is a Christian view only because Christians have always called Jesus the messiah and most Christians, still today, consider Jesus God. If Jesus is the messiah, the unspoken assumption goes, and if Jesus is God, then the messiah must be God. But this is Christian theology with no support in ancient Jewish thinking. The messiah was not God. He was one appointed by God or sent by God. There is only one God, and the messiah is the one God has "anointed" to be his special representative and to do his special work.

The word *messiah* is Hebrew and means "anointed one." As I pointed out earlier, the Greek translation of the term is *christos* so that *Jesus Christ* literally means "Jesus the Messiah." The origin of the term goes back into the ancient history of Israel, to the time when the nation was ruled by kings, who were said to have been specially favored, "anointed," by God. In fact, the king was literally anointed during his inauguration ceremonies, when oil was poured on his head as a way of showing that he was specially favored by God, as seen in such passages as 1 Samuel 10:1 and 2 Samuel 23:1. Other persons thought to be God's special representatives on earth, such as high priests, were sometimes anointed as well (see Leviticus 4:3, 5, 16). Even outside the Hebrew Bible, in the Jewish tradition we have records of such anointing ceremonies showing that a person stood under God's special favor (for example, 2 Maccabees 1:10; the Testament of Reuben 6:8). In fact, any leader who was specially used by God could be called his anointed one; even the Persian king Cyrus, who was one of Israel's conquerors, was said by the prophet

Isaiah to have been God's instrument, and is explicitly called his "messiah" (anointed one; Isaiah 45:1).

Most commonly, however, the term was applied to the king of Israel. Within the ancient Israelite traditions there developed the notion that God would always favor the nation by constantly ruling them through his chosen king. A prophecy was given to Israel's greatest king, David, in 2 Samuel 7:11–14, that he would always have a descendant on the throne—that in perpetuity an anointed one would rule the nation. That promise, however, did not come to fruition. In the year 586 BCE, the Babylonian armies under King Nebuchadnezzar invaded the land of Judah, destroyed the city of Jerusalem, burned the Jewish Temple, and removed the king from the throne. For the next several centuries the Jewish people were ruled by foreign powers: the Babylonians, the Persians, the Greeks, then the Syrians.

Some Jewish thinkers, however, recalled the original promise to David that an anointed one, a messiah, would always sit on the throne, and they came to think that the promise would be fulfilled in days to come. In some future time, possibly soon, God would remember his promise and bring a future king like David to rule his people. This future ruler was naturally enough referred to simply as the "messiah." He would be a human, like David, Solomon, and the other kings. But he would be raised up by God to overthrow the enemies of the Jews and establish Israel once again as a sovereign people in the land God had promised them.

Around the time of Jesus there lived some Jews who expected such a messiah. At that period the Jews in Palestine were ruled by the Romans. But it was sometimes thought that God would intervene and raise up a great warrior who would destroy these pagan enemies and reinstate the kingdom of Israel. One of the clearest expressions of this kind of messianic expectation is in a Jewish writing known as the Psalms of Solomon, written probably during the first century BCE. Its powerful expectation of what the coming messiah would be is worth quoting at length:

See, Lord, and raise up for them their king,
the son of David, to rule over your servant Israel
in the time known to you, O God.
Undergird him with the strength to destroy the
    unrighteous rulers,
to purge Jerusalem from gentiles
who trample her to destruction;
in wisdom and in righteousness to drive out
the sinners from the inheritance;
to smash the arrogance of sinners like a potter's jar;
to shatter all their substance with an iron rod;
to destroy the unlawful nations with the word of
    his mouth;
at his warning the nations will flee from his
    presence;
and he will condemn sinners by the thoughts of his
    heart. . . .
And he will have gentile nations serving him under
    his yoke. . . .
And he will purge Jerusalem
and make it holy as it was even from the beginning. . . .
And he will be a righteous king over them, taught
    by God.
There will be no unrighteousness among them in
    his days,
for all shall be holy,
and their king shall be the Lord Messiah.[10]

Obviously we are not dealing here with the expectation of a messiah who would be tortured to death by his enemies the Romans. Quite the opposite: the messiah would destroy the enemy and set up his throne in Jerusalem, where he would rule his people with power, grandeur, and justice.

Is that what Jesus was said to have done? If not, how could he be the messiah?

Other Jews at the time of Jesus held yet other expectations of the future ruler of Israel. Some Jews had come to think that the messiah would not be a mere earthly king. He would be a cosmic figure, a powerful angelic being sent from God to destroy the enemy and set up God's kingdom on earth. This figure was often modeled on the "one like a son of man" in the book of Daniel (for example, 7:13–14). In an apocryphal writing known as 1 Enoch, probably from about the same time, comes this prediction about the future messianic Son of Man:

[The Son of Man] shall never pass away or perish from before the face of the earth. But those who have led the world astray shall be bound with chains; and their ruinous congregation shall be imprisoned; all their deeds shall vanish from before the face of the earth. Thenceforth nothing that is corruptible shall be found; for that Son of Man has appeared and has seated himself upon the throne of his glory; and all evil shall disappear from before his face. (1 Enoch 69)[11]

Yet other Jews from about the time of Jesus expected that the future anointed one would be a powerful priest who would rule over the people of Israel with authority given him by God, as he interpreted the sacred laws of Israel and enforced their obedience in the good kingdom to come. The community that produced the Dead Sea Scrolls expected *two* messiahs, one who would be a ruler-king and over him the priestly messiah.[12]

In short, ancient Jews at the turn of the era held a variety of expectations of what the future messiah would be like. But all these expectations had several things in common. In all of them the messiah would be a future ruler of the people of Israel, leading a real kingdom here on earth. He would be visibly and openly known to be God's special emissary, the anointed one. And he would be high and mighty, a figure of grandeur and power.

And who was Jesus? In all our early traditions he was a lower-class peasant from rural Galilee who was thought by some to be the future ruler of Israel but who instead of establishing the kingdom on earth came to be crucified. That Jesus died by crucifixion is almost universally attested in our sources, early and late. We have traditions of Jesus's bloody execution in independent Gospel sources (Mark, M, L, John, Gospel of Peter), throughout our various epistles and other writings (Hebrews, 1 Peter, Revelation), and certainly in Paul—everywhere in Paul. The crucifixion of Jesus is the core of Paul's message and is attested abundantly in his writings as one of the—if not the—earliest things that he knew about the man.

Who would make up the idea of a crucified messiah? No Jew that we know of. And who were Jesus's followers in the years immediately after his death? Jews living in Palestine. It is no wonder that Paul found their views so offensive. They were claiming that Jesus was God's anointed one, the one who stood under God's special favor, the great and powerful ruler over all Israel. Jesus—the man who was executed for sedition against the state? He's the one blessed of God, his powerful solution to the plight of the chosen people? A crucified criminal? That's worse than being crazy. It's an offense against God, blasphemous. Or so thought Paul. And so he persecuted this tiny sect of Jews and tried to destroy them.

It is hard today to understand just how offensive the idea of a crucified messiah would have been to most first-century Jews. I try to illustrate it to my class by giving an analogy. What would you think if I tried to convince you that David Koresh was God's chosen one through whom he is going to rule the earth? David Koresh? The leader of the Branch Davidians at Waco, who stockpiled guns and abused children, who was killed by the FBI? He's God's chosen one? Yes, he is the Lord of all. What are you, completely nuts? (I get in trouble with my students every time I use this illustration. At the end of term I invariably get a comment or two from students who can't believe that Ehrman thinks David Koresh is the Lord. . . .)

If it is hard to imagine Jews inventing the idea of a crucified messiah, where did the idea come from? It came from historical realities. There really was a man Jesus. Some of the things he said and possibly did make some of his followers wonder if he could be the messiah. Eventually they became convinced: he must be the messiah. But then he ran afoul of the authorities, who had him arrested, put on trial, and condemned to execution. He was crucified. This, of course, radically disconfirmed everything his followers had thought and hoped since he obviously was the furthest thing from the messiah. But then something else happened. Some of them began to say that God had intervened and brought him back from the dead. The story caught on, and some (or all—we don't know) of his closest followers came to think that in fact he had been raised. This reconfirmed in a big way the hopes that had been so severely dashed by his crucifixion. For his reinspirited followers, Jesus truly is the one favored by God. So he *is* the messiah. But he is a different kind of messiah than anyone expected. God had a different plan from the beginning. He planned to save Israel not by a powerful royal messiah but by a crucified messiah.

Since no one would have made up the idea of a crucified messiah, Jesus must really have existed, must really have raised messianic expectations, and must really have been crucified. No Jew would have invented him. And it is important to remember that Jews were saying that Jesus was the crucified messiah in the early 30s. We can date their claims to at least 32 CE, when Paul began persecuting these Jews. In fact, their claims must have originated even earlier. Paul knew Jesus's right-hand man, Peter, and Jesus's brother James. They are evidence that this belief in the crucified messiah goes all the way back to a short time after Jesus's death.

A Suffering Messiah?

But weren't there *any* Jews who expected the messiah to suffer and die? The short answer is that so far as we can tell, there were not. My students often find this hard, even impossible, to believe. They have been raised in Christian churches, where it is taught that the messiah was *supposed* to suffer, and they are guided to such passages as Isaiah 53, in the Old Testament, as proof:

> He was despised and rejected by others,
> a man of suffering and acquainted with infirmity. . .
> Surely he has borne our infirmities
> and carried our diseases;
> yet we accounted him stricken,
> struck down by God, and afflicted.
> But he was wounded for our transgressions,
> crushed for our iniquities;
> Upon him was the punishment that made us whole,
> and by his bruises we are healed (Isaiah 53:3–5)

Students sometimes quote these verses to me and then say with a smug smile, "See! The messiah was predicted to suffer!" My response is always the same: I ask them to show me where in the passage the word *messiah* occurs. The students are typically nonplussed when the see that the word *messiah* does not appear anywhere in this passage. They protest: "But this sounds just like the crucifixion of Jesus! And so does Psalm 22. And Psalm 69." And so on. I ask them in each case to see if the author is talking about the messiah. Each of these passages talks about someone suffering, but that someone is never the messiah.

In Isaiah 53, for example, the sufferer is called not the "messiah" but the "servant of the Lord," and the passage speaks about his sufferings in the past tense, as something that has already happened at the time of writing (six hundred years before Jesus). As interpreters have long noted, if read in context, the author actually tells us who this servant of the Lord is. In Isaiah 49:3 the prophet declares, "And he said to me, 'You are my servant, Israel, in whom I will be glorified.'"

It is Israel who is God's servant, who has suffered for the sins of the people and so brought healing. Isaiah 53 was written during the Babylonian exile when the Babylonian armies had taken the leaders of Judah hundreds of miles away and forced them to live in Babylon. Isaiah is lamenting the exile but indicating that the suffering will bring atonement for the sins of the people, and God will restore their fortunes. He is not talking about the future messiah.

An even more important point is this: there were no Jews prior to Christianity who thought Isaiah 53 (or any of the other "suffering" passages) referred to the future messiah. We do not have a single Jewish text prior to the time of Jesus that interprets the passage messianically. So why do Christians traditionally interpret it this way? For the same reason they think that the messiah had to suffer. In their view Jesus is the messiah. And Jesus suffered. Therefore the messiah had to suffer. And this must not have come as a surprise to God; it must have all been planned. And so Christians found passages in the Hebrew Bible that talked about someone suffering and said that it referred to the suffering of the future messiah, Jesus. Jews roundly and loudly disagreed with these interpretations. And so the arguments began.

Before he converted, Paul was on the side of the non-Christian Jews. The idea of a suffering messiah ran so counter to scripture and the righteous expectations of God's people that it was completely unthinkable, even blasphemous. Paul, though, had a change of mind and later decided that this one who stood under God's curse—since anyone "who hangs on a tree" is cursed—was in fact the Christ. He was cursed by God not for anything he himself had done but for what others had done. He bore the curse that others deserved and so saved them from the wrath of God. Once Paul was convinced of this, he turned from being a persecutor of the Christians to being their most famous advocate, missionary, and theologian. It was a conversion for the ages.

A Mythicist Response

But still, aren't there *any* passages that refer to a suffering messiah? Some mythicists realize that this is a problem because if someone wanted to make up a messiah—as they claim Christians made up Jesus—they would never have made one up who suffered since that is what precisely no one expected. One mythicist who addresses the problem is Richard Carrier, whom I mentioned in an earlier context as one of the two mythicists in the world (that I know of) with a graduate degree in a relevant subject, in his case, a Ph.D. in classics from Columbia. He is one smart fellow. But I'm afraid he falls down on this one. Even smart people make mistakes.

In his recent book, *Not the Impossible Faith: Why Christianity Didn't Need a Miracle to Succeed,* Carrier states that "this idea of a suffering, executed god, would resonate especially with those Jews and their sympathizers who *expected* a humiliated messiah."[13] This statement is problematic on all counts. For one thing, the earliest Christians from, say, the early 30s CE—as we will see later—did not talk about or think of Jesus as God. Second, we know of no Jews who thought, even in their wildest dreams, that God could be executed. And third, of particular relevance to my argument here, there were none who expected a humiliated messiah.

Carrier tries to establish his point about the humiliated messiah first by quoting Isaiah 53. But as I've shown, Isaiah is not speaking about the future messiah, and he was never interpreted by any Jews prior to the first century as referring to the messiah.

Carrier's argument becomes more interesting when he appeals to a passage in chapter 9 of the book of Daniel. This is one of those postdated prophecies so common to the final six chapters of Daniel. By *postdated prophecies* I mean this: the book of Daniel claims to be written by a Hebrew man, Daniel, in the Babylonian exile, around 550 BCE. In actual fact, as critical scholars have long known (Carrier agrees with this), it was written closer to 160 BCE.[14] When the character Daniel in the book "predicts" what is going to happen, the real author, pretending to be Daniel, simply indicates what already did happen. And so it sounds as if the sixth-century prophet knows the future because what he predicted in fact came to pass.

Daniel 9 is a complicated passage that "predicts" in precise detail what will happen to the people of Jerusalem over the course of "seventy weeks" that have been "decreed for your people and your holy city; to finish the transgression, to put an end to sin, and to atone for iniquity." The weeks are interpreted within the text itself to mean seventy "weeks of years"—that is, one week represents seven years. According to verse 25 there will be seven such weeks of years separating the order to rebuild destroyed Jerusalem and the appearance of "an anointed prince." Verse 26 then indicates that sixty-two weeks of years later an "anointed one" shall be "cut off and shall have nothing." Carrier argues strenuously that this shows that the author of Daniel expected that the messiah (the "anointed one") had to be killed ("cut off").

It is an interesting interpretation but highly idiosyncratic. You won't find it in commentaries on Daniel written by critical Hebrew Bible scholars (those who are not fundamentalists or conservative evangelicals), and for some good reasons. To begin with, the anointed prince of verse 26 is obviously not the same as the anointed one mentioned in verse 25. Are they both princes, that is, traditional messianic figures? It is important to recall that the term *anointed one* was sometimes used as a technical term to refer to the future ruler of Israel. But it was not always used that way. Sometimes it simply referred to a king (Solomon) or a high priest or anyone who went through an anointing ceremony. That is, it was not only a technical term but also a common term. It is striking in this passage that the figure in verse 26 is not called a prince or "the" anointed one—that is, the messiah.

And so, in one of the definitive commentaries written on Daniel, by Louis Hartman, a leading scholar of the Hebrew Bible (Carrier does not claim to be one; I don't know offhand if he knows Hebrew and Aramaic, the languages in which the book was written), we read about verse 25:

> Although in the preexilic period [the period in Israel before the Babylonian exile of 586 BCE—four hundred or more years before Daniel was written] the Hebrew term *masiah,* the "anointed one," was used almost exclusively of kings, at least in the postexilic period [after the people returned to the land years later] the high priest received a solemn anointing with sacred oil on entering his office. . . . It seems much more likely, therefore, that the "anointed leader" of 9:25 refers to the high priest, Joshua ben Josadak.[15]

In other words, 9:25 not only is *not* talking about a future messiah, it is talking about a figure from the history of Israel whom we already know about: the priest Joshua described elsewhere in the Hebrew Bible (see, for example, Zechariah 6:11). Verse 26 is referring to someone who lived centuries later, but it too is not referring to a future messiah. As Hartman has argued—along with many, many other Hebrew Bible scholars—the reference to "an" (not "the") anointed one in 9:26 "almost certainly" refers to another figure known from Jewish history, the high priest Onias III, who was deposed from being the high priest and murdered in 171 BCE, several years before the famous Maccabean revolt broke out, an event recounted in 2 Maccabees 4:1–38.[16]

The two who are called "anointed" are not future messiahs. They are both high priests who, in that role, were anointed. And they both lived in the past. Most important of all, this passage was never, so far as we know, interpreted messianically by Jews prior to the advent of Christianity. In other words, there were no Jews in the early 30s who would have resonated with the idea of a suffering messiah based on Daniel 9:26. No one thought that this is what the passage was talking about.

What then are we left with? We do not have a shred of evidence to suggest that any Jews prior to the birth of Christianity anticipated that there would be a future messiah who would be killed for sins—or killed at all—let alone one who would be unceremoniously destroyed by the enemies of the Jews, tortured and crucified in full public view. This was the opposite of what Jews thought the messiah would be. Then where did the idea of a crucified messiah come from? It was not made up out of thin air. It came from people who believed Jesus was the messiah but who knew full well that he had been crucified.

That no Jew would make up such an idea is made crystal clear by Paul himself in one of his letters. When writing to the Corinthians Paul makes the intriguing and compelling statement that the fact that Christians proclaimed a messiah who had been crucified was the single greatest "stumbling block" for Jews (1 Corinthians 1:23) and a completely ridiculous claim to Gentiles (same verse). That is to say, Jews didn't buy it. And why not? Because for Jews this very claim—the heart of the Christians' affirmation of their faith— was absurd, offensive, and potentially blasphemous.

Yet this is what a very small group of Jews, sometime before the year 32, were saying about Jesus. Not that he was God. And not that he was the great king ruling now in Jerusalem. He was the crucified messiah. It is almost impossible to explain this claim—coming at this place, at this time, among this people—if there had not in fact been a Jesus who was crucified.

Conclusion

WHAT CAN WE SAY in conclusion about the evidence that supports the view that there really was a historical Jesus, a Jewish teacher who lived in Palestine as an adult in the 20s of the Common Era, crucified under Pontius Pilate sometime around the year 30? The evidence is abundant and varied. Among the Gospels we have numerous independent accounts that attest to Jesus's life, at least seven of them from within a hundred years of the traditional date of his death. These accounts did not appear out of thin air, however. They are based on written sources—a good number of them—that date much earlier, plausibly in some cases at least to the 50s of the Common Era. Even these sources were not fabricated purely from the minds of their authors, however. They were based on oral traditions that had been in circulation year after year among the followers of Jesus. These oral traditions were transmitted in various areas—mainly urban areas, we might surmise—throughout the Roman Empire; some of them, however, can be located in Jesus's homeland, Palestine, where they originally circulated in Aramaic. It appears that some, probably many, of them go back to the 30s CE. We are not, then, dealing merely with Gospels that were produced fifty or sixty years after Jesus's alleged death as the principal witnesses to his existence. We are talking about a large number of sources, dispersed over a remarkably broad geographical expanse, many of them dating to the years immediately after Jesus's alleged life, some of them from Palestine itself. On the basis of this evidence alone, it is hard to understand how Jesus could have been "invented." Invented by whom? Where? When? How then could there be so many independent strands of evidence?

But that is just the beginning. The reality is that every single author who mentions Jesus—pagan, Christian, or Jewish—was fully convinced that he at least lived. Even the enemies of the Jesus movement thought so; among their many slurs against the religion, his nonexistence is never one of them. Moreover, this is not a view restricted in the Christian sources to Mark. It is the view of all of our authors, for example, the authors of the epistles written both before and after Mark, whose views are based not on a reading of the Gospels but on traditions completely independent of Mark. It is also the view of Q and M and L and John and of all of John's sources. It is the view of the first-century books or letters of 1 Clement, 1 Peter, 1 John, Hebrews—you name it. And it is also the view of the book of Acts, which preserves very primitive traditions in many of its speeches, traditions that appear to date from the earliest years of the Christian movement, even before the followers of Jesus maintained that he was the Son of God for his entire life or even just from his baptism; according to these traditions, he became the son of God at his resurrection. This is the earliest Christology of them all, probably that of the original followers of Jesus, and so stems from the earliest Palestinian Christian communities. Once again we are back in the 30s of the Common Era, and the witness of these sources is unambiguous that Jesus existed.

The same results obtain by a careful study of Paul's letters. Paul came to know about Jesus within just a year or, at most, two of his death. Paul too preserves traditions that stem from the early period of his Christian life, right after his conversion around 32–33 CE. There is no doubt that Paul knew that Jesus existed. He mentions Jesus's birth, his Jewish heritage, his descent from David, his brothers, his ministry to Jews, his twelve disciples, several of his teachings, his Last Supper, and most important for Paul, his crucifixion. Paul indicates that he received some of these traditions from those who came before him, and it is relatively easy to determine when. Paul claims to have visited with Jesus's closest disciple, Peter, and with his brother James three years after his conversion, that is, around 35–36 CE. Much of what Paul has to say about Jesus, therefore, stems from the same early layer of tradition that we can trace, completely independently, in the Gospels.

Even more impressive than what Paul says about Jesus is whom he knew. Paul was personally acquainted, as I've pointed out, with Peter and James. Peter was Jesus's closest confidant throughout his public ministry, and James was his actual brother. Paul knew them for decades, starting in the mid 30s CE. It is hard to imagine how Jesus could have been made up. Paul knew his best friend and his brother.

Paul also knew that Jesus was crucified. Before the Christian movement, there were no Jews who thought the messiah was going to suffer. Quite the contrary. The crucified Jesus was not invented, therefore, to provide some kind of mythical fulfillment of Jewish expectation. The single greatest obstacle Christians had when trying to convert Jews was precisely their claim that Jesus had been executed. They would not have made that part up. They had to deal with it and devise a special, previously unheard of theology to account for it. And so what they invented was not a person named Jesus but rather the idea of a suffering messiah. That invention has become so much a part of the standard lingo that Christians today assume it was all part of the original plan of God as mapped out in the Old Testament. But in fact the idea of a suffering messiah cannot be found there. It had to be created. And the reason it had to be created is that Jesus—the one Christians considered to be the messiah—was known by everyone everywhere to have been crucified. He couldn't be killed if he didn't live.

Jesus certainly existed. My goal in this book, however, is not simply to show the evidence for Jesus's existence that has proved compelling to almost every scholar who has ever thought about it, but also to show why those few authors who have thought otherwise are therefore wrong. To do that I need to move beyond the evidence for the historical Jesus to the claims made about his existence by various mythicists. I will not try to refute every single point made by every single author who has taken that stand. That would require an enormous book, and trust me, it would not be a pleasant read. Instead I will consider the most important issues and the most interesting and significant arguments. In the next chapter I will deal with several mythicist arguments that are, I will claim, irrelevant to the question of whether or not Jesus actually existed. In the chapter that follows I will then consider several of the best-known mythicist proposals for how Jesus came to be created and argue that they too are thoroughly inadequate to establish the mythicist view.

PART II

The Mythicists' Claims

CHAPTER SIX

The Mythicist Case: Weak and Irrelevant Claims

Up to this stage in our quest to see if the historical Jesus actually existed, I have been mounting the positive argument, showing why the evidence is overwhelming that Jesus really did live as a Jewish teacher in Palestine and was crucified at the direction of the Roman governor Pontius Pilate. It will be equally important for us to learn what the historical Jesus said and did, since the mere fact of Jesus's existence does not get us very far. Anyone interested in the history of Jesus very much wants to know the character of his teachings, the nature of his activities, the reasons for his execution, and so on. I will save the exploration of these other critical issues for the end of the book. For now I need to take on a more pressing matter. If Jesus did exist, why do mythicists say that he did not? The present chapter will look at the typical arguments used by mythicists that are, in my judgment, weak and/or irrelevant to the question. In the following chapter I will consider various ways mythicists have reconstructed the original "invention" of Christ and show why these views too are problematic and do not at all compromise the powerful evidence for the existence of the historical Jesus.

Irrelevancies in Historical Argument

ANYONE WHO SPENDS MUCH time dealing with controversial historical issues knows full well that many arguments are simply irrelevant. Just to give an example from the nonmythicist camp—in fact, from the opposite end of the spectrum: it is frequently argued by fundamentalist and conservative evangelical apologists for the Bible that since the New Testament is more frequently attested in ancient sources than any other book from antiquity, it can therefore be trusted. This argument, I'm afraid, contains a non sequitur. It is true that we have far more manuscripts for the books of the New Testament than for Homer, Plato, Aristotle, Euripides, Cicero, Marcus Aurelius—name your ancient author. But that has absolutely no bearing on the question of whether the New Testament books can be trusted. It is relevant only to the question of whether we can know what the New Testament books originally said.

Look at it this way. Both *Das Kapital* by Karl Marx and *Mein Kampf* by Adolf Hitler are better attested than, say, the New Testament Gospel of John. Far better attested. There is no comparison. We have far, far more copies of each that were produced closer to the time of the originals than we do for any of the books of the New Testament, including John. Does the fact that both books are extremely well attested have any bearing on whether you can trust what either one has to say? Are the author's opinions therefore reliable? Are his teachings to be followed simply because we have a lot of copies of his work? The same applies to the Gospel of John or any other book of the New Testament. The fact that we have more copies of John than of, say, Plato's Republic has no bearing on whether we can trust it more or not. It only has a bearing on the question of whether we can reasonably think that we know what the author originally wrote. Whether what he wrote is right or not has to be judged on other grounds.

Fundamentalists and conservative evangelical Christians are not the only ones who make irrelevant arguments to score points with the reading public. So too—to return to our original side of the spectrum—do mythicists. In this chapter I will consider several arguments typically made by mythicists in their effort to show that Jesus did not exist. My thesis is that most of these points are weak and some are irrelevant to the question.

Claim 1: The Gospels Are Highly Problematic as Historical Sources

MYTHICISTS SOMETIMES LIKE TO revel in the historical problems posed by the Gospels: we do not have the original texts of the Gospels, and there are places where we do not know what the authors originally said; the Gospels are not authored by the persons named in their titles (Matthew, Mark, Luke, and John) but were written by people who were not followers of Jesus living forty to sixty years later in different parts of the world; the Gospels are full of discrepancies and contradictions; and the Gospels report historical events that can be shown not to have happened.

Some scholars may disagree with some of these claims—conservative evangelicals will disagree with all of them—but I personally think they are absolutely right. And I think that these issues create genuine problems for the study of the New Testament, the history of the early Christian church, and the life of the historical Jesus. But I also think they are for the most part irrelevant to the question of whether or not there was a historical Jesus, for reasons I will explain. But first it is important to delve into the issues a bit.

We Do Not Have the Original Texts of the Gospels

To begin with, even though the Gospels are among the best attested books from the ancient world, we are regrettably hindered in knowing what the authors of these books originally wrote. The problem is not that we are lacking manuscripts. We have thousands of manuscripts. The problem is that none of these manuscripts is the original copy produced by the author (this is true for all four Gospels—in fact, for every book of the New Testament). Moreover, most of these manuscripts were made over a thousand years after the original copies, none of them is close to the time of the originals—within, say, ten or twenty years—and all of them contain certifiable mistakes.

I do not need to explicate all these problems here, as I have written about them in more detail elsewhere.[1] My point in this context is that for the question of whether or not Jesus existed, these problems are mostly irrelevant. The evidence for Jesus's existence does not depend on having a manuscript tradition of his life and teachings that is perfectly in line with what the authors of the New Testament Gospels really wrote. Suppose, for example, that it is true that the famous story of Jesus and the woman taken in adultery was not originally part of the Gospel of John (the only Gospel in which the story occurs) even though it is found in the vast majority of manuscripts produced in the Middle Ages. What does that tell us? It tells us that the story was probably not originally in John; in turn, that probably means that it is not something that actually happened in the life of Jesus. But so what? That doesn't mean Jesus didn't live. It simply means this event never happened, as far as we can tell.

Think of an analogy. Suppose Barack Obama's birth certificate turns out to have been altered away from what it really said. (I don't believe it was, not for a second, but suppose it was.) What relevance would that have for the question of whether Barack Obama was born? One would probably want to look for other evidence of

whether he came into the world, and the wording of the birth certificate is irrelevant to the question.

The manuscripts of the New Testament do indeed have large
numbers of variations in them: alternative ways of wording a verse
or a passage; omissions of words or sentences; additional insertions
of words and sentences here and there. But the problem is not of
such a scope as to make it impossible to have any idea what the ancient Christian authors wrote. If we had no clue what was originally
in the writings of Paul or in the Gospels, this objection might carry
more weight. But there is not a textual critic on the planet who
thinks this, since not a shred of evidence leads in this direction.
And I don't know even of any mythicist who is willing to make this
claim. As a result, in the vast majority of cases, the wording of these
authors is not in dispute. And where it is, it rarely has anything at all
to do with the question of whether Jesus existed.

We Do Not Know the Authors of the Gospels

It is also true that we do not know who wrote the Gospels. Although they are attributed to two of Jesus's disciples (Matthew the
tax collector and John the beloved disciple) and to two companions
of the apostles (Mark the secretary for Peter and Luke the traveling
companion of Paul) these ascriptions are almost certainly wrong.
Something similar obtains for most of the rest of the New Testament. Of the twenty-seven books found in the New Testament,
only eight of them almost certainly go back to the authors to whom
they are traditionally ascribed. Either the others are all misattributed
to people who did not in fact write them, or they were actually
forged, that is, written by authors claiming to be famous people
while knowing full well they were someone else.

Again, I have dealt with this issue more fully elsewhere and do
not need to go into all the details here.[2] The one thing we can say
with some assurance about the Gospel writers is that even though

Jesus's own followers were lower-class Aramaic-speaking peasants from rural Galilee, who were almost certainly illiterate, the Gospels were written by highly educated, Greek-speaking Christians who lived outside Palestine. They were not Matthew, Mark, Luke, and John.

But once again, this is irrelevant to the question of whether Jesus lived. In 1983 the famous, or rather infamous, Hitler Diaries came to public view, and they were immediately authenticated by experts. But they were soon shown to be forgeries, and the forger, a German scoundrel named Konrad Kujau, was then caught red-handed. He had been paid millions for the volumes and had done it for the money. The fact that he forged these sources about Hitler, however, has no bearing on the question of whether Hitler existed. That has to be decided on other grounds. In the case of the Gospels and Jesus, even though we don't know who the authors of these books were, we can still use them as historical sources for knowing about Jesus, as I argued in the earlier chapters.[3] The Gospels are valuable to this end whether they were written by Matthew, Mark, Luke, and John or by Fred, Harry, Sam, and Jeff.

The Gospels Are Filled with Discrepancies and Contradictions

It is absolutely true, in my judgment, that the New Testament accounts of Jesus are filled with discrepancies and contradictions in matters both large and small. Anyone who doubts that simply has to compare very carefully a story found in one of the Gospels with the same story found in another. You can pick any set of stories you like. Compare the genealogy of Jesus found in Matthew with the one found in Luke. They simply cannot be reconciled (they are both genealogies of Joseph, but who is his father, grandfather, great-grandfather?). Neither can the stories of Jesus's birth (did his parents flee with him to Egypt, as in Matthew, or did they instead return to Nazareth a month after he was born, as in Luke?).[4] Neither can those of his death (was he crucified the afternoon before the Passover meal was eaten, as in John, or the morning after it was eaten, as in Mark?) or of his resurrection (were his disciples instructed to go north to Galilee and it was there that they met Jesus raised from the dead, as in Matthew, or were they instructed not to leave Jerusalem so that they stayed put, not only to see Jesus raised but to spend months there, as in Luke?).

Sometimes the discrepancies are not simply about small details but about big issues. Did Jesus call himself God? It seems a rather important issue because if he did, one would have to figure out what to make of his claim. Was he crazy? Hopelessly self-important? Or possibly right? It is striking, however, that of all the Gospels, only John, the last to be written, reports that Jesus called himself God. If the historical Jesus really did spend his ministry revealing his divine identity to his disciples, as he does in John, isn't it a little strange that Matthew, Mark, and Luke never get around to saying so? Did they think it was unimportant? Or did they just forget that part?

Once again I have dealt with the discrepancies and the contradictions of the New Testament Gospels in another context and so do not need to delve more deeply into them here.[5] At this point it is enough to reiterate that these issues are more or less irrelevant to the question of whether Jesus actually lived. The contradictions in our sources will make it difficult, or at least interesting, when we want to know what he really said and did. But the case that I built for the existence of Jesus in the previous chapters does not hinge on the Gospels being internally consistent or free from discrepancy. Again, think of an analogy. You will get very different accounts of the presidency of Bill Clinton depending on whom you ask. But the differences have no bearing on whether he existed.

The Gospels Contain Nonhistorical Materials

It is true that the Gospels are riddled with other kinds of historical problems and that they relate events that almost certainly did
not happen. Think of Luke's account of Jesus's birth. Unlike the
Gospel of Matthew, Luke indicates that Jesus's parents lived originally in Nazareth, in the northern part of Galilee (Bethlehem is in
the south, near Jerusalem). According to Luke's story, a tax was im-
posed on "all the world" by Caesar Augustus, and everyone had to
register for a census. Since Joseph's distant ancestor David was born
in Bethlehem, that is where he had to register. While he was there
his betrothed, Mary, gave birth.

There is no way this can be historically correct. There was no
worldwide (or even empire-wide) census in the days of Augustus, let
alone a census in which everyone in the Roman Empire had to register in the town that their ancestors had come from a thousand years
earlier, as I explain in another context.[6] And certainly no such census
could have happened when "Quirinius was the governor of Syria," as
Luke claims, if Jesus was born when Herod was king: Quirinius did
not become governor until ten years after Herod's death.

So too it is completely implausible that when Jesus was put on
trial at the end of his life, Pilate offered to release one of his two
chief prisoners, Barabbas or Jesus, as was allegedly his custom at
Passover (see Mark 15:6–15). We have no historical record of any
such custom being carried out by Pilate or anyone else. And it defies
imagination that the ruthless Pilate, not known for currying favor
among the crowds, would be willing to release a violent and dangerous insurrectionist every year just because the crowds wanted him
to do so. This scene, like the census, almost certainly didn't happen.
But that has little bearing on whether Jesus existed. It simply means
that this alleged episode did not happen.

Back to our analogies. There are lots of stories about George
Washington that may not have happened. Did he really cut down

the cherry tree? Did he really have wooden teeth? Did he really stand in the prow of the boat as his troops crossed the Delaware? Did he really get sick after fleeing in his skivvies out the window of his lover's house when her husband came home, and did he die as a result? Some of these things may have happened (well, not the cherry tree), some of them not. But whether they did or not has little bearing on whether Washington lived. He did live, and we can say some things about him with certainty. So too with Jesus.

Are All the Stories of the Gospels Filled with Legendary Material?

The legendary character of the Gospel accounts of Jesus are stressed by almost all mythicists, but by none with the rigor and passion of Robert Price, whose recent *The Christ-Myth Theory and Its Problems* echoes, in this respect, many of the themes and restates many of the conclusions that he reached in his earlier work, *The Incredible Shrinking Son of Man*.[7] I will address important aspects of Price's case against the historical Jesus in the next chapter. For now I want to stress that his emphasis—hammered home page after page—that the Gospel accounts contain legendary material, when seen in a more balanced light, is only marginally relevant to the question of whether Jesus existed.

Price's argument is sophisticated, and it is a little difficult to explain in lay terms the basic methodological point that forms its backbone. In part it relates to what I mentioned earlier when talking about the form critics, German authors from the beginning of the twentieth century like Martin Dibelius and Rudolf Bultmann. In their view, as we saw, communities shaped the traditions that they passed along about Jesus so that these traditions took specific "forms" depending on the context (the *Sitz im Leben*—the "situation in life") in which they were being told. Stories of Jesus's controversies over the Sabbath took one shape or form, stories of his miracles another form, and so on. One of the implications of this view is that early Christian communities told stories about Jesus only when these stories were relevant to their own communal life situations. Why tell stories that have no relevance? In the logic of Price's argument, this is the first point: communities tell stories only when they advance their own self-interests in one way or another.

His second point comes from developments in scholarship that happened in the wake of form criticism, especially among the students of Rudolf Bultmann. These students wondered if there was any way to get *behind* the stories that had been molded and shaped in the early Christian communities, to see if any surviving traditions escaped the Christian storytellers' influences. Suppose there existed stories about Jesus that show no signs of having been created by the communities that told them, stories, for example, that appear to stand at odds with what the early Christian communities would have wanted to say about Jesus. Traditions dissimilar to what Christians were saying about Jesus would not have been created or formulated by the early Christian storytellers. And so those traditions, if they existed, would involve stories that were told not simply because they were useful in the life situation (*Sitz im Leben*) of the communities in which they were passed along. Stories like that were probably told simply because they were stories about Jesus that really happened.

This is a standard principle used by scholars today to establish which of the stories in the Gospels almost certainly go back to the historical Jesus as opposed to being made up by later storytellers talking about his life in light of their community's concerns and needs. The principle is called the "criterion of dissimilarity." If there is a tradition that does not coincide with what we know about the concerns, interests, and agenda of the early Christian communities—or in fact stands at odds with these concerns—then that tradition is more likely to be authentic than a saying that does coincide with the community's interests. (I will give some examples in a moment.)

Price's modus operandi is to go through all the traditions of the Gospels and show that each and every story of Jesus can be shown to meet some need, concern, or interest of the early Christians, so there are *no* stories that can be shown to go back to a historical figure, Jesus. In other words, the first building block in every case trumps the second so that there are no historically accurate materials in the Gospels.

My own view is that this is completely wrong, for several reasons. For one thing, it is a misuse of the criterion of dissimilarity to use it to show what did *not* happen in the life of Jesus. The criterion is designed to be used as a positive guide to what Jesus really said and did and experienced, not as a negative criterion to show what he did not. That is to say, suppose Jesus in the Gospels predicts that he will go to Jerusalem and be crucified and then raised from the dead. Would this prediction pass the criterion of dissimilarity? Absolutely not! This is something that the community of Christians may well have wanted to put on Jesus's lips. Since it does not pass the criterion, we cannot use this criterion to indicate that Jesus really made this prediction. But can we use it to say that he did not make the prediction? Once again, absolutely not! The criterion may make us suspicious of this or that tradition, but it cannot demonstrate on its own merits whether or not it is historical. In other words, by its very character the criterion does not and cannot indicate what Jesus did *not* do or say, only what he *did* do or say.

My second point is related. This criterion—and others we will consider in a later chapter—is designed to consider probabilities, not certainties. And, as Price himself acknowledges, this is all the historian can do: establish what probably happened in the past. To demand a criterion that yields certainty is to step outside historical research. All we can establish are probabilities. And there are a number of traditions about Jesus that easily pass the criterion of dissimilarity, making their historicity more probable than their non-historicity.

I need to add, as a third point, that the probabilities that one establishes by using one criterion can be strengthened by appealing to others. For example, we saw in earlier chapters that in addition to the surviving Gospels (seven from a hundred years of his death), there are multiple independent witnesses to the life of Jesus, including the many written and oral sources of the Gospels and a large number of other independent Christian writings. Suppose a tradition about Jesus is found in only one of these sources (the visit of the magi to Jesus, for example, found only in Matthew, or the parable of the Good Samaritan, found only in Luke). It is conceivable that the source "made up" that story. But what if you have the same or very similar stories in two independent witnesses? Then neither one of them could have made it up since they are independent, and it must then be earlier than both of them. What if a story or kind of story is found in a large number of sources? That kind of story is far more likely to be historically accurate than a story found in only one source. If you can find stories that are independently attested in multiple sources *and* that pass the criterion of dissimilarity, you can establish, then, a higher level of probability that you are dealing with a historical account. It may have legendary features, but the heart of the story may be historical.

Let me give three quick examples. We saw in an earlier chapter that it is highly improbable that the earliest Palestinian Jewish followers of Jesus would have made up the claim that the messiah was crucified. This passes the criterion of dissimilarity. And it is a claim found multiply attested throughout our tradition (Mark, M, L, John, Paul, Josephus, Tacitus). Conclusion? If what we want are strong probabilities, this is a highly probable tradition. Jesus was crucified.

Something of far less significance, at least to most people, is the question of Jesus's brothers. The independent sources of Mark, John, Paul, and Josephus all say that he had brothers, and in all but John, one of these brothers is named James. The stories in which

Jesus's brothers appear are not tendentious, promoting any particular Christian agenda. So the tradition that Jesus had brothers passes dissimilarity as well as multiple attestation. Conclusion: Jesus probably had brothers, one of whom was named James.

A final example, which will become more important later in this chapter. Jesus is said to have come from Nazareth in multiple sources (Mark, Q, John, L, M). And nowhere in any of these stories is there any hint that the author or his community has advanced its own interests in indicating Nazareth as Jesus's hometown. In fact, just the opposite: the early Christians had to explain *away* the fact that Jesus came from Nazareth, as seen, for example, in John 1:45–46 and in the birth narratives of Matthew and Luke, which independently of one another try to show that even though Jesus came from Nazareth, he really was born in Bethlehem. And why the concern? Because the Old Testament prophet Micah said the savior would come from Bethlehem, not Nazareth (Micah 5:2). Moreover, John reflects a more general embarrassment about Nazareth ("Can anything good come out of Nazareth?"). Nazareth was a little one-horse town (not even that; it was more like a one-dog town) that no one had ever even heard of, so far as we can tell, before Christianity. The savior of the world came from *there?* Not from Bethlehem? Or Jerusalem? Or Rome? How likely is that? And so we have a multiply attested tradition that passes the criterion of dissimilarity. Conclusion: Jesus probably came from Nazareth.

I have explained these criteria used by scholars in part to show why Price's opposing views are problematic. Contrary to Price, we do indeed have several traditions that probably reflect the life of the historical Jesus. In later chapters I will show there are many more. But at this stage I want to conclude by making an even larger methodological point: the question of whether many, most, or all the traditions about Jesus have been colored by legend is for the most part irrelevant to the question of whether Jesus existed.

You could make the case that every person who talks about

another person puts his or her own slant on the story. Every story includes bias. We are humans, not machines, and we slant things the way we see them, necessarily. What that means, though, is that almost everything we say about another person is tinted with legend (our biases). It was no different with Jesus. People who told stories about him tinted his life with legend. Sometimes the legend completely took over, and the stories told were legendary through and through, with no historical core. Other times a historical core was shaped by a legendary interest. But there were indeed some stories with historical cores, and a scholar's ability to show that even these stories are shaped by legend does not have any bearing on the question of whether Jesus existed. For one thing, we have the cores themselves. Moreover, and this is my key point, the shaping of a story is not the same thing as the inventing of a story. You can shape a tradition about Jesus any way you want so that it looks highly legendary. But that has no bearing on the question of whether beneath the legendary shaping lies the core of the historical event.

And—another key point that I want to keep pressing—the evidence of the historical Jesus does not in the least depend exclusively on whether this, that, or the other Gospel story is historically accurate. It is based on other considerations, which I set out in the earlier chapters, including the witness of Paul and the speeches of Acts, which long predate the Gospels.

In short, the problems that the Gospels pose for scholars—the fact we do not have the original texts, that we do not know their actual authors, that they are full of discrepancies, that they contain nonhistorical, legendary materials—are not all that significant for the particular question we are posing, whether or not Jesus existed. These problems may seem significant (and altogether relevant). But when you dig deeper into the matter and think about it more closely, it is clear that they are not.

Claim 2: Nazareth Did Not Exist

ONE SUPPOSEDLY LEGENDARY FEATURE of the Gospels relates closely to what I have just argued and is in fact one of the more common claims found in the writings of the mythicists. It is that the alleged hometown of Jesus, Nazareth, in fact did not exist but is itself a myth (using the term as the mythicists do). The logic of this argument, which is sometimes advanced with considerable vehemence and force, appears to be that if Christians made up Jesus's hometown, they probably made him up as well. I could dispose of this argument fairly easily by pointing out that it is irrelevant. If Jesus existed, as the evidence suggests, but Nazareth did not, as this assertion claims, then he merely came from somewhere else. Whether Barack Obama was born in the United States or not (for what it is worth, he was) is irrelevant to the question of whether he was born.

Since, however, this argument is so widely favored among mythicists, I want to explore it more deeply. It is not a new argument. All the way back in 1906 Schweitzer addressed it when discussing the mythicists of his own day.[8] Among the modern advocates of the view are several we have already mentioned. Frank Zindler, for example, in a cleverly titled essay, "Where Jesus Never Walked," tries to deconstruct on a fairly simple level the geographical places associated with Jesus, especially Nazareth. He claims that Mark's Gospel never states that Jesus came from Nazareth. This flies in the face, of course, of Mark 1:9, which indicates that this is precisely where Jesus came from ("Jesus came from Nazareth in Galilee"), but Zindler maintains that that verse was not originally part of Mark; it was inserted by a later scribe. Here again we see history being done according to convenience. If a text says precisely what you think it could not have said, then all you need to do is claim that originally it must have said something else.[9]

Zindler maintains that some early Christians understood Jesus to be the "branch" mentioned in Isaiah 11:1, who would come from the line of David as the messiah. The term *branch* in Hebrew (which does not have vowels) is spelled *NZR,* which is close (kind of close) to *Nazareth.* And so what happened, in Zindler's view, is that later Christians who did not understand what it meant to call Jesus the *NZR* (branch) thought that the traditions that called him that were saying he was from a (nonexistent) town, Nazareth.

Zindler does not marshal any evidence for this view but simply asserts it. And he does not explain why Christians who did not know what *NZR* meant simply didn't ask someone. Even more important, he doesn't explain why they made up the name of a nonexistent town (in his view) to locate Jesus or how they went from "Jesus is the *NZR*" to "Jesus *came from* Nazareth." The view seems completely implausible, especially given the fact, which we have seen, that multiple independent sources locate Jesus in Nazareth. Moreover, there is the additional evidence, which we will see momentarily, that Nazareth did in fact exist as a small Jewish town in the days of Jesus.

G. A. Wells advances a different argument to much the same end. In his view the key to understanding the nonexistence of Nazareth lies in the four occasions in which Mark indicates that Jesus was a "Nazarene" (1:24; 10:47; 14:67; 16:6). According to Wells, Mark misunderstood what this meant. What it originally meant was that Jesus belonged to a pre-Christian Jewish sect called the Nazarenes, who were similar to certain Old Testament figures (like strong-man Samson) called Nazirites, who took vows to be specially set apart for God (they couldn't touch corpses, drink wine, or cut their hair). Mark didn't know this, though, and wrongly assumed that the term *Nazarene* must have indicated Jesus's place of origin, and so Mark made up "Nazareth" as his hometown.[10]

Once again one looks in vain for any evidence or clear logic to support this view. Why would Mark invent a town that didn't exist to explain how Jesus could be a Nazarene, when what the term originally meant was that he was a Nazirite? Moreover, Mark must have known the Old Testament. He does quote it on a number of occasions. Why wouldn't he know what a Nazirite was? And if the sectarians that Jesus associated with were Nazirites, why did they call themselves Nazarenes (a word that is not etymologically related)? Moreover, it should be stressed that there are multiple traditions about Nazareth (Mark, M, L, John). Nazareth was not invented by Mark.

One of the things that these two examples show is that modern scholars seem to have no clue what *Nazarene* means or where the name of the town Nazareth could have come from if it is not original. So how can we posit some kind of ancient Christian motivation to invent Nazareth if we have no idea what led Christians to do so or even what the root of the term really meant? The problem is compounded by the fact, already mentioned, that Nazareth did exist in the days of Jesus, in the location that Mark and the other Gospels suggest it did.

The most recent critic to dispute the existence of Nazareth is René Salm, who has devoted an entire book to the question, called *The Myth of Nazareth*.[11] Salm sees this issue as highly significant and relevant to the question of the historicity of Jesus: "Upon that determination [that is, on the existence of Nazareth] depends a great deal, perhaps even the entire edifice of Christendom."[12] Like so many mythicists before him, Salm emphasizes what scholars have long known: Nazareth is never mentioned in the Hebrew Bible, in the writings of Josephus, or in the Talmud. It first shows up in the Gospels. Salm is also impressed by the fact that the early generations of Christians did not seek out the place but rather ignored it and seemed not to know where it was (this is actually hard to show; how would we know this about "every" early Christian, unless all of them left us writings and told us everything they knew and did?).

Salm's basic argument is that Nazareth did exist in more ancient times and through the Bronze Age. But then there was a hiatus. It ceased to exist and did not exist in Jesus's day. Based on archaeological evidence, especially the tombs found in the area, Salm claims that the town came to be reinhabited sometime between the two Jewish revolts (between 70 CE and 132 CE), as Jews who resettled following the destruction of Jerusalem by the Romans relocated in northern climes. Salm, like Zindler, wants to insist that Mark did not indicate that Jesus came from Nazareth: Mark 1:9, for him, is a later insertion.

Salm himself is not an archaeologist: he is not trained in the highly technical field of archaeology and gives no indication that he has even ever been on an archaeological dig. He certainly never has worked at the site of Nazareth. Still, he bases almost his entire case on archaeological reports about the town of Nazareth. In particular, he is impressed by the fact that the kind of rock-cut tombs that have been uncovered there—called *kokh* tombs, otherwise known as *locula* tombs—were not in use in Galilee the middle of the first century and thus do not date to the days of Jesus. And so the town did not exist then.

This is a highly problematic claim. It is hard to understand why tombs in Nazareth that can be dated to the days after Jesus indicate that there was no town there during the days of Jesus. That is to say, just because later habitation can be established in Nazareth, how does that show that the town was not inhabited earlier? Moreover, Salm fails to stress one of the most important points about these special rock-cut tombs: they were expensive to make, and only the wealthiest families could afford them.[13] There is nothing in any of our records to suggest that Nazareth had any wealthy families in the days of Jesus. And so no one in town would have been able to purchase a kokh tomb. So what does the fact that none were found from the days of Jesus indicate? Precisely nothing. The tombs that poor people used in Palestine were shallow graves, not built into rock like kokh tombs. These poor-person graves almost never survive for archaeologists to find.

I should also point out that these kokh tombs from later times were discovered on the hillside of the traditional site of Nazareth. Salm, however, claims that the hillside would have been uninhabitable in Jesus's day so that, in his opinion, the village that eventually came into existence (in the years after 70 CE) would have been located on the valley floor, less than a kilometer away. He also points out that archaeologists have never dug at that site.

This view creates insurmountable problems for his thesis. For one thing, there is the simple question of logic. If archaeologists have not dug where Salm thinks the village was located, what is his basis for saying that it did not exist in the days of Jesus? This is a major flaw: using forceful rhetoric, almost to the point of indiscretion, Salm insists that anyone who thinks that Nazareth exists has to argue "*against* the available material evidence." But what material evidence can there be, if the site where the evidence would exist has never been excavated? And what evidence exactly is being argued against, if none has been turned up?

There is an even bigger problem, however. Many compelling pieces of archaeological evidence indicate that in fact Nazareth did exist in Jesus's day and that, like other villages and towns in that part of Galilee, it was built on the hillside, near where the later rock-cut kokh tombs were built. For one thing, archaeologists have excavated a farm connected with the village, and it dates to the time of Jesus.[14] Salm disputes the finding of the archaeologists who did the excavation (remember that he himself is not an archaeologist but bases his views on what the real archaeologists—all of whom disagree with him—say). For one thing, when archaeologist Yardena Alexandre indicated that 165 coins were found in this excavation, she specified in the report that some of them were late, from the fourteenth or fifteenth century. This suits Salm's purposes just fine. But as it turns out, among the coins were some that date to the Hellenistic, Hasmonean, and early Roman period, that is, the days of Jesus. Salm objected that this was not stated in Alexandre's report, but Alexandre has verbally confirmed that in fact it is the case: there were coins in the collection that date to the time prior to the Jewish uprising.[15]

Salm also claims that the pottery found on the site that is dated to the time of Jesus is not really from this period, even though he is not an expert on pottery. Two archaeologists who reply to Salm's protestations say the following: "Salm's personal evaluation of the pottery . . . reveals his lack of expertise in the area as well as his lack of serious research in the sources."[16] They go on to state, "By ignoring or dismissing solid ceramic, numismatic [coins], and literary evidence for Nazareth's existence during the Late Hellenistic and Early Roman period, it would appear that the analysis which René Salm includes in his review, and his recent book must, in itself, be relegated to the realm of 'myth.'"[17]

Another archaeologist who specializes in Galilee, Ken Dark, the director of the Nazareth Archaeological Project, gave a thoroughly negative review of Salm's book, noting, among other things, that "there is no hint that Salm has qualifications—nor any fieldwork experience—in archaeology." Dark shows that Salm has misunderstood both the hydrology (how the water systems worked) and the topography (the layout) of Nazareth and points out that the town could well have been located on the hill slopes, just as other nearby towns were, such as Khirbet Kana. His concluding remarks are damning: "To conclude: despite initial appearances this is not a well-informed study and ignores much evidence and important published work of direct relevance. The basic premise is faulty, and Salm's reasoning is often weak and shaped by his preconceptions. Overall, his central argument is archaeologically unsupportable."[18]

But there is more. As it turns out, another discovery was made in ancient Nazareth a year after Salm's book appeared. It is a house that dates to the days of Jesus. The discovery was reported by the Associated Press on December 21, 2009. I have personally written the principal archaeologist, Yardena Alexandre, the excavations director at the Israel Antiquity Authority, and she has confirmed the report. The house is located on the hill slopes. Pottery shards connected to the house range from roughly 100 BCE to 100 CE (that is, the days of Jesus). There is nothing in the house to suggest that the people inhabiting it over this time had any wealth: there are no glass items or imported products. The vessels are made of clay and chalk.

The AP story concludes that "the dwelling and older discoveries of nearby tombs in burial caves suggest that Nazareth was an out-of-the-way hamlet of around 50 houses on a patch of about four acres . . . populated by Jews of modest means." No wonder this place is never mentioned in the Hebrew Bible, Josephus, or the Talmud. It was far too small, poor, and insignificant. Most people had never heard of it, and those who had heard didn't care. Even though it existed, this is not the place someone would make up as the hometown of the messiah. Jesus really came from there, as attested in multiple sources.

Again I reiterate the main point of my chapter: even if Jesus did not come from Nazareth, so what? The historicity of Jesus does not depend on whether Nazareth existed. In fact, it is not even related to the question. The existence (or rather, nonexistence) of Nazareth is another mythicist irrelevancy.

Claim 3: The Gospels Are Interpretive Paraphrases of the Old Testament

A NUMBER OF MYTHICISTS argue that the New Testament Gospels are little more than reworkings and paraphrases of passages of the Old Testament applied to an invented figure Jesus. Within Jewish tradition this approach to interpreting a text by paraphrasing, expanding, and reapplying it is called *Midrash;* if the text is a narrative rather than a set of laws, the Midrash is called *haggadic* (as opposed to *halakhic*). And so Robert Price has recently argued that "the whole gospel narrative is the product of *haggadic Midrash* upon the Old Testament."[19] The logic behind this assertion is that if the stories told about Jesus in the Gospels have been modeled on those of Old Testament figures, we are dealing with literary fictions, not historical facts, and that Jesus, as a result, is a made-up, fictional character.

Robert Price and Haggadic Midrash

There are significant problems with this view, as I will explain in a moment, but the ultimate problem again is one of scope and relevance. The fact that a story about a person has been shaped according to the mold of older stories and traditions does not prove that the core of the story is unhistorical. It simply shows how the story came to take its shape.

Take as an example the way the story of Jesus is told in the early chapters of the Gospel of Matthew. It has long been recognized that Matthew wants to portray Jesus as a "new Moses," and so it is no surprise to find that the things that happen to Jesus in Matthew closely parallel the Old Testament traditions about Moses. Just as the ruler of the land, the Egyptian pharaoh, sought to destroy Moses as an infant (Exodus 1), so too the ruler of the land, the Jewish king Herod, sought to kill the infant Jesus (Matthew 2). Jesus and his family escape by going to Egypt, the land of Moses. Just as Moses brought the children of Israel out of Egypt to come to the Promised Land (Exodus 13–14), so too Jesus returned from Egypt to Israel. Matthew emphasizes the point by quoting the prophet Hosea's declaration of the salvation of Israel: "Out of Egypt have I called my son" (Hosea 11:1, quoted in Matthew 2:16), only now the "son" is not the nation of Israel but its messiah, Jesus. To escape Egypt, the Israelites had to cross the Red Sea at the exodus. The first thing that happened to the adult Jesus is that he too entered and then came out of the water at his baptism (Matthew 3). The Israelites were in the wilderness for forty years being tested by God, and so too Jesus went into the wilderness for forty days to be tempted (Matthew 4). The Israelites traveled to Mount Sinai, where they were given the Law of Moses; Jesus immediately went up to a mountain and delivered his Sermon on the Mount, where he provided an interpretation of the laws of Moses (Matthew 5–7).

In point after point, Matthew stresses the close parallels between the life of Jesus and the life of Moses. And his reason for doing so is clear: for Matthew, Jesus *is* the new Moses, who provides the authoritative interpretation of the Law of God to the people who choose to follow him. This portrayal is distinct to Matthew: the other Gospels do not include all of these parallels (no king sets out to kill the child; there is no flight to Egypt, no Sermon on the Mount, and so forth). It is the way Matthew personally shaped the story, for reasons of his own.

But the fact that Matthew shaped the story in this way has nothing to do with the question of whether or not Jesus existed. What the shape of the story makes us suspect are the many details, molded in such a way as to allow Matthew to make a theological point about Jesus (the new Moses). The historical existence of the object of the story is a completely different issue.

That is because stories are always shaped, not just by the biblical authors, but by everyone who tells them. And so we in the modern world shape the stories we tell in a number of typical ways. We have the rags-to-riches story, the feel-good war story, the downfall-of-the-great-man story. The shape of the story is not related to the question of whether the figure in the story actually existed.

It would be easy, for example, to tell the story of the demise of Richard Nixon in terms of Shakespearian tragedy. Many of the facts fit the mold well enough, and the facts that don't fit can easily be bypassed or altered to make them fit. Does our ability to shape the story in the way we want mean that Watergate didn't happen or that Richard Nixon never lived? No, it just means that Nixon's story is amenable to a certain kind of shape.

So too with Jesus. Some of the followers of Jesus believed he was the new spokesperson of God, like Moses of old, and so they told stories about him to make the connections with Moses obvious. Many other followers considered him to be a prophet of God and the Son of God. And so they naturally talked about him in the ways they talked about other Hebrew prophets, such as Elijah and Elisha and Jeremiah.

A good example of how this works appears in the story of Jesus and the widow of Nain in Luke 7:11–17, which is similar in many ways to a story told about the prophet Elijah and his encounter with another widow, this one from Zarephath, also in the northern part of the land of Israel (1 Kings 17:17–24). Elijah learns that the only son of the widow has died, and he tells the mourning mother to give him the corpse. He raises the child from the dead and returns him to his mother, who proclaims, "Now that I know that you are a man of God and that the world of the LORD in your mouth is truth." So too Jesus comes to Nain and learns that the only son of a widow has died. He tells her not to mourn, he goes up to the corpse, and he raises the young man from the dead. And the crowd's reaction is similar: "A great prophet has risen among us and God has looked favorably on his people." The crowd, in other words, realizes that Jesus has just performed a feat like his predecessor Elijah, and that he too, therefore, is a great prophet of God.

When a story about Jesus so closely parallels a passage in the Old Testament, it is reasonable to assume that the storyteller—in this case, Luke or his source—has shaped the story in light of its scriptural parallel. But is it fair to say, as Price does, that "the whole gospel narrative" is nothing but a midrash on scripture? That is going too far, as can be seen by the fact that in a number of cases the examples Price cites are far from obvious. For instance, as in the story of the widow of Zarephath in 1 Kings 17, Price indicates that the story in which Jesus heals Peter's mother-in-law (Mark 1:29–31) is drawn from 1 Kings 17:8–16, where Elijah provides miraculous quantities of food for the widow and her son in the time of famine.

Unlike the earlier account I mentioned, however, here there are so many differences between the two episodes and so few similarities that it is hard to see how one was drawn from the other. The Elijah story is about a widow; Mark says nothing about a widow. The Elijah story is about the prophet feeding a starving family. The Jesus story is about him healing a woman who is ill, who then feeds him (not the other way around). The Elijah story is about a prophet helping a non-Jew; the Jesus story is about a Jew. It is hard to see that one of the stories is modeled on the other.

Or take a second story, Jesus healing the paralytic in Mark 2, which Price says is based on an episode in 2 Kings 1:2–17, Elijah healing King Ahaziah. Really? Simply read the stories for yourself. The differences are so pronounced that it is hard to see one as the source for the other.

The overarching problem is this: Price, as we saw earlier, was correct in stressing that historians deal not with certainties but only with probabilities. But he seems to have jettisoned this view when actually making historical judgments. In his view, virtually any story about Jesus with the remotest tie to a text of the Old Testament is written off as a midrash. But where are the probability judgments? To illustrate the problem, consider two stories, one that can plausibly be thought to have been made up to provide a parallel to a text in the Old Testament, and the other not.

The story of Jesus's triumphal entry into Jerusalem has long been recognized by scholars as historically problematic. It is told in an especially interesting way in Matthew's version (Matthew 21:1–11). Near the end of his life Jesus decides to make his fateful trip to Jerusalem; he instructs his disciples to find a donkey so that he can ride into town. In fact, in Matthew, the disciples are instructed to find two animals, a donkey and its colt. They bring the animals to Jesus, and he straddles the two and rides into Jerusalem to the acclamation of the crowds, who spread cloaks and branches on the road before him, shouting, "Hosanna to the son of David! Blessed is the one who comes in the name of the Lord!" We are told that this extraordinary entrance scene was to fulfill a prophecy of scripture: "Look, your king is coming to you, humble, and mounted on a donkey, and on a colt, the foal of a donkey," a quotation from the Old Testament prophet Zechariah (9:9).

In the other Gospels, when Jesus rides into town it is only on one animal, a donkey. Matthew has read the prophecy in Zechariah in an overly literalistic way, not realizing the poetic character of the passage. In the Hebrew Bible, poetry is written in sense lines, in which the statement of the first line either is contrasted with a statement in the second line or, instead, is restated in the second line in different words. Zechariah described the arrival of the holy one in two different ways in the two lines: he would come on a donkey, and on a colt, the foal of a donkey. This is a standard form of Hebrew poetry. But Matthew read the passage literally, thinking that Zechariah was imagining two different animals (a donkey and a colt), and so when he wanted Jesus to fulfill this prophecy, he had him straddling the two animals, a rather uncomfortable and somewhat undignified entrance into the city, one might think.

This entire scene is built around the fulfillment of a prophecy, which may make it historically suspect. But there are other reasons for doubting that it happened the way Matthew describes it. If it is true that the crowds were shouting that Jesus was the messiah now arriving in the holy city, why didn't the authorities immediately take notice and have him arrested both for causing a disturbance and for claiming to be the Jewish king (when only Rome could appoint the king)? Instead, according to Matthew and the other Gospels, Jesus spent an unmolested week in Jerusalem and only then was arrested and put on trial. But it defies belief that the Roman authorities who were in town precisely in order to prevent any mob actions or uprisings would have failed to intervene if the crowds shouted in acclamation for a new ruler arriving in town.

Jesus almost certainly came to Jerusalem, as we will see later, but not like this. The story has been made up (or adopted) in order to show that he fulfilled the prophecy of Zechariah.

Take now a second instance where the heart of the story—as I will argue in a later chapter—is almost certainly historical despite the literary embellishments around it. At the beginning of Jesus's ministry he is said to have been baptized by John the Baptist. The accounts in the Gospels are clearly amplified beyond historical plausibility: in the earliest version, Mark's, when Jesus comes out of the water, the heavens are said to rip apart, the Holy Spirit is said to descend upon him as a dove, and a voice comes from heaven: "You are my beloved son in whom I am well pleased" (Mark 1:9–11). The scene, as narrated, is designed to show that here, at the beginning of his ministry, Jesus is acknowledged by God as his unique son and anointed by the Holy Spirit from heaven to empower him for his preaching and miracles.

But the embellishments do not mean that the event itself is made up, as we will see later. How does Price explain the appearance of the baptism account in the Gospels? In his view,

> The scene in broad outline may derive from Zoroastrian traditions of the inauguration of Zoroaster's ministry. Son of a Vedic priest, Zoroaster immerses himself in the river for purification, and as he comes up from the water, the archangel Vohu Mana appears to him, proffering a cup and commissions him to bear the tidings of the one God Ahura Mazda, whereupon the evil one Ahriman tempts him to abandon this call. (67)

Is this explanation really at the same level of historical probability as the explanation of the triumphal entry? Zoroastrianism? Vohu Mana? Ahura Mazda? These were the influences that determined how the story of Jesus's baptism were told? For one thing, how can Price say that the entire Gospel is a haggadic midrash on the Old

Testament if what he means is that it is a paraphrase of Zoroastrian scripture? Even if it is not historical, the story of Jesus's baptism must go back to the very earliest Christian communities in Aramaic-speaking Palestine. How many Aramaic-speaking Palestinian Jews were influenced by accounts of Zoroaster's initiation in the presence of the archangel Vohu Mana?

In short, many of Price's explanations of where the Gospel stories came from are simply implausible. But my bigger point is that in many instances they are also irrelevant. Even if later storytellers chose to talk about Jesus's baptism in light of something that once happened to Zoroaster—which seems highly unlikely, but if they actually did—this has no bearing on the question of whether Jesus existed and, in this case, very little bearing on the question of whether he really was baptized by John the Baptist. Just because a story is molded by a storyteller or author in light of his own interests does not mean that the story at its core is nonhistorical or that the person about whom it is told did not live. There is other, quite abundant, evidence that Jesus lived. And as we will see, there are solid reasons for thinking he was baptized. None of this evidence hinges on whether he began his ministry like Zoroaster.

Thomas Thompson and the Messiah Myth

Thomas Thompson recently published a book that advances a view similar to Price's but approaches the matter from a slightly different angle. In *The Messiah Myth: The Near Eastern Roots of Jesus and David,* Thompson argues that just as Old Testament notables such as Abraham, Moses, and David were legendary, not historical figures, so too with Jesus, whose stories in the Gospels are not the result of oral traditions dating back to near his own time but are literary fictions invented by the Gospel writers and their predecessors.[20]

Thompson is a trained scholar of the Hebrew Bible and is well known in those circles for being what is called a minimalist, meaning that he thinks there is a very small amount of historical information in the Hebrew Bible. I do not need to enter into that debate here, as I am interested instead in how he transferred his understanding of the Old Testament traditions to the Gospel stories about Jesus. His book on Jesus (and David) consists of little more than a close reading of the Gospels, and he argues that the Gospels try to formulate their stories about Jesus in light of traditions found in the Old Testament. In his view the Gospel stories are constructed specifically as literary texts by authors who wanted to put their views of Jesus in written form. They are not, therefore, based on oral traditions that go back to near the time of Jesus himself. This is especially the case because in his view Jesus did not exist but was a literary invention of the early Christians.

Thompson's book is not easy for a layperson to follow. It involves a close reading of texts, a reading that at times is excessively thick and virtually impenetrable. Those without training in biblical studies are not likely to be able to follow his argument let alone be persuaded by it. But his basic view is clear. The Gospel stories have literary functions that depend heavily on intertextual influences (meaning they are based on other texts—in this case, those of the Hebrew Bible). To understand these stories, the interpreter has to understand where the stories came from. From this assertion Thompson leaps to the conclusion that since the Jesus traditions are textual and literary, they are therefore not rooted in oral traditions and have no basis in actual history. To read the stories as historical narratives, in his opinion, is therefore to misread them.

In my judgment this view goes too far (way too far) and is based on a non sequitur. To say that our Gospel stories are based in many instances (he would say all, but that is surely an exaggeration) on earlier literary texts does not necessarily mean that the stories were invented as written traditions instead of existing first as oral traditions. Even people telling stories, as opposed to writing them, could be influenced by earlier writings that were in broad circu-

lation. And it needs to be remembered always that we have solid
and virtually incontrovertible evidence that the stories of Jesus were
circulated orally before being written down. For one thing, there
is no other way to explain how Christianity spread throughout the
Roman world, as followers of Jesus converted other people to believe, not by showing them books (almost all of them were illiterate) but by telling stories about Jesus. Moreover, we have a number
of authors who explicitly tell us that stories about Jesus were being
transmitted orally. Paul says that he is passing on traditions he has
heard (1 Corinthians 11:22–24; 15:3–5); Luke indicates that his predecessors based their accounts on oral traditions (1:1–4); the author
of the Fourth Gospel indicates that he had an oral source for some of
his stories (19:35); and even later the church father Papias indicates
that he interviewed people who had been companions of Jesus's
disciples.

These oral traditions about Jesus did not arise twenty, thirty, or
forty years after the traditional date of his death. On the contrary,
as we have seen, they began in Aramaic-speaking Palestine, and we
can give reasonably hard dates: at the very latest they started in the
early 30s, a year or two after Jesus allegedly died. They almost certainly started even earlier.

But apart from this question of whether the Gospel stories are
purely literary inventions (rather than written accounts of earlier oral
traditions), with Thompson as with Price we have to ask whether the
view he sets forth is all that relevant to the question of Jesus's historical existence. It is one thing to say that a story has been shaped in
light of an account in the Hebrew Bible. It is another thing to say that
the event never happened at all or, even more, that the person about
whom the story is told never existed. The fact that stories are molded
in certain ways does not necessarily mean that there is no historical
information to be found in the stories. That has to be decided on
other grounds.

An analogy may yet again be useful. Today the historical novel is a widely accepted genre of literature. Over the past few years I have read *Sarah's Key,* by Tatiana de Rosnay, based on events in France during the Holocaust; *A Tale of Two Cities,* by Charles Dickens, about the French Revolution; and *Romola,* by George Eliot, about Savonarola in fifteenth-century Florence. These books are all shaped as novels. They are not meant to be disinterested historical accounts of the Holocaust, French history, or a famous Italian heretic. But to deny that they have some connection with historical events or the persons involved in these events is to miss a basic literary premise. No one would claim that the French Revolution never happened because it is discussed in a work of fiction created by Charles Dickens or that the Holocaust was made up because there is a novel about it. One instead needs to look for other evidence.

So too with the Gospels of the New Testament. They do indeed contain nonhistorical materials, many of which are based on traditions found in the Hebrew Bible. And to understand the gospel stories you do indeed need to understand the intertexts on which they are based. But that has little bearing on the question of whether or not Jesus actually existed. It has to do rather with how reliable some of the stories told about him are. To decide whether Jesus existed, you need to look at other evidence, as we have done.

Claim 4: The Nonhistorical "Jesus" Is Based on Stories About Pagan Divine Men

THIS FINAL ARGUMENT, UBIQUITOUS among the mythicists, is analogous to the preceding, but now rather than arguing that Jesus was made up based on persons and prophecies from the Jewish Bible, it is claimed that he was invented in light of what pagans were saying about the gods or about other "divine men," superhuman creatures thought to have been half mortal, half immortal. As was the case with the earlier claim, I think there is a good deal to be said for the idea that Christians did indeed shape their stories about Jesus in light of other figures who were similar to him. But I also think that this is scarcely relevant to the question of whether or not he existed.

The Claim and Its Exposition

In my textbook on the New Testament, written for undergraduates, I begin my study of the historical Jesus in a way that students find completely surprising and even unsettling. I tell them that I want to describe to them an important figure who lived two thousand years ago.

Even before he was born, it was known that he would be someone special. A supernatural being informed his mother that the child she was to conceive would not be a mere mortal but would be divine. He was born miraculously, and he became an unusually precocious young man. As an adult he left home and went on an itinerant preaching ministry, urging his listeners to live, not for the material things of this world, but for what is spiritual. He gathered a number of disciples around him, who became convinced that his teachings were divinely inspired, in no small part because he himself was divine. He proved it to them by doing many miracles, healing the sick, casting out demons, and raising the dead. But at the end of his life he roused opposition, and his enemies delivered him over to the Roman authorities for judgment. Still, after he left this world, he returned to meet his followers in order to convince them that he was not really dead but lived on in the heavenly realm. Later some of his followers wrote books about him.

But, I tell my students, I doubt if any of you has ever read any of these books. In fact, I say, I don't think you even know this man's name. He was Apollonius of Tyana, a pagan philosopher, a worshipper of the pagan gods. His story was written by a later follower named Philostratus, and we still have the book today, *The Life of Apollonius of Tyana*.[21]

The followers of Jesus, of course, argued that Apollonius was a fraud and a charlatan and that Jesus was the Son of God. The followers of Apollonius argued just the opposite, that it was Jesus who was the fraud. And these were not the only two divine men in antiquity. A number of divine men were thought to have roamed the earth, some of them in the recent past, people born to the union of a mortal (human) and an immortal (god), who could do spectacular deeds and who delivered amazing teachings, who at the end of their lives ascended to heaven to live with the gods.

My students, of course, have a hard time getting their minds around the fact that in the ancient world Jesus was not the only one "known" to be a miracle-working son of God. There were others. Mythicists, as you might imagine, have had field day with this information, arguing that since these others were obviously not real historical persons, neither was Jesus. He, like them, was invented.

But there is a problem with this view. Apollonius, for example, really was a historical person, a Pythagorean philosopher who lived some fifty years after Jesus. I don't really think that Apollonius's mother was impregnated by a God or that Apollonius really healed the sick or raised the dead. But he did exist. And so did Jesus. How do we know? We don't base our judgments on the way later followers made Apollonius and Jesus out to be semi- or completely divine. We base our judgments on other evidence, as we have seen. The fact that Christians saw Jesus as a divine man (or rather, for them, as the only true divine man) is not in itself relevant to the question of whether he existed. Still, since this is a major point among the mythicists, I need to give it some consideration.

I will be dealing with a very similar point in the next chapter, where I consider arguments of the mythicists that do strike me as highly relevant to the question of Jesus's existence. There I will ask whether Jesus was invented like one of the dying-rising gods of the ancient world. Here, however, I am more interested in the mythological parallels to the traditions of Jesus (his birth, his miracles, his ascension, and so forth) and their relevance to the question of whether he existed. My view is that even though one can draw a number of interesting parallels between the stories of someone like Apollonius and Jesus (there are lots of similarities but also scores of differences), mythicists typically go way too far in emphasizing these parallels, even making them up in order to press their point. These exaggerations do not serve their purposes well.

A terrific example of an exaggerated set of mythicist claims comes in a classic in the field, the 1875 book of Kersey Graves, *The World's Sixteen Crucified Saviors: Christianity Before Christ*. Early on his "study" Graves states his overarching thesis:

> Researches into oriental history reveal the remarkable fact that stories of incarnate Gods answering to and resembling the miraculous character of Jesus Christ have been prevalent in most if not all principal religious heathen nations of antiquity; and the accounts and narrations of some of these deific incarnations bear such a striking resemblance to that of the Christian Savior—not only in their general features but in some cases in the most minute details, from the legend of the immaculate conception to that of the crucifixion, and subsequent ascension into heaven—that one might almost be mistaken for the other.[22]

Grave goes on to list thirty-five such divine figures, naming them as Chrisna of Hindostan, Budha Sakia of India, Baal of Phenicia, Thammuz of Syria, Mithra of Persia, Cadmus of Greece, Mohamud of Arabia, and so on. Already the modern, informed reader sees that there are going to be problems. Buddha, Cadmus, and Muhammad? Their lives were remarkably like that of Jesus, down to the details? But as Graves goes on:

These have all received divine honors, have nearly all been worshiped as Gods, or sons of Gods; were mostly incarnated as Christs, Saviors, Messiahs, or Mediators; not a few of them were reputedly born of virgins; some of them filling a character almost identical with that ascribed by the Christian's Bible to Jesus Christ; many of them, like him, are reported to have been crucified; and all of them, taken together, furnish a prototype and parallel for nearly every important incident and wonder-inciting miracle, doctrine, and precept recorded in the New Testament, of the Christian's savior.[23]

This is certainly an impressive statement, and one can see how an unwary reader may easily be taken in. But note, for starters, the exaggeration of the last two lines ("nearly *every* important incident . . ."). Such sensationalist claims are repeated elsewhere throughout the book, as when, for example, we are told that pagan sources provide parallels for "nearly every important thought, deed, word, action, doctrine, principle, precept, tenet, ritual ordinance or ceremony. . . . Nearly every miraculous or marvelous story, moral precept, or tenet of religious faith [told about Jesus]."

Graves then sets out these fantastic (not to say fantastical) parallels in forty-five chapters, including discussions of such things as messianic prophecies, immaculate conceptions, virgin mothers, the visit of angels, shepherds, and magi to see the newborn infant, birth on December 25, crucifixions, descents to hell, resurrections, ascensions, atonements, doctrines of the trinity, and on and on. Possibly the most striking thing about all of these amazing parallels to the Christian claims about Jesus is the equally amazing fact that Graves provides not a single piece of documentation for any of them. They are all asserted, on his own authority. If a reader wants to look up the stories about Buddha or Mithra or Cadmus, there is no place to turn. Graves does not name the sources of his information. Even so, these are the kinds of claims one can find throughout the writings of the mythicists, even those writing today, 140 years later. And as with Graves, in almost every instance the claims are unsubstantiated.

Just to pick a more recent example, I might mention the assertions of Frank Zindler, in his essay "How Jesus Got a Life."[24] Zindler is not as extreme as Graves, but he does make unguarded claims without providing the reader any guidance for finding the supporting evidence. In Zindler's view, Christ's biography started as a set of astrological and comparative mythological speculations in a pagan mystery cult, based to a large extent on the ancient "mystery religion" of Mithraism. According to Zindler, the cult figure of the Mithraists, the Persian god Mithras, was said to have been born on December 25 to a virgin; his cult was headed by a ruler who was known as a pope, located on the Vatican hill; the leaders of the religion wore miters and celebrated a sacred meal to commemorate the atoning death of their savior God, who was said to have been raised from the dead on a Sunday. Sound familiar?

The cult was centered, Zindler claims, in Tarsus (the hometown of the apostle Paul). But then the astrologers involved with the cult came to realize that the zodiacal age of Mithra was drawing to a close since the equinox was moving into Pisces. And so they "left their cult centers in Phrygia and Cilicia . . . to go to Palestine to see if they could locate not just the King of the Jews but the new Time Lord" (that is, they invented Jesus).[25] Zindler says this in all sincerity, and so far as I can tell, he really believes it. What evidence does he give for his claim that the Mithraists moved their religion to Palestine to help them find the king of the Jews? None at all. And so we might ask: what evidence could he have cited, had he wanted to do so? It's the same answer. There is no evidence. This is made up.

Scholars of the Mithraic mysteries readily admit that, as with most mystery religions, we do not know a good deal about Mithraism—or at least nearly as much as we would like to know. The

Mithraists left no books behind to explain what they did in their religion and what they believed. Almost all of our evidence is archaeological, as a large number of the cult's sacred shrines (called *mithraea*) have been uncovered that include a bull-slaying statue (called a *tauroctony*). These statues portray what was evidently the central act within the mythology of the group. The cult figure Mithras is astride a kneeling bull, his bent knee on its back, pulling its head toward him while he himself looks away and plunges a knife into its neck. A dog is shown lapping up the blood from the wound, which has an ear of wheat coming out with it; also present is a snake, and a scorpion is seen biting the bull's scrotum. On either side of the statue is a human torchbearer, one holding his torch upward in the normal position, the other holding his downward.

There are enormous debates among Mithraic scholars about what all this means. It clearly involves the study of the zodiac, and a number of interesting theories have been propounded. Unfortunately, we do not have Mithraic texts that explain it all to us, let alone texts that indicate that Mithras was born of a virgin on December 25 and that he died to atone for sins only to be raised on a Sunday.[26]

As I pointed out earlier, the reason a religion like Mithraism is called a mystery cult by scholars is that the followers of the religion were bound by a vow of secrecy and so never revealed the mysteries of their religion, either their practices or their beliefs.[27] It is true that later writers sometimes indicated what, in their opinion, took place in the religion. But these later writers were not involved personally in the cult, and historians are highly reluctant to take them at their word as if they had real sources of information. They, like their modern counterparts, were often simply speculating.

This is true as well of some of our Christian sources who claim that there were similarities between their own religion and the mystery religions. These later authors, such as the church father Tertullian, started making such claims for very specific reasons. It was not that they had done research and interviewed followers of these religions. It was because they wanted pagans to realize that Christianity was not all that different from what other pagans said and did in their religions so that there would be no grounds for singling out Christians and persecuting them. The Christian sources that claim to know something about these mysteries, in other words, had a vested interest in making others think that the pagan religions were in many ways like Christianity. For that reason—plus the fact that they would not have had reliable sources of information—they generally cannot be trusted.

Many mythicists, however, take what these later sources say at face value and stress the obvious: Christian claims about Jesus were a lot like those of other cult figures, down to the details. But they have derived the details from sources that—in the judgment of the scholars who are actually experts in this material—simply cannot be relied upon.

Other Problems with the Parallels

There are other problems with the mythicists' claims that Jesus was simply invented as another one of the ancient divine men. In many instances, for example, the alleged parallels between the stories of Jesus and those of pagan gods or divine men are not actually close. When Christians said that Jesus was born of a virgin, for instance, they came to mean that Jesus's mother had never had sex. In most of the cases of the divine men, when the father is a god and the mother is a mortal, sex is definitely involved. The child is literally part human and part deity. The mortal woman is no virgin; she has had divine sex.

In other cases the parallels are simply made up. Where do any of the ancient sources speak of a divine man who was crucified as an atonement for sin? So far as I know, there are no parallels to this central Christian claim. What has been invented here is not the Christian Jesus but the mythicist claims about Jesus. I am not saying that I think Jesus really did die to atone for the sins of the world. I am saying that the Christian claims about Jesus's atoning sacrifice were not lifted from pagan claims about divine men. Dying to atone for sin was not part of the ancient pagan mythology. Mythicists who claim that it was are simply imagining things.

My main objection to this line of argumentation, however, is the one with which I began. There certainly are similarities between what pagans were saying about their divine men and what Christians were saying about Jesus, as we have seen in the case of Apollonius. But the parallels are not as close and as precise as most mythicists claim. Nowhere near as close. True, some similarities are significant. But that is not relevant to the question of whether there really was a Jewish teacher Jesus who was crucified under Pontius Pilate. As we saw earlier with respect to parallels to Old Testament figures, when Christians told stories about Jesus, they shaped the stories in light of stories they already knew.

Jewish Christians in particular may have been inclined to portray Jesus in Old Testament terms. As soon as Christianity moved outside Judaism, however, and became a religion largely made up of converts from among the pagans, these new converts told stories about Jesus in terms that made sense to them. They increasingly shaped the stories so that Jesus looked more and more like the divine men commonly talked about in the Roman world, men who were supernaturally born because of the intervention of a god, who did miracles, who healed the sick and raised the dead, and who at the end ascended to heaven. If you wanted to describe a son of God to someone in the ancient world, these were the terms you used. You used the vocabulary and conceptions found in the idiom of the day. What other idiom could you use? It was the only language available to you.

The fact that Jesus was cast in the mold of pagan divine men does indeed create a difficult situation for historians who want to get beyond the idiom of the stories to the historical reality that lies behind them. But the mere fact that the idiom is being used does not mean that there is no reality there. The question of whether Jesus is portrayed as a Jewish prophet or as a pagan divine man is completely independent of the question of whether he existed.

Robert Price and the Mythic Hero Archetype

Robert Price in his recent book, *The Christ-Myth Theory*, uses parallels to pagan divine men in a more sophisticated way. Price argues that an ideal archetype of the "mythic hero" was "shared by cultures and religions worldwide and throughout history."[28] This ideal type comprises twenty-two characteristics, many of which apply to Jesus. Like many of these other figures from around the world, Jesus was made up according to type.

I do not need to belabor my criticism of this view since many of the points I made earlier apply here as well. I can say, though, that when social scientists talk about an "ideal type," they are not referring to an actually existing entity but to a scholarly construct that is useful for classifying phenomena. Anyone who is "true to type" is not necessarily "made up" to fit the type. This is significant because some of the figures that Price uses to establish the type were certainly actual persons, such as the famous Peregrinus discussed by the ancient author Lucian of Samosata (as Price admits on page 46). Jesus too could be true to type and be a real person. Here again, then, we need to differentiate between two questions: (a) How was Jesus talked about and portrayed by his later followers, and (b) did he really exist as a historical figure?

Price knows that these are separate questions, and he anticipates the objection by claiming that unlike other figures who really lived, such as Peregrinus, with Jesus we have no "neutral" information about his life. In Price's view, "Every detail [of the Gospel stories] corresponds to the interest of mythology and epic." And so the whole thing looks like it is made up.

This is another place where I seriously part company with Price. It simply is not true that all the stories in the Gospels, and all the details of stories, promote the mythological interests of the early Christians. The claim that Jesus had brothers named James, Joses, Judas, and Simon, along with several sisters, is scarcely a mythological motif; neither is the statement that he came from the tiny hamlet of Nazareth or that he often talked about seeds.

Price goes on to say that one other thing that makes historical figures stand out from those who are completely true to type is that they have left a "footprint on . . . profane history." That is, we have records of Caesar Augustus and Apollonius of Tyana, who are mentioned in other (profane) sources.

The first thing to stress by way of response is that it really is not fair to use Caesar Augustus as the criterion by which we evaluate whether one of the other sixty million people of his day actually existed. If I wanted to prove that my former colleague Jim Sanford really existed, I would not do so by comparing his press coverage to that of Ronald Reagan. Moreover, in the ancient context I do not even know what the term *profane* (as opposed to *sacred*) is supposed to mean. The ancient world did not divide the sacred from the profane or even imagine these as discrete categories. And even if they had, why would a profane historical source be more valuable than a nonprofane one (whatever that is)? And which of the two is Philostratus, our chief source of information about Apollonius? Philostratus clearly sees Apollonius as an important religious figure, and he holds deep religious convictions about him. Does that mean Philostratus is not a valuable source? The same could be said about many of the sources for Augustus, who was widely seen as a superhuman being who eventually came to be deified.

Here again, however, my biggest problem with this mythicist approach is the question of relevance. Yes, early Christians told stories about Jesus in light of what they thought about other divine men in their environment—or used to think before they converted.

Modern critical historians have noted these parallels, which are nowhere near as numerous as the mythicists have typically contended.
And scholars have long discussed why the parallels create problems
for knowing exactly what Jesus really said and did. The early storytellers shaped their stories about Jesus according to the models available to them, making up details—and sometimes entire stories—or
altering features here and there. But the fact they did so does not
have any bearing on whether Jesus really existed. That has to be
decided on other grounds.

Or to put the matter more concretely: what if it were true, historically, that the followers of Mithras portrayed him as having been
born on December 25, as wearing a halo, and as having followers
who were headed by a pope on Vatican Hill? What does that have
to do with whether there lived a Jewish preacher from Nazareth
named Jesus who was crucified by Pontius Pilate? This entire set of
arguments, as with those that I noted earlier, is simply not relevant
to the question of whether or not there was a historical Jesus.

CHAPTER SEVEN

Mythicist Inventions: Creating the Mythical Christ

TEACHING COURSES ON THE New Testament in the Bible Belt is a real honor and pleasure. For one thing, one never needs to worry about getting enough enrollment. My classes are always bursting at the seams, with dozens of students who cannot get into the course desperately begging to be let in. And it's not because of me. It's because of the subject. I've known some truly awful teachers in my time at universities in the South, professors of biblical studies who still had full classes every term. Students in this part of the world are eager to study the New Testament—both Christians who want to learn about it from a different perspective than what they absorbed in church and Sunday school and non-Christians who realize just how important the Bible is for their society and culture.

Because of where I teach, almost all my students come from conservative Christian backgrounds and already have both a vested interest in and a firm set of opinions about the subject matter. That makes biblical studies unlike almost any other academic discipline in the university, and it is why courses in the field are perfect for a liberal arts education. Students who take courses in other areas of the humanities—classics, philosophy, history, English, you name it—do not usually hold fixed ideas about the subject. As a result, they simply are not shocked by what they learn, for example, about the lives of Plato, Charlemagne, or Kaiser Wilhelm, and they do not come to class with deeply held opinions about other classics, *King Lear, Bleak House,* or *The Brothers Karamazov.* But they do have set opinions about the Bible—what it is and how it should be understood. These opinions can be challenged in class, and when they are, students are forced to think. Since one of the goals of a liberal arts education is to teach students how to think, courses in biblical studies are perfect for a liberal arts education, especially in a region such as the South, where the vast majority of students think they already know what the Bible is about.

At a reputable university, of course, professors cannot teach simply anything. They need to be academically responsible and reflect the views of scholarship. That is probably why there are no mythicists—at least to my knowledge—teaching religious studies at accredited universities or colleges in North America or Europe. It is not that mythicists are lacking in hard-fought views and opinions or that they fail to mount arguments to back them up. It is that their views are not widely seen as academically respectable by members of the academy. That in itself does not make the mythicists wrong. It simply makes them marginal.

As we saw in the previous chapter, some of the arguments that mythicists typically offer in support of their view that Jesus never existed are in fact irrelevant to the question. Other arguments are completely relevant but not persuasive. Those are the views that the present chapter will address, each of them involving ways mythicists have imagined, or rather invented, their mythical Christ. I will try to present these views fairly and then show why scholars in the rel-

evant fields of academic inquiry simply do not accept them. I begin
with the most commonly advocated view of them all.

Did the Earliest Christians Invent Jesus as a Dying-Rising God, Based on Pagan Myths?

ONE OF THE MOST widely asserted claims found in the mythicist
literature is that Jesus was an invention of the early Christians who
had been deeply influenced by the prevalent notion of a dying-
rising god, as found throughout the pagan religions of antiquity.
The theory behind this claim is that people in many ancient religions
worshipped gods who died and rose again: Osiris, Attis, Adonis,
Tammuz, Heracles, Melqart, Eshmun, Baal, and so on. Originally,
the theory goes, these gods were connected with vegetation and
were worshipped in fertility cults. Just as every year the crops die
in winter but then come back to life in the spring, so too with the
gods who are associated with the crops. They die (when the crops
do) and go to the underworld, but then they revive (with the crops)
and reappear on earth, raised from the dead. They are worshipped
then as dying-rising deities.

Jesus, in this view, was the Jewish version of the pagan fertility
deity, invented by Jews as a dying and rising god. Only later did
some of the devotees of this Jewish deity historicize his existence
and begin to claim that he was in fact a divine human who had once
lived on earth, who had died and then rose again. Once the histo-
ricizing process began, it continued rapidly until stories were told
about this God-man, and eventually a whole set of narratives were
invented by authors like Mark, the author of our first Gospel. These
narratives were not based on real history, however; they were based
on myths that have been historicized.

This view of the invention of Jesus is nearly ubiquitous among
mythicists (one who takes a different line, as we will see below, is

G. A. Wells). We have already seen it set forth in the book of Kersey Graves of 1875. More recently, Robert Price claims in his just published book that he himself, once a former evangelical preacher, became a mythicist precisely when he realized that there were significant parallels between the traditions of Jesus and the stories of other dying and gods.[1]

Problems with the View

There are two major problems with this view that Jesus was originally invented as a dying-rising god modeled on the dying and rising gods of the pagan world. First, there are serious doubts about whether there were in fact dying-rising gods in the pagan world, and if there were, whether they were anything like the dying-rising Jesus. Second, there is the even more serious problem that Jesus could not have been invented as a dying-rising god because his earliest followers did not think he was God.

Dying and Rising Gods in Pagan Antiquity

Even though most mythicists do not appear to know it, the onetime commonly held view that dying-rising gods were widespread in pagan antiquity has fallen on hard times among scholars.

No one was more instrumental in popularizing the notion of the dying-rising god than Sir James George Frazer (1854–1941). Frazer did in his day what Joseph Campbell did in the second half of the twentieth century: he convinced thousands of people that at heart many (or most) religions are the same. Whereas Campbell was principally revered by popular audiences, especially for such books as *The Hero with a Thousand Faces* and *The Power of Myth,* Frazer's studies made their greatest impact upon scholars. Particularly influential was his view of dying and rising gods.

Frazer's important book was called *The Golden Bough,* which went through a number of editions, each time growing larger and larger. Already in the first edition of 1890 Frazer had set out his view of pagan deities who died and then rose again; by the third edition of 1911–15 Frazer devoted all of part 4 to the topic. In it Frazer claimed that Eastern Mediterranean divinities such as Osiris, Dumuzi (or Tammuz), Attis, and Adonis were all dying and rising gods. In each case we are dealing, Frazer averred, with vegetative gods whose cycle of life, death, and resurrection replicates and explains the earth's fertility. Frazer himself did not draw explicit connections between these divinities and Jesus, but it is perfectly clear from his less-than-subtle ways of discussing these other gods what he had in mind. He thought that the Christians picked up this widespread characterization of the pagans and applied it to their myths about Jesus.[2]

Although such views about pagan gods were widely held in some circles for years, they met with devastating critique near the end of the twentieth century. There are, to be sure, scholars here or there who continue to think that there is some evidence of dying and rising gods. But even these scholars, who appear to be in the minority, do not think that the category is of any relevance for understanding the traditions about Jesus.

This is true of the most outspoken advocate for the onetime existence of such gods, Tryggve N. D. Mettinger, whose book *The Riddle of the Resurrection: "Dying and Rising Gods" in the Ancient Near East* tries to revive the major thesis of Frazer. On the basis of a highly detailed and nuanced study of evidence, Mettinger claims that "the world of ancient Near Eastern religions actually knew a number of deities that may be properly described as dying and rising gods."[3] He does go on to stress, however, that the vocabulary of resurrection (that is, of a dead person being revived to live again) is used in only one known case: Melqart (or Heracles). As examples of such pagan deities in pre-Christian times, Mettinger names, in addition to Melqart, Dumuzi and Baal. Like Frazer before him, he argues that the dying and rising of these gods have "close ties to the seasonal cycle of plant life."[4]

Having read Mettinger's book carefully, I do not think that it will provide much support for the mythicist view of pagan dying and rising gods. For one thing, even though Mettinger claims that such views were known in Palestine around the time of the New Testament, he does not provide a shred of evidence. He instead quotes passages from the Old Testament (his field of expertise): Ezekiel 8:14; Zechariah 12:11; and Daniel 11:37. But you can look at these passages yourself. None of them mentions the dying and rising of a god. So how do they prove that such a god was known in Palestine? What is more, none of them dates from anywhere near the time of the New Testament but are from hundreds of years earlier. Can anyone cite a single source of any kind that clearly indicates that people in rural Palestine, say, in the days of Peter and James, worshipped a pagan god who died and rose again? You can trust me, if there *was* a source like that, it would be talked about by everyone interested in early Christianity. It doesn't exist.

What is particularly striking about Mettinger's study of older deities (not in the time of the New Testament but centuries earlier) is just how ambiguous the evidence is, even in cases that he argues for most strenuously. He has to offer an exceedingly nuanced and philologically detailed argument to make the point that *any* of these deities was thought by anyone at all as dying and rising. So how strong and prevalent a category was it if in fact there are few unambiguous sources, even if we restrict ourselves to centuries before the matter becomes relevant to us?

It is worth emphasizing that even Mettinger himself does not think that his sparse findings are pertinent to the early Christian claims about Jesus as one who died and rose again. The ancient Near Eastern figures he talks about were closely connected with the seasonal cycle and occurred year in and year out. Jesus's death and resurrection, by contrast, were considered a onetime event. Moreover—this is a key point for him—Jesus's death was seen as being a vicarious atonement for sins. Nothing like that occurs in the case of the ancient Near Eastern deities.

But there is an even larger problem. Even if—a very big *if*—there was an idea among some pre-Christian peoples of a god who died and arose, there is nothing like the Christian belief in Jesus's resurrection. If the ambiguous evidence is interpreted in a certain way (Mettinger's), the pagan gods who died did come back to life. But that is not really what the early teachings about Jesus were all about. It was not simply that his corpse was restored to the living. It is that he experienced a resurrection. That's not the same thing.

The Jewish notion of resurrection is closely tied to a worldview that scholars have labeled Jewish apocalypticism. In the next chapter I will explain more about what that worldview entailed. For now it is enough to note that many Jews in the days of Jesus believed that the world we live in is controlled by powers of evil. That is why there is so much pain and misery here on earth: drought, famine, epidemics, earthquakes, wars, suffering, and death. Jews who held to this view, however, believed that at some future point God would intervene to overthrow the forces of evil in control of this world and set up his good kingdom on earth. In that future kingdom there would be no more pain, misery, suffering, or death. God would destroy everything and everyone opposed to him and would reward those who had been faithful to him. These rewards would not only come to those who happened to be living at the time, however. Faithful Jews who had suffered and died would be raised from the dead and given a reward. In fact, death itself would be destroyed, as one of the enemies of God and his people. At the future resurrection, the faithful would be given eternal life, never to die again.

Many Jews who believed in a future resurrection thought it would come very soon, possibly within their own lifetimes. God would crash into history to judge this world, overthrow all his enemies, including sin and death, and raise his people from the dead. And it would happen very soon.

When the earliest Christians claimed that Jesus had been raised from the dead, it was in the context of this Jewish notion of the soon-to-come resurrection. The earliest Christians—as seen from the writings of our first Christian author, Paul—thought that Jesus's resurrection was important, in no small part, because it signaled that *the* resurrection had begun. That is to say, they thought they were living at the end of this wicked age, on the doorstep of the coming kingdom. That is why Paul talked about Jesus as the "firstfruits" of the resurrection. Just as farmers gathered in the firstfruits of their crop on the first day of harvest and then went out and harvested the rest of the crop the next day (not centuries later), so too Jesus is the firstfruits of what is now imminent: the resurrection of all the dead, to face judgment if they sided with evil or to be rewarded if they sided with God.

The idea of Jesus's resurrection did not derive from pagan notions of a god simply being reanimated. It derived from Jewish notions of resurrection as an eschatological event in which God would reassert his control over this world. Jesus had conquered the evil power of death, and soon his victory would become visible in the resurrection of all the faithful.

As I already suggested, Mettinger himself does not think that the idea of pagan dying and rising gods led to the invention of Jesus. As he states, "There is, as far as I am aware, no *prima facie* evidence that the death and resurrection of Jesus is a mythological construct, drawing on the myths and rites of the dying and rising gods of the surrounding world."[5]

More common among scholars, however, is the view that there is scarcely any—or in fact virtually no—evidence that such gods were worshipped at all. No one was more instrumental in the demise of the views so elegantly set forth by Frazer in *The Golden Bough* than Jonathan Z. Smith, an eminent historian of religion at the University of Chicago. Most significant was an article that Smith produced for the influential *Encyclopedia of Religion,* originally edited by Mircea Eliade.[6] After thoroughly reexamining Frazer's claims about pagan dying and rising gods, Smith states categorically:

> The category of dying and rising gods, once a major topic
> of scholarly investigation, must be understood to have been
> largely a misnomer based on imaginative reconstructions and
> exceedingly late or highly ambiguous texts. . . .
>
> All the deities that have been identified as belonging to the
> class of dying and rising deities can be subsumed under the two
> larger classes of disappearing deities or dying deities. In the first
> case the deities return but have not died; in the second case the
> gods die but do not return. There is no unambiguous instance
> in the history of religions of a dying and rising deity.[7]

Smith backs up these claims by looking at the evidence for such gods as Adonis, Baal, Attis, Marduk, Osiris, and Tammuz or Dumuzi. With respect to ancient reports of the Greek Adonis, for example, there were in antiquity two forms of myth, which only later were combined into a kind of megamyth. In the first form two goddesses, Aphrodite and Persephone, compete for the affections of the human infant Adonis. Zeus (or in some of the myths Calliope) decides in Solomon-like fashion that Adonis will spend part of each year with each divinity, half the year with Aphrodite in the realms above, with the other gods, and the other half with Persephone, the goddess of the underworld. There is nothing here to suggest either death or resurrection for Adonis. Part of the year he is in one place (the realm of the living) and part in the other (the realm of the dead).

The other more familiar form of the myth comes from the Roman author Ovid. In this account the young man Adonis is killed by a boar and is then mourned and commemorated by the goddess

Aphrodite in the form of a flower. In this version, then, Adonis definitely dies. But there is nothing to suggest that he was raised from the dead. It is only in later texts, long after Ovid and after the rise of Christianity, that one finds any suggestion that Adonis came back to life after his death. Smith argues that this later form of the tradition may in fact have been influenced by Christianity and its claim that a human had been raised from the dead. In other words, the Adonis myth did not influence Christian views of Jesus but rather the other way around. Yet even here, Smith points out, there is no evidence anywhere of some kind of mystery cult where Adonis was worshipped as a dying-rising god or in which worshippers were identified with him and his fate of death and resurrection, as happens, of course, in Christian religions built on Jesus.

Or take the instance of Osiris, commonly cited by mythicists as a pagan parallel to Jesus. Osiris was an Egyptian god about whom a good deal was written in the ancient world. We have texts discussing Osiris that span a thousand years. None was as influential or as well known as the account of the famous philosopher and religion scholar of the second Christian century, Plutarch, in his work *Isis and Osiris*. According to the myths, Osiris was murdered and his body was dismembered and scattered. But his wife, Isis, went on a search to recover and reassemble them, leading to Osiris's rejuvenation. The key point to stress, however, is that Osiris does not—decidedly does not—return to life. Instead he becomes the powerful ruler of the dead in the underworld. And so for Osiris there is no rising from the dead.

Smith maintains that the entire tradition about Osiris may derive from the processes of mummification in Egypt, where bodies were prepared for ongoing life in the realm of the dead (not as resuscitated corpses here on earth). And so Smith draws the conclusion, "In no sense can the dramatic myth of his death and reanimation be harmonized to the pattern of dying and rising gods."[8] The same can be said, in Smith's view, of all the other divine beings often pointed to as pagan forerunners of Jesus. Some die but don't return; some disappear without dying and do return; but none of them die and return.

Jonathan Z. Smith's well-documented views have made a large impact on scholarship. A second article, by Mark S. Smith, has been equally informative. Mark Smith is a scholar of the ancient Near East and Hebrew Bible who also opposes any notion of dying and rising gods in the ancient world.[9] Mark Smith makes the compelling argument that when Frazer devised his theory about dying and rising gods, he was heavily influenced by his understanding of Christianity and Christian claims about Christ. But when one looks at the actual data about the pagan deities, without the lenses provided by later Christian views, there is nothing to make one consider them as gods who die and rise again. Smith shows why such views are deeply problematic for Osiris, Dumuzi, Melqart, Heracles, Adonis, and Baal.

According to Smith, the methodological problem that afflicted Frazer was that he took data about various divine beings, spanning more than a millennium, from a wide range of cultures, and smashed the data all together into a synthesis that never existed. This would be like taking views of Jesus from a French monk of the twelfth century, a Calvinist of the seventeenth century, a Mormon of the late nineteenth century, and a Pentecostal preacher of today, combining them all together into one overall picture and saying, "That's who Jesus was understood to be." We would never do that with Jesus. Why should we do it with Osiris, Heracles, or Baal? Moreover, Smith emphasizes, a good deal of our information about these other gods comes from sources that date from a period *after* the rise of Christianity, writers who were themselves influenced by Christian views of Jesus and "who often received their information second-hand."[10] In other words, they probably do not tell us what pagans themselves, before Christianity, were saying about the gods they worshipped.

The majority of scholars agree with the views of Smith and Smith: there is no unambiguous evidence that any pagans prior to Christianity believed in dying and rising gods, let alone that it was a widespread view held by lots of pagans in lots of times and places. But as we have seen, scholars such as Mettinger beg to differ. What can we conclude from this scholarly disagreement for the purposes at hand, the question of whether Jesus was invented as a dying and rising god? There are several key points to emphasize. First, it is important to realize that the reason there are disagreements among scholars (at least with someone like Mettinger) is that the evidence for such gods is at best sparse, scattered, and ambiguous, not abundant, ubiquitous, and clear. If there were any such beliefs about dying and rising gods, they were clearly not widespread and available for all to see. Such gods were definitely not widely known and widely discussed among religious people of antiquity, as is obvious from the fact that they are not clearly discussed in any of our sources. On this everyone should be able to agree. Even more important, there is no evidence that such gods were known or worshipped in rural Palestine, or even in Jerusalem, in the 20s CE. Anyone who thinks that Jesus was modeled on such deities needs to cite some evidence—any evidence at all—that Jews in Palestine at the alleged time of Jesus's life were influenced by anyone who held such views. One reason that scholars do not think that Jesus was invented as one of these deities is precisely that we have no evidence that any of his followers knew of such deities in the time and place where Jesus was allegedly invented. Moreover, as Mettinger himself acknowledges, the differences between the dying and rising gods (which he has reconstructed on slim evidence) and Jesus show that Jesus was not modeled on them, even if such gods were talked about during Jesus's time.

But there is an even more important reason for thinking that Jesus was not invented as a Jewish version of a dying and rising god. The earliest Christians did not think that Jesus was God.

Jesus as God

That the earliest Christians did not consider Jesus God is not a controversial point among scholars. Apart from fundamentalists and very conservative evangelicals, scholars are unified in thinking that the view that Jesus was God was a later development within Christian circles. Fundamentalists disagree, of course, because for them Jesus really is God, and since he is God, he must have known he was God, and he must have told his followers, and so they knew from the beginning that he was God. This view is rooted in the fundamentalist doctrine of the inerrancy of scripture, where everything that Jesus is said to have said, for example in the Gospel of John, is historically accurate and beyond question. But that is not the view of critical scholarship. Whether or not Jesus really was God (a theological, not a historical, question), the earliest followers did not think so. As I indicated at the very beginning of this book, the questions of how, when, and why Christians came to regard Jesus as God will be the subject of my next book, not this one. But I do need to stress the point here: this was a later development in Christian thinking.

It is striking that none of our first three Gospels—Matthew, Mark, and Luke—declares that Jesus is God or indicates that Jesus ever called himself God. Jesus's teaching in the earliest Gospel traditions is not about his personal divinity but about the coming kingdom of God and the need to prepare for it. This should give readers pause. If the earliest followers of Jesus thought Jesus was God, why don't the earliest Gospels say so? It seems like it would have been a rather important aspect of Christ's identity to point out. It is true that the Gospels consistently portray Jesus as the Son of God. But that is not the same thing as saying that he was God. We may think it is since for us the son of a dog is a dog, the son of a cat is a cat, and the son of a god, therefore, is a god. But the Gospels were not written by people living in the twenty-first century with modern understandings (or even in the fourth century with fourth-century understandings). The Gospels were written in a first-century context and were ultimately guided by Jewish understandings, especially as these were mediated through the Jewish scriptures, the Old Testament. The Old Testament speaks of many individuals and groups who were considered to be son(s) of God. In no instance were these persons God.

And so, for example, the king of Israel was explicitly said to be "the son of God" (for example, Solomon, in 2 Samuel 7:11–14). This certainly did not make the king (especially Solomon) God. He was instead a human who stood in a close relationship with God, like a child to a parent, and was used by God to mediate his will on earth. So too the nation of Israel was sometimes called "the son of God" (for example, Hosea 11:1). This did not make the nation divine; Israel was instead the people through whom God mediated his will on earth. When the future messiah was thought of as the son of God, it was not because he would be God incarnate but because he would be a human particularly close to God through whom God worked his purposes. Jesus, for the Gospels of Matthew, Mark, and Luke, is that human.

This is the view, of course, that the Gospel writers inherited from the oral and written traditions on which they based their accounts. Jesus is not called God in Q, M, L, or any of the oral accounts that we can trace from the synoptic Gospels. But we can go yet earlier than this. As I pointed out, we have very primitive views of Jesus expressed in such pre-Pauline traditions as the one he cites in Romans 1:3–4, where Jesus is said to have become the son of God (not God) at his resurrection. That is, at Jesus's resurrection God adopted him into sonship. So too with the speeches of Acts, which we examined earlier (see Acts 2:36; 13:32 33). God exalted Jesus and made him his son, the Christ, at the resurrection.

This is in all probability the earliest understanding of Jesus among his followers. While he was living they thought that perhaps he would be the future messiah (who also, as we have seen, was not God). But this view was radically disconfirmed when he was arrested by the authorities, put on trial, and then tortured and crucified. This was just the opposite fate from the one that the messiah was supposed to enjoy. For some reason, however, the followers of Jesus (or at least some of them) came to think that he had been raised from the dead. This reconfirmed in a major way what they had thought of Jesus—that he was someone special before God. But it also forced his followers to rethink who he was. Some began to think of him as the messiah who had to suffer for sins, who had gone obediently to his death knowing that God wanted him to do so, but who was raised by God from the dead to show that he really was the one who enjoyed God's special favor. And so God exalted him to heaven, where he is now waiting to return in order to bring in God's kingdom as the coming messiah.

One passage that mythicists often appeal to, however, may on the surface seem to suggest that Paul, writing before the Gospels, understood Jesus as God who died and rose again (comparable to dying and rising pagan deities). This is the much-debated "hymn"—as it is called—found in Philippians 2:6–11. There is probably no other passage in the entire New Testament, and certainly none in the writings of Paul, that has had as much interpretive ink spilled over it. Scholars have written large books just on these six verses alone.[11] Even though mythicists typically treat it as unambiguous evidence of their views, the reality is that there is almost nothing unambiguous in the passage. Every word and phrase has been pored over and debated by scholars using the most sophisticated tools of analysis that are available. And still there is no consensus on what the passage means. But one thing is clear: it does not mean what mythicists typically claim it means. It does not portray Jesus in the guise of a pagan dying and rising god, even if that is what, on a superficial reading, it may appear to be about.

First I need to quote the passage in full. (It is important to rec-

ognize that scholars have heated and prolonged debates about even
how to translate many of the key terms.)

> Have this mind in yourselves which is also in Christ Jesus,
> who although he was in the form of God,
> did not regard being equal with God something to be
>   seized.
>
> But he emptied himself,
> taking on the form of a slave,
> and coming in the likeness of humans.
>
> And being found in the appearance as a human
> he humbled himself
> and became obedient unto death, even the death of the
>   cross.
>
> Therefore also God highly exalted him [literally:
>   hyperexalted him],
> and gave to him the name
> that is above every name.
>
> That at the name of Jesus,
> every knee should bow
> of things in heaven, and on earth, and under the earth.
>
> And every tongue should confess
> that Jesus Christ is Lord
> to the glory of God the Father.

Here then is one of the most intriguing accounts of Christ in the
New Testament. I cannot even begin to give a full interpretation of

the passage here. But I can say something about the passage, broadly, before making a couple of key interpretive points.

There is wide agreement that the passage appears to be poetic— possibly some kind of hymn (this is what everyone used to think) or a creed (this is more plausible)—and that Paul appears to be quot- ing it rather than composing it. But even this is debated, as scholars dispute whether it was written by someone else before Paul drafted this letter to the Christians in Philippi or whether Paul himself was its author.[12] It is debated how to divide the passage. In my transla- tion I have divided it in half, with the first half consisting of three stanzas of three lines, each talking about the descent or humbling of Christ, and the second half consisting of three stanzas of three lines, each talking about the ascent or exaltation of Christ. That is one possibility. Many, many others have been proposed by fine scholars, many of whom have studied this passage far more than I have, even though I have studied, thought about, ruminated on, and read about this passage for well over thirty years.[13]

For the purposes of my discussion here I simply want to make a couple of very basic points. One interpretation of the passage— the one that will strike many first-time readers as the only obvious one—is that it portrays Christ as a preexistent divine being who came to earth, was crucified, and was then exalted back to heaven. That may be the right way to read the passage, but as I've said, it is hotly debated. Even if that is the best way to read the passage, how- ever, it does not support the idea that originally Christ was seen as a dying-rising god, for several reasons.

First, even though it says that before humbling himself Christ was in the "form of God," that does not mean that he was God. Divinity was his "form," just as later in the passage he took on the "form" of a "slave." That does not mean that he was permanently and always a slave; it was simply the outward form he assumed. Moreover, when it says that he "did not regard equality with God something to be seized," it is hotly debated whether that means that he did not want to "retain" what he already had or to "grab" something that he did not have. In favor of the latter interpretation is the fact that after he humbled himself, Christ is said to have been hyperexalted, that is, exalted even higher than he was before. That must mean that before he humbled himself he was not already equal with God. Otherwise, how could he later be exalted even higher? What would be "higher" than God? That would suggest that even though he was originally in God's form, he was not fully God at the beginning; being fully God was something that he refused to grasp.

But if Christ was in the form of God without being equal with God, what was he? Here scholars have had a field day. One of the most popular interpretations of the passage may not have occurred to you at all. A large number of scholars think that the passage does not imagine Christ existing as a divine being with God in heaven, coming to earth to die, and then being exalted even higher afterward. They think instead that the passage is talking about Christ as the "second Adam," one who was like the first man, Adam, as described in the book of Genesis, but who acted in just the opposite way, leading to just the opposite result.[14]

In the book of Genesis, when God creates "man," Adam is said to have been made in the "image" of God (Genesis 1:26). The terms *image* and *form* are sometimes used synonymously in the Old Testament. Is Christ in the "form" of God the same way that Adam was? If so, what did Adam do? He wanted to be "equal with God," and so he grabbed for the fruit of the tree of the knowledge of good and evil. Christ, by contrast, did not think that equality with God "was something to be grabbed." His actions were just the opposite of Adam's. Because of sin, Adam was destined to die—as were all of his descendants. Christ, by contrast, explicitly chose to die for the sake of those who had to die because of Adam. And because he did not grab for equality with God but died out of obedience, God did just the opposite for Christ that he did for Adam. Adam and his descendants were cursed. Christ was highly exalted above all else. So high was he exalted that it is at the name of Jesus that every knee shall bow and every tongue will confess.

This final part of the passage is actually a quotation from Isaiah 45:23, which says that it is to God alone that every knee shall bow and tongue confess. However you interpret the rest of the passage, this conclusion is stunning. Christ will receive the adoration that is by rights God's alone. That is how highly God exalted him in reward for his act of obedience.

If this interpretation is correct, then the beginning of the passage is describing Christ not as a preexistent divine being but as very much as a human being. But even if it is not correct, the passage begins by describing Christ, not as God, but as a being in the form of God. Another option is that this is describing Christ as a preexistent angelic being. Angels in the Old Testament are God's messengers who can appear like God, as in passages in the Old Testament where an "angel of the Lord" appears and is actually called God (as in Exodus 3—the passage about Moses and the Burning Bush). In these cases, though, the angels may appear like God (in the "form" of God), but they are not actually God. They are God's messengers, his angels. It is striking that a number of Jewish traditions speak of an angel being exalted to the level of God, sitting on a throne next to that of the Almighty.[15]

However one interprets the beginning of this passage in Philippians, one thing is clear. It does not describe a dying and rising god. Thinking that it does so requires the reader to ignore what the text actually says in the second stanza. What is most significant is that Christ—whether a preexistent divine being, Adam, or an angel (I prefer the final interpretation myself)—"emptied himself" before dying on the cross. That is to say, he deprived himself of whatever status he had when he was in the "form of god," and he took on a completely different form, that of a "slave." It is not as a god that he dies, but as a slave. And he is not raised as God. He is exalted to a position worthy of equal worship with God only *after* he is raised. That is when he is awarded divine attributes and given divine worship. This passage is thus not talking about a god who dies and then is raised, it is talking about the death of a humbled slave and his exaltation to a position of divine authority and grandeur.

The most important point I want to make, however, is this. Even those scholars who think that Paul inherited this hymn (or creed) do not think that it was the oldest form of belief about Jesus. Even if it predates Paul, it does not represent the earliest Christian understanding of Christ. However we interpret this passage, the earliest Christian traditions point in a completely different direction, emphasizing Jesus's full humanness and saying nothing at all about his being God. The divinity of Christ is a relative latecomer to the scene of Christian theological reflections.

The broad views about Jesus in the early Christian traditions are otherwise clear. As I indicated, the earliest view was almost certainly that God exalted Jesus and made him his son when he raised him from the dead (this is roughly the view of the Philippians hymn as well, of course). And so the speeches of Acts, which must date well before any of our Gospels, and almost certainly predate the writings of Paul himself, indicate that it was at the resurrection that Jesus was made the Lord, the Christ, the Son of God (Acts 2:36; 13:32–33).[16] That is the view of the creed that Paul quotes in Romans 1:3–4 as well.

Some Christians were not content with the idea that Jesus was the Son of God only at his resurrection, however, and came to think that he must have been the Son of God for his entire public ministry. And so we have traditions that arose indicating that Jesus became the Son of God at his baptism. That may be the view still found in our earliest Gospel, Mark, who begins his narrative with Jesus being baptized and hearing the voice of God from heaven declaring him his son. In Mark Jesus is certainly not God. In fact, in one passage he clearly indicates that he is not to be thought of as God (Mark

10:17–18; a man calls Jesus "good," and Jesus objects because "no one is good but God alone").

Eventually some Christians came to think that Jesus must have been the Son of God not only during his public ministry but for his entire life. And so they began telling stories about how he was *born* as the Son of God. We find this view in Matthew and Luke, where Jesus's mother is in fact a virgin so that he is in a more literal sense the Son of God because the Spirit of God is responsible for making Mary pregnant (see Luke 1:35).

As time went on, even this view failed to satisfy some Christians, who thought that Jesus was not simply a being who came into the world as the Son of God but someone who had existed even before being born. This is a view not suggested by either Matthew or Luke (they appear to think that when he came into existence at conception). And so we come to our final canonical Gospel, the Gospel of John, which indicates that Jesus is the Word of God who existed with God from eternity past, through whom God created the world, who has now become a human (John 1:1–18). But I need to stress: this is a view found only in our last Gospel.[17] It eventually became the standard view among Christians and was written into Christian statements of faith: Christ is himself God. But it was not the earliest Christian view, not by a long shot. Christians, then, did not invent Jesus as a dying and rising god. In the oldest form of the faith they did not consider him to be God. That belief developed only later.

Instead, as we have seen, the earliest Christians considered Jesus to be the crucified messiah. Even though Jesus is never explicitly called God in any of our early Gospels—or in the traditions they were based on or even in Paul—he was almost everywhere called something else. He was called the Christ. Even the Philippians hymn, Paul tells us, is about "Christ Jesus." So frequently was Jesus called Christ in the oldest Christian traditions that already by the time of Paul, "Christ" had become Jesus's name (Jesus Christ, not

Jesus God). Jesus is called Christ in Paul, Mark, M, L, John, Josephus, Pliny, Tacitus, and so on. It is important to remember what
this term meant in ancient Judaism. It referred—however it was
interpreted—to a future powerful deliverer of God's people from
their enemies.

And so the key question to ask of the early traditions is not why
the earliest Christians called Jesus God (since they didn't), but why
they called him the Christ. He was, after all, known by everyone
to have been crucified, and the messiah—whatever else you might
say about him—was not supposed to be crucified. Just the opposite.
The early Christians did not ask why God had been crucified. They
asked why Christ had been crucified. They did not derive the ideas
of Jesus's death from pagan myth. They knew he had died, and they
believed, in Jewish apocalyptic fashion, that he had been raised. But
the fact that they called him the Christ shows they did not derive
the ideas of his death from Jewish legend and myth either since Jews
had no conception of a crucified messiah. Thus the conclusion that
has been reached by historians far and wide appears to be the right
one: Jesus must have really existed and must have really been crucified. Those who believed in him thought that he was the messiah
anyway. And they redefined what the term *messiah* meant in order
to make sense of it. They did not invent the idea of Jesus, however.
Had they done that, they never would have invented him as a crucified messiah. They were forced to come up with the idea of the crucified messiah because they knew there really was a man Jesus who
was crucified, yet they wanted to maintain that he was the messiah.

And so Jesus was not invented as a Jewish version of the pagan
dying and rising god. There are very serious doubts over whether
any pagans believed in such gods. Few scholars wonder if Jews believed in them, however. There is no evidence to locate such beliefs
among Palestinian Jews of the first century. But even more important, Christians did not see Jesus as a dying and rising god because
they at first did not even see him as God. The divinity of Christ was

a later theological development. The earliest Christians saw him as a dying and rising messiah.

Was Jesus Invented as a Personification of Jewish Wisdom?

NO ONE HAS BEEN a more enduring spokesperson for a mythicist view of Christ than G. A. Wells. For over thirty-five years Wells has insisted that the Christ of Christian tradition did not exist but was invented. He does not think, however, that the majority of mythicists are right that Christ was invented as a Jewish version of some pagan dying-rising gods. In his opinion the myths used to generate Christ were Jewish. Specifically, Christ was created as a personification of the mythical figure known in Jewish texts as "Wisdom."

As we will see in greater detail later, Wells also disagrees with most other mythicists because he thinks that there really was a man Jesus. But for Wells, Jesus had very little, or nothing, to do with the myth about Christ. He was not the Galilean preacher and healer of the first century. That figure is the creation of the Gospel of Mark. Jesus was a completely unknown and obscure Jewish figure who lived over a hundred years earlier. Christ, by contrast, was an invention of a Jewish sect of the first century.[18]

In rough outline this view is similar to that earlier held by Archibald Robertson, who suggested the following: "May not a solution of the dispute [between those who insist that Jesus did not exist and those who claim he did] lie in recognition of the fact that the two parties are arguing on different subjects—that there are indeed, two different Jesuses, a mythical and an historical, having nothing in common but the name, and that the two have been fused into one?"[19] In Robertson's view, Paul was "a Gnostic missionary who, even if he knew anything of a Messiah executed in Palestine, cared nothing for him or his followers." For Robertson, it is Mark who effected the fusion of the two Jesuses. And so the historical Jesus did exist. But "we know next to nothing about this Jesus."

Wells takes this ball and runs with it, a considerable distance. Wells thinks that the early Christians who invented Christ were particularly influenced by Jewish traditions that spoke of God's Wisdom as if it existed as an actual divine entity, distinct from but obviously closely related to, God himself. Wisdom preexisted with God and was used by God to create the world. Wells is right that this is indeed a known figure from Jewish traditions, appearing as far back as the book of Proverbs in the Old Testament. The most famous passage occurs in Proverbs 8, where Wisdom itself is speaking:

> The Lord created me at the beginning of his work,
> the first of his acts of long ago.
> Ages ago I was set up,
> at the first, before the beginning of the earth. . . .
> Before the mountains had been shaped,
> before the hills, I was brought forth. . . .
> When he established the heavens I was there,
> when he drew a circle on the face of the deep,
> when he made firm the skies above,
> when he established the fountains of the deep. . . .
> Then I was beside him, like a master worker;
> And I was daily his delight, rejoicing before him always.

In a book of Jewish tradition not found in the canon of the Hebrew Bible (but included in the Apocrypha), called the Wisdom of Solomon, we learn the following about Wisdom:

> She is a breath of the power of God
> and a pure emanation of the glory of the Almighty. . . .
> For she is a reflection of eternal light,
> a spotless mirror of the working of God,

> and an image of his goodness. . . .
> She reaches mightily from one end of the earth to the
>   other,
> and she orders all things well. . . .
> For she is an initiate in the knowledge of God,
> and an associate in his works. (Wisdom of Solomon 7–8)

Here we have a figure who was preexistent with God, who perfectly reflects God, who was used by God to create the world. This, for Wells, sounds a good deal like what we find in a passage celebrating Christ in one of the letters attributed to Paul in the New Testament:

> For he is the image of the invisible God, the firstborn of all
> creation; for all things were created in him—things in heaven
> and on earth, the visible and the invisible, whether thrones
> or dominions or rulers or authorities. All things were created
> through him and for him. And he is before all things and
> all things subsist in him. And he is the head of the body, the
> church, he who is the beginning, the firstborn from the dead,
> that he might be preeminent in all things. Because in him
> all the fullness was pleased to dwell and, through him, to
> reconcile all things to himself, having made peace through the
> blood of his cross, whether things on earth or in the heavens.
> (Colossians 1:15–20)

This passage, which Wells points out is very similar to the Philippians hymn, which we just considered (Philippians 2:6–11), portrays Christ as the Wisdom of God, the image of God himself who created all things, who comes to earth and dies for the sake of reconciling all things back to God. In Wells's view, the idea that Christ was crucified came to Paul as he reflected on the traditions of Wisdom that he inherited through the Jewish traditions. Before Paul, "some Christians . . . did not share his view that Jesus was crucified." But in the Wisdom of Solomon we hear of the wise man who suffered a "shameful death" (see Wisdom of Solomon 2:12–20). "It may well have been musing on such a passage that led Paul (or a precursor) to the idea, so characteristic of his theology, that Christ suffered the most shameful death of all."[20]

The key point for Wells, however, is that Paul explicitly calls Christ the "Wisdom of God" in 1 Corinthians 1:23–24: "We preach Christ crucified, which is a scandal to the Jews and foolishness to the Gentiles; but to those who are called, both Jews and Gentiles, Christ is the power of God and the wisdom of God." And later in the same book Paul says, "We speak wisdom to those who are mature, but it is a wisdom not of this age nor of the rulers of this age who are passing away. But we speak a wisdom of God that has been revealed in a mystery, which God foreknew before the ages unto our glory, which none of the rulers of this age knew. For if they had known, they would not have crucified the Lord of glory" (1 Corinthians 2:6–8).

According to Wells, then, Paul held to the view that Wisdom had become incarnate in Christ. The myth of Christ as Wisdom made incarnate was eventually historicized—that is, made into a real, historical, human being—when the Gospels were written toward the end of the first century.

Despite the inherent intrigue of this proposal, it is, I am afraid, riddled with problems, which may be why most other mythicists have not latched on to it. For one thing, while it is true that Paul calls Jesus the Wisdom of God in 1 Corinthians, this is not the normal way that he refers to him and is certainly not the way he first thought of him. There is no reason to privilege this conception over the many others that can be found in Paul. Within this passage alone, for example, Paul calls Jesus both the "Christ" and the "power of God." Why should we think that Paul (or his predecessor) *first* imagined Christ to be incarnate Wisdom—especially since he does not call Jesus this anywhere else in his writings? And what does he call him? Typically, he calls him Christ. This, not Wisdom, was Paul's earliest understanding of Jesus upon his conversion.

Paul calls Christ the wisdom of God in the Corinthians passage because he is trying to make a specific point, that the crucifixion of the messiah is a stumbling block for Jews and foolish for Gentiles. We have already seen the reason Jews stumbled over the claim that the messiah was crucified: this was not at all what was supposed to happen to the messiah. But for Paul, rather than showing that Christ was "weak" when he was crucified, the cross shows forth God's true "power." So too Gentiles thought that the idea of an executed criminal as the revealer of God was ridiculous. But for Paul it was, by contrast, a sign of God's "wisdom." That is why Jesus is the wisdom of God, not because he is an embodiment of the Jewish traditions about the Wisdom figure.

Moreover, it is important to note how Paul phrases this entire passage: his emphasis throughout is precisely on "Christ" and his crucifixion. This is an important point because Wells himself admits that the Jewish traditions about Wisdom include no reference to Wisdom ever being or becoming the messiah. There is no way to move, then, from the idea that God's Wisdom became incarnate to the notion that this one was specifically the messiah. It is quite easy, however, to move in the other direction. If Christ was crucified—the main point Paul makes about him—it may seem to be "foolish," but God's ways are not ours, and for God this evident foolishness is in fact "wisdom." Paul, in other words, did not start out as a Christian thinking that Wisdom had become incarnate; he started out thinking that Christ had been crucified.

It should not be objected—as Wells does—that the poetic passage in Colossians that I quoted at length shows that Paul understood

Christ as Wisdom incarnate. There is a fatal objection to this view. Paul almost certainly did not write the letter to the Colossians. It is one of the forgeries in Paul's name, written after his death, as critical scholars have recognized for a very long time.[21] And to argue that the passage derives from a pre-Pauline tradition is problematic. Colossians is *post*-Pauline, so on what grounds can we say that a passage in it is *pre*-Pauline?

In short, the idea that Jesus is in some sense God's Wisdom stands on the margins of Paul's thinking. It is certainly not the first thing that popped into his mind when he became a follower of Jesus. It was a later theological reflection. The first and primary thing that Paul came to think of Jesus was that he was the messiah, and a crucified messiah at that. This is the tradition about Jesus that we can trace back to the time even before Paul converted to be a follower of Jesus sometime around the year 32 or 33. The Christians who proclaimed this view did not originally think of Christ as incarnate Wisdom based on the books of Proverbs and the Wisdom of Solomon. They thought of Christ as the one who had been crucified.

And this was not based on the reflection that a wise man was said to have died a "shameful death" in a passage of the Wisdom of Solomon, a book that did not become part of the Jewish scriptures. It was based on the fact that everyone knew that Jesus had been crucified. Those who believed he was the messiah therefore concluded that the messiah had been crucified. And as a result they redefined what it meant to be the messiah. It meant one who suffered for the sins of others. This view seemed ridiculous to most hearers. But the followers of Jesus argued that it was one of those paradoxical truths that showed that God's ways are not human ways and that what seems foolish to humans is wisdom for God. Once they began to make that claim, years after Paul had been converted, they began to press it even more and (possibly) came to think of Jesus as God's Wisdom itself, the one through whom God made the world. But this was not the earliest belief of the Christians or of Paul.

Was Jesus an Unknown Jew Who Lived in Obscurity More Than a Century Before Paul?

G. A. WELLS HAS argued that Paul did not understand Jesus to be a real flesh-and-blood Jew who recently lived as a teacher in Palestine and was crucified by the Roman authorities in the recent past. Instead, Wells contends, Paul understood Jesus to have been a supernatural being who lived in utter obscurity some 150 years or so earlier, who was crucified not by the Romans but by the demonic forces in the world.[22] In part Wells derives this view from Paul's first letter to the Corinthians, where, as we have just seen, he refers to God's wisdom: "We speak a wisdom of God that is hidden in a mystery, which God foreordained before the ages for our glory, which none of the rulers of this age knew. For if they had known, they would not have crucified the Lord of glory" (1 Corinthians 2:7–8).

The fact that the "rulers" did not grasp the hidden mystery of who Christ was shows that he lived in utter obscurity. He was not a well-known teacher. Moreover, for Wells, Paul gives no indication that Jesus lived in the recent past. Paul simply indicates, says Wells, that Jesus started to "appear" to people in the recent past, after his resurrection (appearing to Paul himself, for example). But that does not mean he had recently lived. On the contrary, even though Jesus was a descendant of King David, Paul gives "no indication in which of the many centuries between David and Paul" that Jesus lived.[23] Wells argues that 1 Thessalonians 2:15 cannot be used to establish Paul's views of a recent Jesus, when the text speaks of the Judeans "who killed both the Lord Jesus and the prophets, and drove us out, and are displeasing to both God and all humans." In Wells's view, this passage is an insertion into Paul's letter, not something Paul himself wrote—a view that I discussed (and dismissed) earlier.

In short, for Paul, Jesus lived a completely unknown and obscure life over a century earlier. He was executed during the reign of the ruthless Jewish king Jannaeus (ruled 103–76 BCE), who was known to have crucified some eight hundred of his Jewish opponents. Paul knew nothing of Jesus's life and did not care to know anything of his life. All he knew was that Jesus had now, in recent times, begun to appear to people, showing that he was alive again. Those who believed in him could be united with him by mystical baptism in light of the approaching end. It was twenty-five to thirty years after Paul that the story of Jesus began to be historicized into Gospel traditions, as eventually written down first by the Gospel of Mark.

For Wells, if Paul had thought Jesus had died recently, he surely would have mentioned something about a crucifixion in Jerusalem under Pontius Pilate. Indications that Paul did not think that Jesus had lived recently can be found in such passages as Colossians 1:15, which speaks of Christ as "the image of the invisible God, the first-born of all creation." For Wells, "such passages do not read like allusions to a near-contemporary being."[24]

There are numerous problems with this view. To begin with, as we have seen, Paul did not write the letter to the Colossians. It can scarcely be used to establish Paul's views. But even if we thought that Paul wrote it, the passage in question says nothing at all about when Christ existed as a human, whether in the recent or the distant past. This is the kind of weak assertion that Wells typically makes. He provides no solid ground for thinking that Paul imagined Jesus to have lived in the remote past—certainly nothing to suggest that his life ended during the reign of King Jannaeus. The fact that Paul does not mention that Jesus died in Jerusalem under Pontius Pilate is not in the least odd. What occasion did Paul have to mention something that everyone knew? That this was common knowledge should be clear from our Gospel sources, which did not begin to historicize Jesus two or three decades after Paul but spoke of the historical Jesus already by the early 30s, within at least a year of the traditional date of his death, before Paul was even converted, as we have seen.

There are solid reasons for thinking that Paul understood Jesus to have died recently. I can start with that basic confession of faith that Paul lays out in 1 Corinthians 15:3–5, a confession that was passed along to him by those who came before, as he himself states: "For I delivered over to you as of first importance what I also received, that Christ died for our sins in accordance with the scriptures, and that he was buried; and that he was raised on the third day in accordance with the scriptures and that he appeared to Cephas and then to the twelve."

Several points are worth emphasizing here. This ancient creed is a neatly balanced, poetical statement, with two halves. In both halves it makes a claim about Christ (he died; he was raised), indicates that the claim is "in accordance with the scriptures," and then offers an empirical proof: that he died is proved by the fact that he was buried; that he was raised is proved by the fact that he appeared to Cephas (Peter) and then to the twelve (apostles).

The reason the passage is highly relevant to our discussion here is that Paul gives no indication at all that a hundred years or more passed between Jesus's resurrection and his appearance to the apostles. Quite the contrary; to insert a century-long hiatus into the formulation seems to be a bizarre interpretive move. What in the statement could possibly make one inclined to do so? No, Paul is expressing a straight chronological sequence of events: Jesus died; he was buried; three days later he was raised; and he then appeared to the apostles.

In Wells's view Jesus died over a century earlier and presumably was raised then, since Paul does say that the resurrection took place three days (not a century) after the death. But quite apart from this view being completely ungrounded and counterintuitive, it works precisely against the logic involved in Paul's view of the resurrection of Jesus. For Wells, the fact that Jesus has started to appear to people now, a century later, shows to Paul that the end of the age is drawing to a close. But what is the logic in that? Why would the sudden appearance of a long-dead man show Paul anything other than that he was seeing things? By contrast, if the death and burial and resurrection and appearances were all recent, then Paul's theological understanding of the resurrection makes perfect sense.

Paul's theology in fact was very much based on the fact (for him it was a fact) that Jesus was raised, and raised quite recently (not that he simply started appearing recently). If you were to ask Christians today what the significance of the resurrection of Jesus was, you might get a wide range of answers, from the rather uninformed "you can't keep a good man down" to the more sophisticated "it shows that he really was the Son of God." If you were to ask the apostle Paul the question, he would give a response that almost no one today would give. For Paul, the fact that Jesus was (recently) raised from the dead shows clearly that the end of the age is imminent.

The logic is tied to the apocalyptic understanding of the resurrection that I described earlier in this chapter. Paul was a Jewish apocalypticist even before he became a follower of Jesus. As such, Paul believed that God would soon intervene in history, overthrow the forces of evil, and bring in a good kingdom on earth. In thinking this, Paul was much like all the other apocalypticists from the time that we know about, for example, the authors of the Dead Sea Scrolls and of the various Jewish apocalypses. At this soon-to-arrive cataclysmic end of the age, a judgment would be rendered on all people, leading to judgment of some and condemnation of others. This would apply to both the living and the dead, at the future resurrection. The idea of the "resurrection of the dead" was an apocalyptic idea shared by a wide range of Jews, like Paul, even before he was converted. The key point is this: the resurrection was to happen at the end of this age.

For Paul, Jesus's resurrection—this end-of-the-age event—showed that the end had already begun. That, as we saw, is why Paul calls Jesus the "firstfruits of the resurrection" in 1 Corinthians 15:20.

After the farmer gathers the firstfruits on the first day of harvest, when does he gather the rest? Does he wait a hundred years? No, he goes out the next day. If Jesus is called the firstfruits of the resurrection it is because all the others who are dead will soon—very soon—be raised as well. We are living at the end of time.

The fact that Paul thinks of Jesus as the firstfruits shows beyond reasonable doubt that he thought the resurrection was a recent event. It is not that Jesus—killed a hundred or more years earlier—had started to appear to people (including "apostles" who never knew him) here at the end. It is that he has been raised here at the end. The culmination of the end is therefore imminent. That is why Paul intimates that he will be alive when Jesus returns (see 1 Thessalonians 4:13–18). The recent resurrection of God's messiah is a clear indication that the end of all things is virtually here.

And so both the literary character of 1 Corinthians 15:3–5 and the logic of Paul's understanding of the resurrection show that he thought that the life, death, and resurrection of Jesus were recent events. I should stress that this is the view of all of our sources that deal with the matter at all. It is hard to believe that Paul would have such a radically different view from every other Christian of his day, as Wells suggests. That Jesus lived recently is affirmed not only in all four of our canonical Gospels (where, for example, he is associated with John the Baptist and is said to have been born during the reign of the Roman emperor Augustus, under the rulership of the Jewish king Herod, and so on); it is also the view of all of the Gospel sources—Q (which associates Jesus with John the Baptist), M, L—and of the non-Christian sources such as Josephus and Tacitus (who both mention Pilate). These sources, I should stress, are all independent of one another; some of them go back to Palestinian traditions that can readily be dated to 31 or 32 CE, just a year or so after the traditional date of Jesus's death.

Was Jesus Crucified in the Spiritual Realm Rather Than on Earth?

ONE OF THE STAUNCHEST defenders of a mythicist view of Christ, Earl Doherty, maintains that the apostle Paul thinks that Jesus was crucified, not here on earth by the Romans, but in the spiritual realm by demonic powers. In advancing this thesis, Doherty places himself in an ironic position that characterizes many of his mythicist colleagues. He quotes professional scholars at length when their views prove useful for developing aspects of his argument, but he fails to point out that not a single one of these scholars agrees with his overarching thesis. The idea that Jesus was crucified in the spiritual realm is not a view set forth by Paul. It is a view invented by Doherty.

It is rather difficult to respond to a book like Doherty's recent massive tome, *Jesus: Neither God nor Man*. It is an 800-page book that is filled with so many unguarded and undocumented statements and claims, and so many misstatements of fact, that it would take a 2,400-page book to deal with all the problems. His major theses are set forth in a brief preface that lists "The Twelve Pieces of the Jesus Puzzle." Many of the claims are problematic, and I have dealt with a number of them already. One particular piece is especially unconvincing: in Doherty's view, Paul (and other early Christians) believed that the "Son of God had undergone a redeeming 'blood' sacrifice" not in this world but in a spiritual realm above it.[25]

Doherty's reason for this remarkable statement involves what he calls "the ancients' view of the universe" (was there one such view?). According to Doherty, authors who were influenced by Plato's way of thinking and by the mythology of the ancient Near East believed that there was a heavenly realm that had its counterpart here on earth. "Genuine" reality existed, not here in this world, but in that other realm. This view of things was especially true, Doherty avers, in the mystery cults, which Doherty claims provided "the predominant form of popular religion in this period."[26] (This latter claim, by the way, is simply not true. Most religious pagans were not devotees of mystery cults.)

In the first edition of Doherty's book, he claimed that it was in this higher realm that the key divine events of the mysteries transpired; it was there, for example, that Attis had been castrated, that Osiris had been dismembered, and that Mithras had slain the bull.[27] In his second edition he admits that in fact we do not know if that is true and that we do not have any reflections on such things by any of the cult devotees themselves since we don't have a single writing from any of the adherents of the ancient mystery cults. Yet he still insists that philosophers under the influence of Plato—such as Plutarch, whom we have met—certainly interpreted things this way.

In any event, in both editions of his book Doherty claims that the myths of the mystery cults and of Christianity took place in this upper, spiritual realm. In particular, Christ was crucified up there, by the demons, not down here, by humans. As he states, "The essential element of *The Jesus Puzzle* interpretation of early cultic Christ belief, and the one which has proven the most difficult for the modern mind to comprehend and accept, is that Paul's Christ Jesus was an entirely supernatural figure, crucified in the lower heavens at the hands of the demons spirits."[28] Like Wells before him, Doherty refuses to allow that 1 Thessalonians—which explicitly says that the Jews (or the Judeans) were the ones responsible for the death of Jesus—can be used as evidence of Paul's view: it is, he insists, an insertion into Paul's writings, not from the apostle himself. (Here we find, again, textual studies driven by convenience: if a passage contradicts your views, simply claim that it was not actually written by the author.) More telling for him is the passage I already quoted above from 1 Corinthians 2:6–8, which indicates that the "rulers of this age" were the ones who "crucified the Lord of glory." For Doherty these are obviously not human rulers but demonic forces. Thus for Paul and other early Christians, Christ was not a human crucified on earth but a divine being crucified in the divine realm.

But is this really what Paul thought—the Paul who knew Jesus's own brother and his closest disciple Peter, who learned of traditions of Jesus just a year or two after Jesus's death? Is this why Paul persecuted the Christians—not for saying the (earthly) messiah was crucified by the Romans but for saying that some kind of spiritual being was killed in heaven by demons? And why exactly was that so offensive to Paul? Why would it drive him to destroy the new faith, as he himself says in Galatians 1 that he did?

There are a host of reasons for calling Doherty's view into serious question. To begin with, how can he claim to have uncovered "the" view of the world held by "the" ancients, a view that involved an upper world where the true reality resides and this lower world, which is a mere reflection of it? How, in fact, can we talk about "the" view of the world in antiquity? Ancient views of the world were extremely complex and varied, just as today's views are. Would anyone claim that Appalachian snake handlers and postmodernist literary critics all have the same view of the world? Or that Primitive Baptists, high-church Episcopalians, Mormons, atheists, and pagans do? Or Jews, Muslims, and Buddhists? Or Marxists and capitalists? That all of these groups have "the" modern view of the world? To talk about "the" view of the world in any century is far too simplistic and naive.

It is true that Plato and his followers had a certain view of reality where, roughly speaking, this material world is but a reflection of the world of "forms." But Platonism was simply one of the ancient philosophies popular at the time of Christianity. Also popular was Stoicism, with a completely different, nondualistic sense of the world; Stoicism lacked the notion that this realm is an imitation of the higher realm. So too did Epicureanism, which thought in fairly modern fashion that the material world is all there is. Why should we assume that the mystery cults were influenced by just one of these philosophies? Or for that matter by any of them? What evidence does Doherty cite to show that mystery religions were at heart Platonic? Precisely none.

When, in his second edition, Doherty admits that we do not know what the followers of the mystery cults thought, he is absolutely correct. We do not know. But he then asserts that they thought like the later Platonist Plutarch. How can he have it both ways? Either we know how they thought or we do not. And it is highly unlikely that adherents of the mystery cults (even if we could lump them all together) thought like one of the greatest intellectuals of their day (Plutarch). Very rarely do common people think about the world the way upper-class, highly educated, elite philosophers do. Would you say that your understanding of how language works matches the views of Wittgenstein? Or that your understanding of political power is that of Foucault?

In the case of someone like Plutarch there is, in fact, convincing counterevidence. Philosophers like Plutarch commonly took on the task of explaining away popular beliefs by allegorizing them, to show that despite what average people naively believed, for example, about the gods and the myths told about them, these tales held deeper philosophical truths. The entire enterprise of philosophical reflection on ancient mythology was rooted precisely in the widely accepted fact that common people did not look at the world, or its myths, in the same way the philosophers did. Elite philosophers tried to show that the myths accepted by others were emblematic of deeper spiritual truths.

I hardly need to emphasize again that the early followers of Jesus were not elite philosophers. They were by and large common people. Not even Paul was philosophically trained. To be sure, as a literate person he was far better educated than most Christians of his day. But he was no Plutarch. His worldview was not principally dependent on Plato. It was dependent on the Jewish traditions, as these were mediated through the Hebrew scriptures. And the Hebrew scriptures certainly did not discount the events that transpire here on earth among very real humans. For the writers of the Hebrew Bible, the acts of God did not transpire in some kind of ethereal realm above us all. They happened here on earth and were deeply rooted in daily, historical, real human experience. In the same way, the early Christians, including Paul, thought of Jesus crucified the way they thought of other prophets who had suffered. He was crucified here on earth, by humans.

In short, since we know almost nothing about what adherents of the mystery cults believed, we simply cannot assume that they thought of the world like Plutarch and other upper-crust elite philosophers. One thing that we do know about them, however, is where they were located and thus, to some extent, where they exerted significant influence. We know this from the archaeological record they have left behind. Among all our archaeological findings, there is none that suggests that pagan mystery cults exerted any influence on Aramaic-speaking rural Palestinian Judaism in the 20s and 30s of the first century. And this is the milieu out of which faith in Jesus the crucified messiah, as persecuted and then embraced by Paul, emerged.

There are no grounds for assuming that Paul, whose views of Jesus were taken over from the Palestinian Jewish Christians who preceded him, held a radically different view of Jesus from his predecessors. Paul tells us about his background. He was raised a highly religious Jew, and he was a Pharisee. Were Pharisaic Jews influenced by the mystery cults? Did they spend their days plumbing the depths of the myths about Attis and Osiris? Did they look deeply into the mysteries of Isis and Mithras? It is an easy question to answer. These mystery cults are never mentioned by Paul or by any other Christian author of the first hundred years of the church. There is not a stitch of evidence to suggest that mystery cults played any role whatever in the views of the Pharisees or, for that matter, in the views of any Jewish group of the first century: the Sadducees, the Essenes (who produced the Dead Sea Scrolls), the revolutionaries who wanted to overthrow the Romans, the apocalyptic prophets like John the Baptist (and their followers), or the common people. So not only do we not know whether mystery cults were influenced by "the" (alleged) ancient view of the world—whatever that might be—there is not a shred of evidence to suggest that these cults played the least role in the development of early views of Jesus. Rather, we have plenty of reasons, based on our early Jewish sources, that just the opposite was the case.

That in no small part is why not a single early Christian source supports Doherty's claim that Paul and those before him thought of Jesus as a spiritual, not a human, being who was executed in the spiritual, not the human, sphere. That is not the view of Mark, Matthew, Luke, or John. It is not the view of any of the written sources of any of these Gospels, for example, M and L. It is not the view of any of the oral traditions that later made their way into these Gospels. And it is not the view of the epistles of the New Testament, including Hebrews—the one book of the New Testament that may well reflect some Platonic influence—which unabashedly stresses that Christ "came into the world" (10:5), declares that he made a bloody sacrifice in this world (10:12), and says that "in the days of his flesh he offered up prayers and petitions to the one who was able to save him from death, with strong cries and tears" (5:7). This is not heavenly but earthly suffering. Or consider the book of 1 John, which is quite emphatic not only that Jesus shed his blood (1:7) as an "expiation for sins" (2:2) but also that he was a real, fleshly human being who could be heard, seen, felt, and handled when he was "manifested" here on earth (1:1–3).

So too with Paul. Paul indicates that Jesus was born (in this world) of a woman and as a Jew (Galatians 4:4); he repeatedly stresses that Jesus experienced a real bloody death (for example, Romans 3) and that he was bodily raised from the dead (1 Corinthians 15). This resurrection was not in the heavenly realm for Paul. It was here on earth. That is why Jesus appeared, not to heavenly beings in the upper realm, but to human beings in this one (1 Corinthians 15:5–8). If his resurrection took place here on earth, where was his crucifixion? Paul leaves little doubt about that. Jesus had a last meal with his disciples on the "night" in which he was handed over to his fate. Do they have nights in the spiritual realm? This is a description of something that happened on earth. But even more, Paul stresses that Jesus was buried between his death and his (earthly) resurrection. Surely he means he was buried in a tomb, and that would be here on earth.

The early Christians, Paul included, had a thoroughly apocalyptic understanding of the world, inherited from a Jewish worldview attested long before them, in which this created order would be transformed by the power of God when he brought his kingdom here, to this earth. The kingdom was not an ethereal place in some spiritual realm. For apocalypticists—from the Jewish author of the famous "War Scroll" discovered among the Dead Sea Scrolls to the Christian author of the book of Revelation—the future kingdom would be earthly, through and through (Revelation 20–21). Paul and others expected Jesus to return from heaven, into this very realm where we dwell now (1 Thessalonians 4–5), leading to the transformation of both us and the world (1 Corinthians 15). Paul thought Christ was to "return" here because he had "left" here. This is where he was born, lived, died, and was raised. It all happened here on earth, not in some other celestial realm. Jesus was killed by humans. The forces of evil may have ultimately engineered this death (although, actually, Paul says God did); the demons (whom Paul never mentions) may have inspired the authorities to do the dirty deed, but it was they who did it.

In sum, there is no evidence to support Doherty's contention that for Paul and the Christians before him Jesus's death took place in the spiritual rather than the earthly world, effected by demons instead of humans. But there are many other reasons to reject this view.

Did Mark, Our First Gospel, Invent the Idea of a Historical Person, Jesus?

WE HAVE SEEN THAT most mythicists maintain that the early Christians believed in a divine Christ modeled on pagan dying-rising gods or, in the case of G. A. Wells, in a Christ who was Wisdom made incarnate. It is widely thought among those who hold such views that the Jesus of the Gospel tradition—the Jewish teacher and prophet of Galilee who did miracles and then was crucified by the Romans—is an invention of our first Gospel, Mark. The later Gospels then derived their views, and many of their stories, from him. This view is suggested in several places by Wells[29] and is stated quite definitively by Doherty: "All the Gospels derive their basic story of Jesus of Nazareth from one source: the Gospel of Mark, the first one composed. Subsequent evangelists reworked Mark in their own interests and added new material."[30] Throughout this study I have addressed this issue piecemeal in the context of other discussions. Here I would like to tackle it head-on to show that it is almost certainly not correct.

To begin with, there are solid reasons for doubting that the Gospel of John is based on Mark or on either of the other two earlier Gospels, even though the matter is debated among scholars.[31] But the reality is that most of the stories told about Jesus in the synoptic Gospels are missing from John, just as most of John's stories, including his accounts of Jesus's teachings, are missing from the synoptics. When they do tell the same stories (for example, the cleansing of the Temple, the betrayal of Judas, the trial before Pilate, the crucifixion and resurrection narratives) they do so in different language (without verbatim overlaps) and with radically different conceptions.[32] It is simplest to assume that John had his own sources for his accounts. And I should stress yet again that even if John did know the earlier

Gospels, they did not provide him with most of his stories about Jesus as these, generally, are not found in those other books.

I should stress as well that some of these sources lying behind John stem from the early years of the Jesus movement, as is evident in the fact that some of them still betray their roots in Aramaic-speaking circles of Palestine. This puts them (some of them) in the early days of the movement, decades before Mark was written.[33]

Whatever one decides about the Gospel of John, it is clear that Matthew and Luke used narratives of Jesus's life and death that were independent of Mark. The sources I have called M and L contain accounts, not only of Jesus's words and deeds but also of his Passion, that differ from those in Mark. Even more telling, Luke explicitly informs us that "many" authors before him had produced accounts of the things Jesus said, did, and experienced. Mark by itself is not "many." Other Gospels, in addition to Mark, were produced. It is regrettable that some of Luke's other predecessors did not survive, but there is no reason to think he is lying when he says that he knows about them. And when he summarizes his Gospel at the beginning of his second volume, the book of Acts, it is clear that in his mind a full narrative of "the things accomplished among us" (as he describes the accounts of his predecessors in Luke 1:1) include not only what Jesus said and did but also the accounts of his Passion, up to the narrative of the ascension (Acts 1:1–4). Mark did not make up this kind of narrative. There were others. Luke writes his simply because he thinks he can do a better job.

In addition, Luke indicates that these kinds of narratives were based on what was being told by "eyewitnesses and ministers of the word" (1:2). In other words, Luke admits that even before there were written accounts of Jesus's life and death, these stories were being passed along orally, from the very beginning. The apostle Paul knew several of the people who passed along such stories, as we have seen, as he mentions traditions that he inherited from believers before him (1 Corinthians 11:22–24; 15:3–5) and names several of Jesus's close intimates as personal acquaintances: the disciples Cephas and John, along with Jesus's brother James.

The idea that Christians were telling stories of Jesus's life, death, and resurrection before Luke, before Mark, and before Paul is held by virtually all scholars of the New Testament, and for compelling reasons. As I earlier pointed out, the only way the early Christians—starting in the months after Jesus's death—could have propagated their beliefs, converting first Jews and then Gentiles to believe in Jesus, was by telling stories about him. Before he converted, Paul had heard some of these stories, at least those about Jesus's crucifixion but almost certainly other stories as well. If he was offended that this Jew in particular was the one being called the messiah, it means he must have known something about Jesus in particular (it is *possible* of course that all Paul knew was that followers of Jesus were calling him a crucified messiah and that he knew absolutely nothing else, but that does require a bit of a stretch of the imagination). In any event, Paul certainly knew other stories about Jesus soon after he converted in 32–33 CE, as he provides information about Jesus's birth, teachings, family, ministry, Last Supper, and crucifixion in his later writings, long before Mark wrote.

In addition, we have remnants of some of the early traditions of Jesus that were circulating orally, outside the Gospels, and only later written down. We have looked already at the speeches in the book of Acts. These speeches show clear signs of having derived from the earliest Christian communities since their Christological views are so "primitive" in relation to the views of Paul and the later Gospels. In several of these speeches it is clear that the storytellers believed that Jesus had become the Son of God and messiah at the time of the resurrection (not, say, at his baptism or his birth). These speeches must come from exceedingly early times. And in them we find summaries of Jesus's life and death, where it is clear that he was a Jewish teacher and miracle worker who was crucified by the Romans at the instigation of the Jews (see, for example, Acts

2:22–28; 3:11–26; 13:26–41). This is not a story invented by Mark; it was in circulation from the earliest period of Christian storytelling.

That traditions of Jesus's life and death were circulating in the early years of the Christian community independently of Mark can also be shown, somewhat ironically, from sources that are even later than Mark. We have already seen that writings unconnected to Mark, such as the letter to the Hebrews and the book of 1 John, stress both the earthly life of Jesus and the fact that he experienced a bloody death, which for these authors functioned as an atonement for sins. Whether or not Jesus's death was an atonement is a theological question, but the historical fact remains that these authors believed that Jesus both lived and died. Thus they based their exhortations and theological reflections on these historical data and on the stories that conveyed them, all independent of Mark.

Even in the Gospel of Mark there is evidence of traditions that long predate Mark and involve both Jesus's life and death. This we have seen from the fact that even though Mark was a Greek-speaking Christian, a number of his stories show clear signs of being originally told in Aramaic. And so we have seen that some of the sayings found in Mark make sense only when translated back into Aramaic (for example, "Sabbath was made for man, not man for the Sabbath, therefore the Son of Man is lord of the Sabbath"). Even more clearly, it is shown by the fact that some stories were passed down to Mark with their key Aramaic words left untranslated so that Mark, or more likely a predecessor, had to provide Greek speakers with a translation. Notably, this occurs in stories that involve both Jesus's public ministry (Mark 5:41) and his Passion (Mark 15:34).

There is no reason to think that Mark was the one who first imagined putting a ministry of Jesus together with an account of his death and that all other accounts of Jesus's life and death are dependent on his. The writings of Paul, speeches of Acts, the Gospel of John, the sources M and L, the comments of Luke, and other pieces of evidence all suggest quite the contrary, that even though Mark is our earliest surviving Gospel, his was not the first such narrative to be propagated. Luke is no doubt right that there were "numerous" such accounts before him, and there were certainly others after him. They are not all dependent, in all their stories, on Mark.

Conclusion

WE HAVE CONSIDERED SUBSTANTIAL and powerful arguments showing that Jesus really existed (chapters 2–5 above). Many of the arguments made by the mythicists, by contrast, are irrelevant to the question (chapter 6); many of the others are relevant but insubstantial or, quite frankly, wrong (this chapter). There was a historical Jesus, a Jewish teacher of first-century Palestine who was crucified by the Roman prefect Pontius Pilate.

But knowing this is only part of the story. Historians also want to know more about Jesus, about what he stood for, what he said, what he did, what he experienced, and why he was executed. Once we move from the fact of Jesus's existence to the question of who he really was, we move from the remarkably firm ground of virtual historical certainty to greater depths of uncertainty. Scholars debate these latter issues roundly. It will not be my purpose in the chapters that follow to solve the problems once and for all to the satisfaction of everyone who has ever thought about them. My goal instead is simply to explain why the majority of scholars who have dealt with these matters over the past century or so have concluded that the Jesus who existed is not the Jesus of the stained-glass window or the second-grade Sunday school class. The Jesus of popular imagination (there are actually a large number of Jesuses in various popular imaginations) is a "myth" in the sense that mythicists use the term: he is not the Jesus of history.

But there was a Jesus of history, and there is good evidence to suggest what he was like. In very broad terms Albert Schweitzer, with whom I started this story, was probably right. Jesus appears to have been a Jewish apocalypticist who expected God to intervene in the course of history to overthrow the forces of evil and to bring in his good kingdom. And in Jesus's view this would happen very soon, within his own generation. We will see in the following two chapters why this view of Jesus is persuasive.

PART III

Who Was the Historical Jesus?

CHAPTER EIGHT

Finding the Jesus of History

EVERY SPRING SEMESTER AT Chapel Hill I teach my undergraduate course Introduction to the New Testament. My students are smart, interesting, and interested; the majority of them are Bible-believing Christians. We spend a good portion of the semester—over half of it—studying the early Christian Gospels and then the life of the historical Jesus. To most of the students almost everything in the course is a complete revelation. Even though most of them were raised in the church and attended Sunday school for a good portion of their lives, they have never heard anything like what they learn in this class. That is because rather than teaching about the Bible from a theological, confessional, or devotional perspective, I teach the class—as is only appropriate in a state-supported, secular, research university—from a historical point of view.

Many of my students are surprised, dismayed, and sometimes even depressed (or, alternatively, liberated!) as they acquire historical knowledge about the New Testament. They hear, often for the first time, that we do not know who the authors of the Gospels actually were other than that they were almost certainly not the Aramaic-speaking lower-class peasants who made up the earthly disciples of Jesus. They learn that the different Gospels present very different portrayals of who Jesus was, what he stood for, and what he preached and that the New Testament tales of Jesus are full of discrepancies in matters both large and small. Many students are especially taken aback when they realize that even though the Gospels appear to be presenting historical accounts of Jesus's life, much of the material in the Gospels in fact is not historically reliable.

I do not discuss mythicists in the class since, as I've repeatedly indicated, the mythicist view does not have a foothold, or even a toehold, among modern critical scholars of the Bible. But knowing that Jesus really existed is only the beginning of the quest for the historical Jesus. Let's say that he did exist. What then? What was Jesus like? What do we know about his life? What did he stand for? What did he preach and teach? What did he do? What kinds of controversies was he involved in? How did he come to be crucified? These are the questions that my students are particularly keen to address once they realize that the Gospels do not preserve completely accurate eyewitness testimonies. And they are the issues that I will be addressing in this chapter and the one that follows.

Certainties and Uncertainties in the Life of Jesus

As I HAVE REPEATEDLY emphasized, different scholars come to radically different conclusions about how to understand the life of the historical Jesus. This is almost entirely because of the nature of our sources. We have seen that these sources are more than ample to establish that Jesus was a Jewish teacher of first-century Roman Palestine who was crucified under Pontius Pilate. As we will see in a moment, they are also ample for knowing a few more things about his life, as virtually every researcher agrees. But they are not ample when it comes to wanting to know more details, in greater depth, about what he actually said, did, and experienced. Some of the sources are sparse to the point of being completely frustrating. How we wish that Josephus, Tacitus, and, say, the letter of James had much more to say! Others are so slanted in their presentation that they have to be handled like an inordinately hot potato. The Infancy Gospel of Thomas, for example, and the Proto-Gospel of James do not give us much to go on if we want to know about the life of the historical Jesus, even his early life. Paul gives us some good, useful information, but there is not much there if we want extensive descriptions about what Jesus said, did, and experienced. The canonical Gospels are full of information, but they are at odds with one another in one detail after the other, and their overall portrayals of Jesus differ from one another, sometimes radically. As a result, the information they provide needs to be handled with a deft critical touch.

Even given these problems, there are a number of important facts about the life of Jesus that virtually all critical scholars agree on, for reasons that have in part been shown and that in other ways will become increasingly clear throughout the course of this chapter and the next. Everyone, except the mythicists, of course, agrees that Jesus was a Jew who came from northern Palestine (Nazareth) and lived as an adult in the 20s of the Common Era. He was at one point of his life a follower of John the Baptist and then became a preacher and teacher to the Jews in the rural areas of Galilee. He preached a message about the "kingdom of God" and did so by telling parables. He gathered disciples and developed a reputation for being able to heal the sick and cast out demons. At the very end of his life, probably around 30 CE, he made a trip to Jerusalem during a Passover feast and roused opposition among the local Jewish leaders, who arranged to have him put on trial before Pontius Pilate, who ordered him to be crucified for calling himself the king of the Jews.

Nearly all critical scholars agree at least on those points about the historical Jesus. But there is obviously a lot more to say, and that is where scholarly disagreements loom large—disagreements not over whether Jesus existed but over what kind of Jewish teacher and preacher he was. Some scholars have said that he is principally to be thought of as a first-century Jewish rabbi whose main concern was teaching his followers how best to follow the Law of Moses. Others have said that he was a Jewish holy man, like those we learn about from Josephus, a kind of shaman reputed to do spectacular deeds because of his unusual powers. Others have maintained that he is best understood as a political revolutionary who was preaching armed rebellion against the Roman Empire. Still others have claimed that he was a social reformer who urged the Jews of his time to adopt an entirely different lifestyle, for example, by embracing new economic principles as a kind of proto-Marxist or different social relationships as a kind of proto-feminist. Yet others have suggested that he is best seen as a Jewish version of the ancient Greek Cynic philosophers, urging his followers to abandon their attachments to the material things of this world and to live lives of poverty, internally liberated from the demands of life. Others have suggested that he is best seen as a magician, not in the sense that he could do magic tricks but that he knew how to manipulate the laws of nature like other workers of magic in his day.

Each of these views has had serious scholarly proponents.[1] But none of them represents the views of the majority of scholars in modern times. Instead, as I have repeatedly noted, most scholars in both the United States and Europe over the past century have been convinced that Jesus is best understood as a Jewish apocalyptic preacher who anticipated that God was soon to intervene in history to overthrow the powers of evil now controlling this world in order to bring in a new order, a new kingdom here on earth, the kingdom of God. This was essentially the view that Albert Schweitzer popularized in his famous book, *The Quest of the Historical Jesus*. Schweitzer was not the first to articulate this view, but he was the first to bring it to wide public attention.[2] And even though there are no scholars who agree any longer with the details of how Schweitzer worked out his views, there is still broad agreement that the fundamental assumption behind them is correct, that Jesus really did anticipate a cataclysmic break in the course of history when God would judge the world and set it to rights, establishing a rule of peace and justice here on earth, sometime, Jesus thought, within his own generation.

In my discussion here I will not go into great depth either to show why this view of Jesus is so widely seen to be correct or to explicate all the details of Jesus's life that fit so well this way of understanding him. I have already discussed the matter at greater length in my earlier book *Jesus: Apocalyptic Prophet of the New Millennium*. Here I will simply provide a brief overview to accomplish three major tasks: (a) I will show what we can know about ancient Jewish apocalyptic thinking in the days of Jesus since Jesus was not the only apocalypticist of his time (far from it), and we need to know about Jesus's historical context if we expect to learn anything about his life; (b) I will discuss the various criteria that scholars use to determine which of the many traditions about Jesus are probably historically reliable (I have begun doing this already in the earlier chapters); and (c) I will provide an overview of what the rigorous application of these criteria yield, explaining the most important features of Jesus's life that we can know about with relative certainty. The first two tasks will take up the rest of the present chapter; the third will be the topic of the next.

Unity and Diversity in First-Century Judaism

TO MAKE SENSE OF the apocalyptic perspective that appears to have been so prominent among Jews in the days of Jesus, we first need to situate ourselves more broadly in the first-century Jewish world.

As we will see, there were wide-ranging differences among Jews around the time of Jesus. Even so, some very basic things can be said about Judaism as a whole.[3]

To begin with, almost all Jews were monotheists. This does not seem like an extraordinary thing in our day, but in the ancient world it is one of the main features of the Jewish religion that made it so unlike the other religions in the Roman Empire. All other religions were polytheistic; pagans recognized many gods living in all sorts of places and serving all sorts of functions.[4] There were the great gods of the empire (mainly the ones we know about from Greek and Roman myth); there were gods of the different cities, towns, and villages; gods of a field, a forest, a stream, a house, and a hearth. There were gods who controlled the weather, gods who controlled the crops, gods who controlled childbirth and health; there were gods of war, gods of love, gods of personal welfare. All these gods, and many others, deserved worship, and since there were so many of them none of these gods, at least in the period we are talking about, was thought to be jealous of another, in the sense that they alone were to be worshipped. People worshipped all the gods that they wanted and chose to. But not in Judaism. Jews had only one God, and this made Jews different from all other peoples.

The God of the Jews was believed by the Jews (and them alone) to have created the world and ultimately to be sovereign over it. Jews did not insist that other people worship this God, but he was the only God for them. Among the first of the commandments given to the Jews by this God was "You shall have no other gods before me." Jews by and large did not deny that other gods existed, but they were not to be worshipped by the Jews themselves.

In no small measure this was because Jews believed that their God not only created all things but also chose them, the Jewish people, to be uniquely related to him. He was their God, and they alone were his people. God had shown that he chose them way back in the days of Moses when he miraculously brought the children of Israel out of their slavery in Egypt, destroyed their enemies, and then gave them his Law, the Law of Moses delivered on Mount Sinai (see Exodus 1–20 in the Hebrew Bible). Jews believed that in those days God had made a kind of covenant (or peace treaty) with them. The covenantal agreement, at its heart, was very simple. God had chosen Israel. He would be their God, and they would be his people. They showed they were his people by doing what he commanded in the Law he had provided.

The Law was given to the Jewish people not as some kind of onerous burden that they had to bear—as so many Christians today seem to think—but for the opposite reason: to provide guidance to God's people about how they should worship him and relate to one another in their communal lives together. The Law was the greatest gift God had given his people, instructions from on high by the Almighty himself about how to live. What could be greater? People today wonder about how to act, how to behave, what is right to do and what is wrong; people wonder about ultimate reality, the meaning of life, the purpose of existence. Ancient Jews believed that God had told them. It was in the Law that God had given.

This Law was written down and could be found in the five books of Moses, which together are often simply called the Torah, the Hebrew word for law (or direction or guidance or instruction). These books of Genesis, Exodus, Leviticus, Numbers, and Deuteronomy—the first five books of the Hebrew Bible—describe how God created the world, chose Israel to be his people, guided the lives of their ancestors, saved them from their lives of slavery, and gave them the Law. The Law itself is spelled out in great detail in these books—not just the Ten Commandments, but all the laws showing how to serve God and live with one another. Keeping this Law was widely seen as not only the greatest obligation but also the greatest joy. It included directions about circumcision—the "sign" that the Jews were chosen and distinct from all the nations—kosher food laws, Sabbath observance, festivals, and procedures to be followed in worshipping God.

The worship of God involved, among other things, sacrifices of animals and other foodstuffs to God at different times and for various occasions. In the days of Jesus it was almost universally thought that these sacrifices had to be performed at the central sanctuary, as dictated in the Torah, which was located in the capital city of the Jews, Jerusalem. This sanctuary was the famous Jewish Temple, originally built by King Solomon but then destroyed by the Babylonian armies in the sixth century BCE and later rebuilt. In the days of Jesus the Temple was an enormous and spectacular structure that played a major social, political, and economic—not to mention religious—role in the lives of Jews, especially those living in Jerusalem and the surrounding areas of Judea. It was run by priests who inherited their sacred duties from their families. One could not aspire to be priest; one was either born into a priestly family or not. Priests ran the Temple and all its functions, including the sacrifices of animals prescribed in the Torah.

Outside Jerusalem it was not allowed to perform these sacrifices, so Jews from around the world came to Jerusalem, if they could afford the time and expense, to participate in the worship of God at the Temple. This especially happened during the set annual festivals, such as the Passover, a celebration that commemorated God's deliverance of Israel from slavery in Egypt back in the days of Moses. This does not mean, however, that Jews outside Jerusalem could not worship God. They certainly did worship, but not through sacrifices. Instead, communities of Jews throughout the Roman world gathered in synagogues, local meetings where they would hear the sacred scriptures (especially the Torah) read and interpreted and where they would offer up their prayers to God. Jews would gather together in synagogues on their weekly day of rest, the Sabbath, a day set apart from all others.

These are some of the key aspects of what we might call "shared

Judaism" in the days of Jesus: the belief in one God; the covenant he had made with them, including the circumcision of male infants; the Law he had provided; the Temple in Jerusalem where sacrifices were to be made; the observance of Sabbath; and synagogues scattered throughout the world where Jews would meet to discuss their traditions and offer prayers to God.

Different Jews and Jewish groups emphasized different aspects of their shared religion, however, and as is true of almost every large religious group today (Christians, Muslims, Buddhists, you name it) there were wide-ranging and deep disagreements about major points. We know of four such groups in Palestine in the days of Jesus, based on the writings of the Jewish historian Josephus, whom we met before as our principal source of knowledge of first-century Palestinian Judaism. Josephus indicates that there were four major Jewish sects in the days of Jesus: Pharisees, Sadducees, Essenes, and a group that he calls the Fourth Philosophy. It should not be thought that every Jew belonged to one or another of these groups. On the contrary, most people didn't belong to any. It is not, then, like modern political parties in America today ("Are you a Democrat, Republican, or Libertarian?"); it is more like civic organizations or secret societies ("Are you a member of the Elks or the Rotary Club? Were you in Skull and Bones?").[5]

The Pharisees

The Pharisees are probably the best known and least understood of the four Jewish groups mentioned by Josephus. Largely because of the nasty things said about them in parts of the New Testament (for example, Matthew 23), most Christians seem to think that Pharisees' chief defining characteristic was that they were hypocrites. In fact, in English dictionaries you will often find *hypocrite* as one of the definitions of *Pharisee*. I've always thought this is rather odd. Pharisees were not required to be hypocritical.

The Pharisees were a highly religious group that stressed the importance of keeping the Law God had given. There is obviously nothing wrong with that from a religious perspective. If God gave you a law, you are well advised to keep it. The problem with the Law of Moses, however, is that it is not very detailed in places. In fact, it is notoriously vague and ambiguous, not like, for instance, the American legal code. For example, the Ten Commandments indicate that the Sabbath day is to be honored and kept holy, but the Law does not go into great detail about how to do that. The Pharisees were intent on making sure they did what God wanted. But if the Law itself does not say how, then one has to come up with some guidelines.

Suppose it is agreed that honoring the day of rest means that on that day no work should be done, as the Torah states. Fair enough. But what constitutes work? Is it work to harvest your fields? Yes, probably so. So you should not harvest on the Sabbath. What if you don't work all day but just go out into the field to harvest enough to have a bite to eat: is that work? Well, yes, that's virtually the same thing as working all day except you're not doing it as long. So that too should be forbidden even if the Law does not explicitly say so. What about if you are in your grain fields on the Sabbath and you knock off some of the grain just by walking through? Is that the same as harvesting? That's the kind of question that does not have an easy answer: some people might say, no way, and others might say, yes indeed. And so different Jewish teachers argued about such things.

Their arguments were not meant to make life difficult. They were meant to help everyone know how to keep the Law. Keeping the Law was the main thing. The Pharisees developed a number of interpretations of the Law that were intended to make sure that Jews followed what Moses commanded. These interpretations came to be known as the "oral law." Pharisees thought that if you followed the oral law (for example, by not walking through your grain fields on the Sabbath), then you were certain not to violate the written law of Moses. And that was the point of the religion, so it was all to the good.

We don't know as much about Pharisees in the days of Jesus as we would like since none of them left any writings and we have to use later sources—very critically—to figure out what they stood for. But they are significant in the pages of the Gospels because Jesus is often in conflict with them. Jesus apparently did not think that being overly concerned about keeping the Law to the nth degree is what really mattered to God. He did think it was important to do what God commanded, but not in the ways that mattered to the Pharisees. And so they had some serious fallings-out. But it is important to remember that when Jesus opposed Pharisaic interpretations of the Law—for example, over what could and could not be done on the Sabbath—he was not opposing Judaism. He was simply opposing one interpretation of Judaism. Other Jews as well disagreed with the Pharisees.

The Sadducees

The real power players in Palestine in Jesus's day were not the Pharisees—despite their prominence in the Gospels—but the Sadducees. Again we are handicapped in our ability to know much about the group because we have no writings that clearly come from any of them. What is certain, in any event, is that they had a different set of concerns from the Pharisees and that they were the ones who held power in Judea.

The Sadducees were closely connected with the priests who ran the Temple cult, and it is widely thought that many of them were themselves priests. Unlike the Pharisees, most Sadducees were apparently wealthy aristocrats. From their number was chosen the "high priest," who was the ultimate authority for all things religious and civic in Jerusalem. The high priest was the chief liaison with the Roman ruling authorities, and it appears that Sadducees were by and large willing to compromise with the Romans in order to keep the peace and enjoy the freedom of exercising their religious prerogatives. Contrary to what is widely thought, Romans were not much of a physical presence in Palestine, or even in Jerusalem, most of the time during the days of Jesus. The Roman governor, Pilate, had his headquarters on the coast in Caesarea, where he kept his small contingent of troops. The real armies were up in Syria. There was no need for a greater Roman presence in the land so long as there was peace and the taxes kept rolling in.

As was their wont throughout the provinces, the Romans allowed the Jews of Judea to operate more or less under local rule. Except for instances of capital punishment, Romans appear to have let the local authorities do what needed to be done. The local Jewish council, which was authorized to run the political and civic affairs in Jerusalem, was called the Sanhedrin. It was headed by the high priest and appears to have comprised mainly other Sadducees, since these tended to be the wealthy and well-connected Jews.

In terms of religious commitments, the Sadducees placed no stock in the oral laws developed by Pharisees. They were instead interested strictly in what the Torah itself commanded, in particular with respect to the worship of God. Their focus was on the Temple in Jerusalem and on properly following the commandments of Moses concerning how the Temple cult was to be run and its sacrifices carried out. As we will see, even though Jesus apparently had a number of controversies with Pharisees during his public ministry, it was the Sadducees who spelled his demise. He openly showed opposition to the Temple and the sacrifices being performed there, and it was the local ruling authorities—the Sanhedrin and its Sadducees—who took greatest offense. They appear to have been the ones who had Jesus arrested and turned over for trial to the Roman governor Pilate, who was in town to keep peace during the incendiary times of the Passover festival.

The Essenes

Ironically, the one Jewish group from Jesus's day that we are best informed about happens to be the one that is not mentioned in the New Testament. We know about the Essenes from Jewish writers such as Josephus but even more important from an entire library of their own writings first discovered by pure serendipity by a wandering shepherd boy in 1947. These are the famous Dead Sea Scrolls, a collection of writings from roughly the time of Jesus and the preceding years that was apparently produced by and for Essenes. One group of Essenes lived in a monastic-like community in a place known as Qumran, just west of the northern part of the Dead Sea in what is now Israel.[6]

A number of different kinds of books are found among the Dead Sea Scrolls. Some are copies of the Hebrew Bible (older by a thousand years than the copies we had prior to the 1947 discovery); others are commentaries on scripture that indicate that the predictions of the prophets were coming true in the community's own day; others are books of hymns and psalms used in community worship; others are apocalyptic descriptions of what will happen in the end times; others are manuals that describe and prescribe the behavior of members of the community in their social and religious lives together. I should stress that nothing in the Dead Sea Scrolls is directly related to Christianity: Jesus is not mentioned in the scrolls; neither is John the Baptist or any of the early followers of Jesus. The Dead Sea Scrolls are Jewish books through and through, with nothing Christian in them. But they are invaluable for understanding Jesus and his early followers because they are writings produced in Jesus's own day, or in the years immediately preceding, by Jews living in approximately the same location.

The term *Essene* never occurs in the Dead Sea Scrolls. But Qumran was located precisely where other ancient sources indicated that there was an Essene community, and the writings of the

scrolls coincide well with what we otherwise know about the Essenes. Jews in this community were in serious conflict with both
Pharisees and Sadducees. They believed that all other Jews were
corrupt and had misunderstood and misapplied the Jewish Law, to
the degree that they had defiled the Temple and rendered the worship of God there invalid. To preserve their own holiness, this particular group of Essenes (there were other Essenes, but we know less
about them) went off into the wilderness to live a rather monastic
life together, maintaining their own purity, removed from the im-
purity of Jewish society at large.

In no small part they did so because they believed they were
living at the end of the age. God would soon send two messiahs to
deliver his people, one a priest who would instruct all the faithful
about how to follow God's law and the other a political leader who
would run the civic affairs of the people. In the view of the Essenes,
a massive war was soon coming in which God and his people would
emerge triumphant over the filthy Romans, and God's kingdom
would then come to earth.

Jesus himself was not an Essene. Nothing connects either him
or John the Baptist to the group. In fact, just the opposite. John, as
we will see, was concerned not with preserving his own purity but
with preaching repentance to sinners to get them to turn from their
wicked ways. And Jesus scandalized the highly religious Jews invested
in maintaining pure lives removed from the uncleanness of the world
around them because he preferred to associate with sinners, just the
opposite of the Essenes at Qumran. But Jesus did have something in
common with them. He too thought the end of the age was imminent and that God would soon set up his kingdom on earth.

The Fourth Philosophy

The final group of Jews mentioned by Josephus is not given a name.
He calls it simply the Fourth Philosophy (to differentiate it from the

other three). But its overarching views are clear and unambiguous. This was a group made up of Jews who thought that the Roman overlords had wrongfully taken possession of the Promised Land. This group—or these groups, all lumped together by Josephus—believed that God wanted them to take up the sword to oppose the Romans and foment a political and military revolt. This was not a secular movement; it had deep religious roots. In the view of those who adhered to this philosophy, God himself had called for action, and just as he had driven out the foul Canaanites from the land under the leadership of Joshua in the Hebrew Bible (see the book of Joshua), so he would do it again in their own day. God would fight for the faithful Jews, and he would reinstate Israel as a sovereign state in their own land ruled by his own chosen one.

Members of this Fourth Philosophy, then, were not ultimately concerned about the oral laws being developed by the Pharisees to help them keep the commandments of Moses in precise detail, and they did not care about maintaining their own ritual purity in the face of the uncleanness of the world around them, like the Essenes. They were especially opposed to Sadducees, who were seen as collaborators with the foul Romans who had devastated the land and taken what was not theirs. The chief focus of this Fourth Philosophy was, in fact, the land, promised to Israel by God. The land needed to be retaken, and it was to happen as it had in days of old, by military force.

Some scholars, as I have pointed out, thought that Jesus too preached an armed rebellion against the Romans. But that does not seem to be the dominant theme throughout the earliest traditions we have about him. It is not that Jesus was a collaborationist like the Sadducees. Quite the contrary, he too opposed both them and their Roman masters. But he did not appear to think that the solution lay in armed resistance. He appears instead to have been an apocalypticist who thought that God himself would overthrow the Roman armies, not by military action but in a cosmic act of judgment in which a divine savior figure would arrive from heaven to destroy the armies of the enemy and to set up a new kingdom here on earth.

In his apocalyptic views, then, Jesus was probably more like the Essenes than the other Jewish groups. But he was not an Essene, and he held many different views as well. His views were molded, in particular, by his association with John the Baptist, an apocalyptic preacher who anticipated the imminent end of the age. Before discussing that association, we need to learn more generally about Jewish apocalypticism, for it was adhered to and proclaimed by a wide range of Jews in the days of Jesus.

Jewish Apocalypticism

THE WORLDVIEW THAT SCHOLARS call apocalypticism developed in Jewish history before the time of Jesus, and I have discussed the historical details elsewhere.[7] Suffice it to say here that about a century and a half before Jesus was born, a number of Jews became radically distraught with the course of political and military affairs. The nation of Judea had been controlled by foreign powers for centuries—first the Babylonians in the sixth century BCE, then the Persians, then the Greeks, and then the Syrians. In resistance to Syrian atrocities, in 167 BCE an indigenous uprising occurred headed by a Jewish family known as the Maccabees. This Maccabean Revolt eventually led to an independent state of Judea, which lasted for nearly a century until the Romans conquered the land in 63 BCE.

Along with political woes before the revolt came a kind of theological crisis. For centuries certain Jewish prophets had declared that the nation was suffering because God was punishing it for turning away from him (thus prophets such as Hosea, Amos, Isaiah, Jeremiah, and—well, just about all the prophets of the Hebrew Bible). But in this period, under the Syrians, many Jews had turned back to God and were doing precisely what he instructed them to do in the Torah. And yet they were suffering worse than ever. How could that be?

Jewish apocalyptic thinking arose in the context. It came to be thought that the suffering of the people of God was not a punishment for sin inflicted by God himself. On the contrary, it was punishment for righteousness, inflicted by forces of evil in the world, which were aligned against God. The first clear literary expression of such a view is found in the book of Daniel, the last book of the Hebrew Bible to be written (around 165 BCE?). The view eventually became widely popular among Jews, as their woes continued. In the days of Jesus it was a view held by Pharisees, Essenes, and prophetic groups such as the one headed by John the Baptist.

The view is called "apocalyptic" from the Greek word *apocalypsis,* which means a "revealing" or an "unveiling." Jewish apocalypticists believed that God had revealed to them the heavenly secrets that made sense of mundane realities. The short version is that God, for mysterious reasons, had temporarily ceded control of this world over to powerful cosmic forces that are opposed to him, his purposes, and his people. That was why the people of God experienced such pain and misery. But God would soon reassert his sovereignty over this world and destroy the forces of evil to vindicate his people, restore them to a place of privilege, and bring in a good, utopian kingdom that would last forever.

This point of view can be found in a number of Jewish writings from the period, including, for example, the Dead Sea Scrolls and Jewish apocalypses that did not become part of the Bible. An examination of these works shows that most Jewish apocalypticists subscribed to four major tenets of thought.

Dualism

Most basically, apocalypticists were dualists. They believed there were two fundamental components of reality, the forces of good and the forces of evil. The ultimate source for all that was good, of course, was God. But God had a personal enemy, called by various names: the Devil, Satan, Beelzeboul. (Before the development of apocalyptic thought, Jews did not subscribe to the idea of a personal Devil as God's archenemy. He is not found in Jewish scripture. Apocalypticists, by contrast, very much believed he existed.) Moreover, just as God had angels who did his will, the Devil had demons who did his. And there were other cosmic forces in the world—principalities, authorities, and powers. God had the power to give life while the forces of evil had the power of death, not to mention all the pain, misery, and suffering en route to it.

The struggle between the forces of good and evil had radical and dire consequences for humans. A cosmic battle was going on, and the powers of evil were in the ascendancy. That is why this world was such an awful place, with all its famines, droughts, epidemics, earthquakes, poverty, injustice, and war.

This cosmic dualism worked itself out in a historical scenario, also dualistic, involving this age and the age to come. The present age was controlled by the powers of evil: the Devil and his minions. But there would be a future age in which all that is opposed to God would be destroyed and a good kingdom would appear. Then God, along with all that is good, would reign supreme. There would be no more famine, drought, natural disaster, war, or hatred. Those who entered into this new age would be rewarded with eternal peace, joy, and bliss. They would be able to love and serve God without fear, and they would live in harmony in a world of rich abundance forever.

Pessimism

Even though for apocalypticists the long-term picture looked very good, the short-term looked very bleak. Apocalypticists were thoroughly pessimistic about the prospects of life in the present age.

The forces of evil would soon gain greater and greater power, and there was nothing anyone could do to stop them. It would not help to develop new technologies, to reform the welfare state, to build up national defense, to put more cops on the beat or more teachers in the classroom. There would be more disasters, more wars, more hunger, more poverty, more oppression—more and more until at the end of this age, when literally all hell would break out.

But then this age would come to a radical end, and God would reassert himself.

Vindication

Many apocalypticists did not dream of conquering the powers of evil by their own efforts. God would conquer them. This would not happen gradually over a long period of time, as good eventually gained back ground ceded to evil. The end would come suddenly and cataclysmically. God would intervene in the course of human and worldly affairs to overthrow the forces of evil and bring in his good kingdom. He would redeem this world and vindicate both his good name and his people. When things got just as bad as they could possibly get, God would send a savior figure who would make right all that is wrong.

Apocalyptic thinkers called this savior by various titles. We have already seen that some referred to him as a messiah; others, basing their views on the earliest surviving apocalyptic text that we have, the book of Daniel, referred to him as the Son of Man (see Daniel 7:13–14). This cosmic figure would destroy the forces that aligned themselves against God along with all the people on earth who joined with them. In the present age it was the rich and powerful who had obviously sided with the forces that controlled this world. They were the ones, then, who would be destroyed when the Son of Man arrived. The weak, the poor, the oppressed, and the righteous were suffering—in the present age—because they had sided with

God. But they would be vindicated when the end came and God reasserted himself to establish a good kingdom on earth.

This future judgment would apply not only to those who happened to be living at the time, but to the dead as well. At the end of this age, when the Son of Man arrived, there would be a resurrection of the dead. All who had previously died would be revived and returned to their bodies to face judgment. Those who had sided with the forces of evil would be punished, or at least annihilated; those who had sided with God would be rewarded and granted a share of the coming kingdom. Among other things, this meant that no one should think that they could side with the forces of evil and prosper as a result, causing others to suffer so as to become rich and powerful, and then die and get away with it. No one could get away with it. God would raise everyone from the dead, and there was nothing that anyone could do to stop him.

This then is the period in which Jews began to affirm the doctrine of the future resurrection, to occur at the end of this age, as I discussed in the previous chapter. Before apocalyptic thinking came to be in vogue, most Jews thought either that after death a person continued to live on in a shadowy netherworld called Sheol or that the person simply died with his or her body. But not apocalypticists. They believed in a coming eternal life for the righteous, and it would be lived in the body, in the future kingdom of God that was to arrive here on earth.

Imminence

And when was that kingdom going to arrive? Jewish apocalypticists believed it was coming very soon. It was right around the corner. It might happen at any time. Apocalypticists believed that things were as bad as they could possibly get. The powers of evil were out in full force. Now was the time for God to intervene to destroy these powers and set up his good kingdom. "Truly I tell you," as one famous apocalypticist is recorded as saying, "some of you who are standing here will not taste death before you see that the kingdom of God has come in power." These are the words of Jesus, from our earliest surviving Gospel (Mark 9:1). Or as he says later in the same Gospel, when asked when the cosmic cataclysm that he had predicted would occur, culminating in the appearance of the Son of Man: "Truly I tell you, *this generation* will not pass away before all these things take place" (Mark 13:30).

As a Jewish apocalypticist, Jesus believed that the world was controlled by evil powers that were present in full force. But God would cast judgment on this world by sending the Son of Man from heaven. This one would bring about a cataclysmic change in all things, a day of reckoning for all that is evil and for everyone who had sided with evil. And the kingdom would then arrive, in which the powerful and mighty would be taken down and the poor and oppressed would be exalted. This was to happen within Jesus's own generation. Jesus, like many other Jews of his time and place, was an apocalypticist who expected the imminent end of history as he knew it.

But how do we know that Jesus said these words—or in fact, any of the other words of the Gospels? How can we know that he represented an apocalyptic point of view? Or more generally, how can we know anything beyond the mere fact of his onetime existence?

This question takes us directly to the matter of historical method. Scholars have devised criteria for detecting historically authentic tradition, even within such problematic sources as those we have that discuss the life of the historical Jesus. These criteria apply, in fact, to any figure of the past described in any kind of historical source. But our interest here is obviously with Jesus and with what we can establish, with good probability, about what he said and did. In earlier chapters I broached these issues more or less in passing. Now I need to address them head-on. What methods do historians use in order to establish the words and deeds of Jesus, either apocalyptic or otherwise?

Methods for Establishing Authentic Tradition

As I HAVE STRESSED throughout this book, doing history, at least ancient history, means abandoning any hope of absolute certainty. But even though we can rarely be completely certain about a past event, some things are far more certain than others. It is far more certain that Julius Caesar fought the Gallic Wars (he wrote about them and we still have the books) than that Apollonius of Tyana raised a genuinely dead person back to life (apart from the inherent improbabilities of the case—as a miracle—our one source dates from long after the fact and is thoroughly biased). Historians deal for the most part in probabilities, and some things are more probable than others.

Earlier I mentioned the historians' wish list when it comes to sources of information about the past. This wish list certainly applies to the historical Jesus. To establish the historical probability of a saying, deed, or experience of Jesus, we want a large number of independent sources that can be shown not to be incorporating their own biases in the account in question and that corroborate one another's reports without showing any evidence of collaboration. And the closer these sources are in time to the events they narrate, the better.

More specifically, the probability that a tradition about Jesus— or anyone else, for that matter—is historically accurate is increased to the extent that it passes the following criteria.

Contextual Credibility

I spent some time in the preceding pages talking about Judaism during the days of Jesus for one principal reason. If there is a story about Jesus—for example, an account of something that he allegedly said or did—that does not fit into his known historical context, then it can scarcely be historically accurate. I should stress that simply because a tradition can be plausibly situated into Jesus's context does not mean that it is historically reliable. It simply means it is possible. Probability will need to be established on other grounds (that is, those of the following two criteria). But if a tradition does not fit into a first-century Palestinian context, then it almost certainly can be discounted as a later legend.

For example, in an earlier context we saw that scattered through-out the Gospels are sayings of Jesus that at one time must have cir-culated in Aramaic, Jesus's native tongue. Sometimes that is because they make better sense when translated back from the Greek of the Gospels into Aramaic ("Sabbath was made for man, not man for the Sabbath; therefore the Son of Man is lord of the Sabbath," Mark 2:27–28). At other times it is because an Aramaic word or phrase from the original form of the story has been left untranslated, re-quiring the Gospel writer to explain its meaning ("Talitha cumi," which translated means, 'Little girl, arise'" Mark 5:41). Since Jesus lived in rural Palestine, he would have spoken Aramaic, and these sayings can plausibly be connected with him. That does not mean that he said them. But he *may* have said them.

By contrast, if there is a saying that clearly cannot be translated back into Aramaic, then Jesus almost certainly did not say it. That is true of the example I gave earlier from John 3, where Jesus says that a person must be born *anothen* to enter the kingdom. Did he mean "from above" or "a second time"? The entire conversation is predicated on the peculiar meanings of the double entendre, which works in Greek but not in Aramaic. So Jesus almost certainly did not have this conversation, at least as recorded, with Nicodemus.

We will see in the next chapter that there are solid reasons for thinking that Jesus was an apocalypticist. Traditions about Jesus that make sense in an apocalyptic context, therefore, have a chance of being authentic. At the same time, we have nothing to suggest that the beliefs embraced by later Gnostic Christians were present in first-century rural Palestine. And so the Gnostic sayings of Jesus found in such Gnostic Gospels as the Gospel of Philip or the Gospel of Mary almost certainly do not go back to Jesus himself but were placed on his lips by his later (Gnostic) followers.

I need to be clear that of the three criteria of authenticity I will be discussing here, this one alone is negative. It shows, not what Jesus probably *did* say or do, but what he almost certainly did *not*. If a tradition of Jesus passes this first criterion, it is possible. But it is not necessarily probable. To establish probability, we need recourse to the other two criteria. And a tradition is even more probable if it can pass not just one but both of them.

Multiple Attestation

I have repeatedly stressed that a tradition appearing in multiple, independent sources has a greater likelihood of being historically reliable than a tradition that appears in only one. If a saying or deed of Jesus is found in only one source, then it is possible that the source simply made it up. But if a word or action is found in several sources and they did not collaborate with one another, then none of them made it up; the tradition must predate them. If it is found independently in a number of sources, the probability of its being reliable is increased, assuming, of course, that it is contextually credible.

Any story that is found in Matthew, Mark, and Luke, of course, is not multiply attested, even though it is found in three of our sources. Matthew and Luke took a number of their stories from Mark, and so a story found in virtually the same words in all three simply comes from Mark, one source alone. But there are plenty of traditions that are found in different ones of our early independent sources—Mark, Q, M, L, John and its sources, Paul, other authors of other epistles, Thomas, and even Josephus and Tacitus—all from within a century of Jesus's death.

We have already seen a few obvious examples. The crucifixion of Jesus under Pontius Pilate is, of course, contextually credible. The Romans crucified lots of people all the time. And this is one tradition that is abundantly attested—in Mark, M, L, John, and the speeches in Acts, not to mention Josephus and Tacitus. It is alluded to, independently, in 1 Timothy. The crucifixion itself is attested (without Pilate) throughout Paul and in a range of other independent sources: 1 Peter, Hebrews, and so on. This is one of the best attested traditions about Jesus and one, as we will see, that passes the next criterion as well with flying colors.

Or take the issue of Jesus's brothers. As we have seen, in multiple independent sources Jesus is said to have brothers, and most of those sources name one of these brothers as James; this is true of Mark, John (doesn't name James), Paul, and Josephus. Paul, as we have seen, actually knew James. This establishes reasonably good probability in favor of the tradition.

Moreover, again, Jesus is said to have come from Nazareth, not just in Mark and John but also in independent stories from M and L. Here too, as we will see, this tradition passes both of our other criteria and so seems highly probable.

The Criterion of Dissimilarity

The most controversial criterion that scholars use to establish historically probable traditions about Jesus is one we already discussed, the "criterion of dissimilarity." This criterion is rooted in the idea that the biases of a source, and those of the source behind the source, need to be taken into account. So the stories about Jesus the miracle-working five-year-old who could wither his playmates when they irritated him—as found in the Infancy Gospel of Thomas—are not historically reliable, since these stories serve a Christian purpose of showing that Jesus was a powerful Son of God even before his public ministry. We saw how the story of Jesus's birth in Luke does not make historical sense for there is no record of a worldwide census and it could not have been when Quirinius ruled Syria if Jesus was actually born during the reign of King Herod since their reigns did not overlap. And it contradicts Matthew (not that Matthew is necessarily right either; but it is worth knowing that they *both* can't be right). So where did the story come from? It seems most likely that Luke, or his source, simply made it up to make sure that Jesus was born where the prophets—in this case Micah—indicated that the Jewish savior would come from, Bethlehem (see Micah 5:2; quoted in Matthew 2:6).

But when we encounter a story about Jesus that does not support an early Christian agenda or that seems to run contrary to what the early Christians would have wanted to say about Jesus, as we saw, the story is more likely to be historically reliable since it is less likely to have been made up. We saw how the story that Jesus was crucified created enormous headaches for the Christian mission because no Jews would have expected a crucified messiah. This tradition clearly passes the criterion of dissimilarity. Given the additional fact that it is so thoroughly attested in so many of our independent sources, it appears highly probable that in fact Jesus was crucified. That is far more probable than an alternative claim, for example, that he was stoned to death or that he ascended without dying or even that he simply lived out his life and died as an old man in Nazareth, none of which is ever mentioned in our sources.

Or take the details of Jesus's life. The idea that he had brothers does not serve any clear-cut Christian agenda. It is simply taken as a statement of fact by the early authors who mention it (Paul, Mark, John, Josephus). And so Jesus probably had brothers, and one of them happened to be named James. So too with the claim that he came from Nazareth. Since Nazareth was a tiny hamlet riddled with poverty, it is unlikely that anyone would invent the story that the messiah came from there. Given that the story of Jesus coming from Nazareth is widely attested in our sources, it is probable that Jesus came from Nazareth.

I need to reemphasize that both of these latter criteria—multiple attestation and dissimilarity—are best used in a *positive* way to establish traditions that most probably can be accepted as reliable. They are not as useful when used negatively. That is, just because a tradition is found in one source and one source only does not necessarily mean that it is unreliable. But if there is no corroboration elsewhere, it is at least suspect. And if it does not pass the criterion of dissimilarity, it is doubly suspect. So too, if a tradition does not pass the criterion of dissimilarity, that does not necessarily mean it is inaccurate, but it should at least raise doubts. If it is not widely attested as well, it simply cannot be relied on. And as we have seen, in some instances there are solid historical reasons for arguing that a tradition that does not pass the criterion of dissimilarity should be seen not only as less probable but as almost certainly legendary—as in the case of the census that brought Joseph and Mary to Bethlehem or Matthew's account of Jesus's triumphal entry into Jerusalem.

All of the traditions about Jesus, in short, need to be considered in detail on a case-by-case basis to determine if they pass the various criteria and to see if there are other historical grounds for either affirming or denying their historical probability. The likelihood of Jesus having brothers, for example, is increased by the fact that the apostle Paul knew one of them. Conversely, the likelihood of Jesus entering into Jerusalem straddling two donkeys and with the crowd shouting out that he was the messiah is decreased by the circumstance that had such an event really happened (unlikely as it is on its own terms), Jesus would no doubt have been arrested by the authorities on the spot instead of a week later.

The Early History of Jesus

I WOULD LIKE TO conclude this chapter by pointing out what we can say, with some good degree of probability, about Jesus's life before he began his public ministry as an adult.

To begin with the negatives: there is no way a historian can say that Jesus was probably born of a virgin. Quite apart from the question of implausibility (which I think is extraordinarily high), there is the fact that the two sources that mention it each explains the reason for the miraculous birth, and these explanations tip the authors' hands.[8] In Matthew Jesus is born of a virgin because it was predicted in the prophet Isaiah. Or at least that is how Matthew reads Isaiah. In the Hebrew text of Isaiah 7:14 the prophet indicated that a "young woman" would conceive and bear a son. Matthew, however, read the prophet in the Greek translation, which says that a *parthenos* would conceive. *Parthenos* is a Greek word that often, though not always, refers to a young woman who has never had sex. That is not the meaning of the Hebrew word originally used in the passage (*alma*), but Matthew probably did not know this. For him, Jesus had to be born of a virgin to fulfill prophecy, and so he was. At the very least, this makes the birth story of Matthew historically suspect.

Luke has Jesus born of a virgin for a different reason. In his account Jesus really is the Son of God because the Spirit of God is the one who made Mary pregnant. As she herself learns from the angel Gabriel (none of this passes any of our criteria, of course), "The Holy Spirit will come upon you and the power of the Most High will overshadow you; for that reason, the one born of you will be called holy, the Son of God" (Luke 1:35). Luke is invested in showing that Jesus is uniquely God's son, and the virgin birth is the proof.

In any event, historians have no means at their disposal to render a judgment about the virginity of Jesus's mother other than the general probabilities of the case and the fact that the two stories that mention the tradition do so for different, but completely interested, reasons. The stories were almost certainly invented to heighten the importance of Jesus at his birth.

We also have good reasons for doubting that Jesus was born in Bethlehem. Not only is the tradition rooted in the belief that the messiah was to come from the city of David, but the two accounts of how it came about hopelessly contradict each other, as we have seen. What the sources do agree on (at least the ones that mention anything of relevance) is that Jesus came from Nazareth. This is multiply attested, and it passes the criterion of dissimilarity.

Jesus then was born and raised Jewish. His parents lived in rural Galilee. Archaeological work on Nazareth indicates that it was a small hamlet with no evidence of any wealth whatsoever.[9] And so Jesus was almost certainly raised in relative poverty. He had brothers and probably sisters (although these are mentioned in just one passage, Mark 6:3). His family was working class. Our earliest account indicates that Jesus was a *tekton* (Mark 6:3), a word normally translated "carpenter," although it can refer to anyone who works with his hands, for example, a stonemason or blacksmith. It was a lower-class occupation. In that part of the world it meant a hand-to-mouth existence. If it does mean that Jesus worked with wood instead of stone or metal, he would have done so to make, not fine cabinetry, but roughly hewn stuff such as gates or yokes needed in the rural community. Other traditions indicate that it was his father who was the *tekton* (Matthew 13:55). Even if that is correct, it is completely plausible that the oldest son was apprenticed so that Jesus may have applied that craft himself.

If he did, he would have lived a lower-class existence, with little promise for future advancement. After Jesus began his public ministry, we have reports that the people of his hometown had trouble understanding what happened to him, how he could suddenly seem so wise and insightful into the religious traditions of Israel (Mark 6;

Luke 4). This suggests that he was not a wunderkind growing up but an altogether average person. It is widely debated among scholars whether he was literate. For reasons I suggested earlier, it seems most probable that he was not writing-literate, and in fact we have no early record of him writing anything or even knowing how to write. Whether or not he learned to read is an interesting and difficult question. The older view among scholars that Jewish boys were almost always taught how to read has been shown to be wrong. Most were not, and literacy rates in Roman Palestine were shockingly low. But if, as seems probable, Jesus was widely seen among his followers as an expert interpreter of the Torah, this may suggest that he could read and study the texts. Possibly a local teacher taught him on the side. At the end of the day, it is very hard to know.

In any event, these are not the issues that most people interested in the historical Jesus really care about. Of much greater interest, generally, are questions about Jesus's life as an adult. Who was he, really? What did he stand for? What can we say about his public ministry? What did he do? What did he say? And why was he executed by the Romans? I will address these questions in the next chapter, as I explain in greater detail why Jesus is best understood to have been an apocalyptic preacher who anticipated that the end of the age was coming within his own generation.

CHAPTER NINE

Jesus the Apocalyptic Prophet

MOST OF THE UNDERGRADUATE students who take my classes on the New Testament or the historical Jesus seem to learn a lot and to enjoy the experience. Or so they say on their end-of-the-year course evaluations. I regularly do get one complaint from students, however: that I do not present "the other side" of the story. Students learn in class that the early Gospel sources contain historically reliable traditions but also legends about Jesus (what mythicists would call "myths"); they learn that each of the Gospels has a different point of view and presents Jesus in a distinctive way; they hear all about early Jewish apocalypticism; and they see the evidence that Jesus is best understood as an apocalyptical Jewish preacher. But students wish that I would also present "the other side."

I sympathize with the concern, but I also recognize why it is a problem. The semester lasts only fifteen weeks. How can we cover everything that various scholars have said about this, that, and the other thing? To my students' surprise and dismay, I emphasize in class that there is no such thing as "the" other side for any of the topics we discuss. There are *lots* of other sides. That's the nature of scholarship.

With respect to Jesus being an apocalypticist, what would "the" other side be? I could present the evidence that other scholars offer for seeing Jesus as something else. But which other side would I choose: that Jesus was a political revolutionary? A proto-Marxist? A proto-feminist? A countercultural hero? A Jewish holy man? A Jewish Cynic philosopher? A married man with children? The students who want to hear "the" other side, of course, mean that they want me to spend at least half the class presenting their own views about Jesus rather than the scholarly consensus. In almost all instances, here in the South, it means they want me to present a conservative evangelical view. But even within my classes, lots of other views are represented, as I have students who are Jewish, Muslim, Roman Catholic, Mormon, atheist, and so on.

For my class I do have the students read scholars who represent other views. But instead of spending class time discussing Jesus from all these other sides, I present the view that appears to be the most widely held by critical scholars in the field, the one first popularized, as we have seen, by Albert Schweitzer: that Jesus was an apocalyptic prophet who predicted that the end of this evil age is soon to come and that within his generation God would send a cosmic judge of the earth, the Son of Man, to destroy the forces of evil and everyone who has sided with them and to bring in his good kingdom here on earth.

Evidence for Jesus as an Apocalypticist

IT IS, OF COURSE, contextually credible that Jesus was an apocalypticist, as we have evidence that apocalyptic thinking was widespread in his day—among Pharisees,[1] the authors of the Dead Sea Scrolls, the writers of the various Jewish apocalypses of the time, and prophetic leaders such as John the Baptist, about whom I will soon say a few words. We will also see clear instances in which apocalyptic teachings of Jesus pass the criterion of dissimilarity. At the outset, however, I want to stress that the apocalyptic proclamation of Jesus is found widely throughout our earliest sources.[2] In other words, it is multiply attested, all over the map, precisely in the sources that we would normally give the greatest weight to, those that are our oldest. And so, for example, we find the following apocalyptic teachings on Jesus's lips in our four earliest accounts of his life: Mark, Q, M, and L.

Early Independent Sources

From Mark

Whoever is ashamed of me and of my words in this adulterous and sinful generation, of that one will the Son of Man be ashamed when he comes in the glory of his Father with the holy angels. . . . Truly I tell you, there are some standing here who will not taste death until they see that the kingdom of God has come in power. (Mark 8:38–9:1)

And in those days, after that affliction, the sun will grow dark and the moon will not give its light, and the stars will be falling from heaven, and the powers in the sky will be shaken; and then they will see the Son of Man coming on the clouds with great power and glory. And then he will send forth his angels and he will gather his elect from the four winds, from the end of earth to the end of heaven. . . . Truly I tell you, this generation will not pass away before all these things take place. (Mark 13:24–27, 30)

From Q

For just as the flashing lightning lights up the earth from one part of the sky to the other, so will the Son of Man be in his

day. . . . And just as it was in the days of Noah, so will it be
in the days of the Son of Man. They were eating, drinking,
marrying, and giving away in marriage, until the day that Noah
went into the ark and the flood came and destroyed them all.
So too will it be on the day when the Son of Man is revealed.
(Luke 17:24; 26–27, 30; cf. Matthew 24:27, 37–39)

And you, be prepared, because you do not know the hour
when the Son of Man is coming. (Luke 12:39; Matthew 24:44)

From M

Just as the weeds are gathered and burned with fire, so will it
be at the culmination of the age. The Son of Man will send
forth his angels, and they will gather from his kingdom every
cause of sin and all who do evil, and they will cast them into
the furnace of fire. In that place there will be weeping and
gnashing of teeth. Then the righteous will shine forth as the
sun, in the kingdom of their father. (Matthew 13:40–43)

From L

But take care for yourselves so that your hearts are not
overcome with wild living and drunkenness and the cares of
this life, and that day come upon you unexpectedly, like a
sprung trap. For it will come to all those sitting on the face of
the earth. Be alert at all times, praying to have strength to flee
from all these things that are about to take place and to stand
in the presence of the Son of Man. (Luke 21:34–36)

I could quote many other verses, but here I want to make a very
simple point. The oldest attainable sources contain clear apocalyptic
teachings of Jesus, all of them independent of one another. What
is equally striking, however, is a subsidiary issue. The apocalyptic

character of Jesus's proclamation comes to be muted with the passing of time. After the writing of these earlier sources, we find less and less apocalyptic material. By the time we get to our last canonical Gospel, John, we have almost no apocalyptic teachings of Jesus at all. Here Jesus preaches about something else (chiefly his own identity, as the one who has come from the Father to bring eternal life). And when we get to still later Gospels, from outside the New Testament, we actually find instances—such as in the Gospel of Thomas—where Jesus argues against an apocalyptic view (Gospel of Thomas 3, 113).

Why would Jesus be portrayed as an apocalypticist in our earliest sources but as nonapocalyptic or even antiapocalyptic in our later sources? Evidently Jesus came to be deapocalypticized with the passing of time. And it is not hard to understand why. In our earliest sources Jesus is said to have proclaimed that the end of the age would come suddenly, within his own generation, before the disciples themselves died. But over the course of time, the disciples did die and Jesus's own generation came and went. And there was no cataclysmic break in history, no arrival of the Son of Man, no resurrection of the dead. What were later Christians to do with the fact that Jesus predicted that "all these things" would take place in his hearers' lifetimes when in fact the predictions did not come true? They took the obvious next step and changed the tenor and content of Jesus's preaching so that he no longer predicted an imminent end of the age. Over time, Jesus became less and less an apocalyptic preacher. This move to deapocalypticize Jesus was enormously successful. Down through the Middle Ages and on to today, the vast majority of people who have considered Jesus have not thought of him as an apocalyptic preacher. That is because the apocalyptic message that he delivered came to be toned down and eventually altered. But it is still there for all to see in our earliest surviving sources, multiply and independently attested.

There is an even more compelling general reason to think that the historical Jesus was a Jewish apocalypticist. It is that we know how he began his public ministry, and we know what happened in its wake after he died. The relatively certain beginning and the relatively certain ending are keys to understanding what happened in the middle—the proclamation of Jesus itself.

The Beginning and the End as Keys to the Middle

There is little doubt how Jesus began his public ministry. He was baptized by John the Baptist. That is significant for understanding Jesus as an apocalypticist.

That Jesus associated with John the Baptist is multiply attested in a number of our early sources. It is found in both Mark and John, independently of one another; there are also traditions of Jesus's early association with John in Q and a distinctive story from M. Why would all these sources independently link Jesus to John? Probably because there was in fact a link.

Moreover, the baptism of Jesus appears to pass the criterion of dissimilarity. The early Christians who told stories about Jesus believed that a person who was baptized was spiritually inferior to the person who was doing the baptizing, a view most Christians still hold today. And so who would make up a story about Jesus being baptized by someone else? That story would suggest that John was Jesus's superior. Moreover, why was John baptizing? According to our early traditions, it was after people repented, for "the forgiveness of sins" (Mark 1:4). Did Jesus have sins that needed to be forgiven? Who would make up such a tale? The reason we have stories in which Jesus was baptized by John is that this is a historically reliable datum. He really was baptized by John, as attested in multiple independent sources.

That is a crucial finding. What did John stand for, and why would Jesus associate with him as opposed to someone else—a Pharisee, for example, or the Essenes? John the Baptist is known to have preached an apocalyptic message of coming destruction and salvation. Mark portrays him as a prophet in the wilderness, proclaiming the fulfillment of the prophecy of Isaiah that God would again bring his people from the wilderness into the Promised Land (Mark 1:2–8). The Q source gives further information, for here John preaches a clear message of apocalyptic judgment to the crowds that come out to see him: "Who warned you to flee from the wrath to come? Bear fruits worthy of repentance. . . . Even now the ax is lying at the root of the trees; every tree therefore that does not bear good fruit is cut down and thrown into the fire" (Luke 3:7–9).

This is an apocalyptic message. The chopping down of trees is an image of coming judgment, people who did not live as God desired would be "thrown into the fire." And when will that day of judgment come? It is right around the corner. The ax is already set at the root of the tree. The chopping will commence any moment now.

Jesus obviously could have associated with any religious leader of his day. He could have become a Pharisee or practiced the cult in the Temple or joined an Essene community or a band of revolutionaries. Of all the options, he chose John the Baptist. This must mean that he agreed with the particular message John was proclaiming. John's message was one of impending apocalyptic judgment. Jesus started his public ministry subscribing to that view.

We not only know how Jesus started, we also know, with even greater certainty, what happened among his followers after he died. They began to establish communities of believers around the Mediterranean. We have our first glimpse of these communities in the writings of our earliest Christian author, Paul. And it is clear what these communities (and Paul) were like. They were filled with expectations that they—the Christians at the time—would be alive when Jesus returned from heaven as judge of the earth (see, for example, 1 Thessalonians 4:13–5:12 and 1 Corinthians 15). In other words, Christianity started out as an apocalyptic movement after the death of Jesus.

This too is highly significant for our present discussion. At the beginning of Jesus's ministry he associated with an apocalyptic prophet, John; in the aftermath of his ministry there sprang up apocalyptic communities. What connects this beginning and this end? Or put otherwise, what is the link between John the Baptist and Paul? It is the historical Jesus. Jesus's public ministry occurs between the beginning and the end. Now if the beginning is apocalyptic and the end is apocalyptic, what about the middle? It almost certainly had to be apocalyptic as well. To explain this beginning and this end, we have to think that Jesus himself was an apocalypticist.

That is to say, if Jesus *started out* apocalyptically but then in the aftermath of his life the communities of his followers were not apocalyptically oriented, one could easily argue that Jesus moved away from being an apocalypticist after his association with John. But that is not the case: the later communities were in fact apocalyptic in nature and presumably took their cues from him. So too, if Jesus did *not* start out apocalyptically but the later communities were apocalyptic, one could argue that Jesus himself was not an apocalypticist but that later followers of his changed his message to make it apocalyptic. But that cannot be argued either because Jesus did indeed start out apocalyptically. The only plausible explanation for the connection between an apocalyptic beginning and an apocalyptic end is an apocalyptic middle. Jesus, during his public ministry, must have proclaimed an apocalyptic message.

I think this is a powerful argument for Jesus being an apocalypticist. It is especially persuasive in combination with the fact, which we have already seen, that apocalyptic teachings of Jesus are found throughout our earliest sources, multiply attested by independent witnesses.

Jesus, then, is best understood in general terms as an apocalypticist. What can we say specifically about what he taught and did?

The Apocalyptic Proclamation of Jesus

JESUS'S APOCALYPTIC MESSAGE FOCUSED on the coming kingdom of God. The first words he is recorded as saying set the tone for much of his public proclamation: "The time has been fulfilled and the kingdom of God is near. Repent and believe the good news" (Mark 1:15). This is an apocalyptic message. A certain amount of time has been allotted to the current age, and that time is up. Now the new age is soon to arrive, the kingdom of God. Jesus's listeners are to repent in preparation for that coming kingdom.

The Kingdom of God

When people today hear the term *kingdom of God,* they typically think of heaven, as the place where souls go once they die. But that is not what apocalypticists meant, as we have already seen. For Jesus the kingdom was an actual place, here on earth, where God would rule supreme. And so, for example, Jesus speaks about his twelve disciples sitting on twelve thrones as rulers in the coming kingdom (Matthew 19:28; this comes from Q); he talks about eating and drinking in this kingdom; and he talks about people being cast out of the kingdom (more Q: see Luke 13:23–29). The kingdom was a real, tangible place, where love, peace, and justice would prevail.

The Son of Man

This future kingdom would be brought by a cosmic judge whom Jesus called the Son of Man. A number of sayings about the Son of Man are on the lips of Jesus in the early Gospels, and scholars have long puzzled over them. As this is a matter that is confusing to many readers, I need to say a few words about the situation.

In some of the sayings Jesus is alleged to have said, it is clear that he is referring to himself as the Son of Man. On occasion, for example, he talks about his present life in these terms: "Foxes have lairs and birds have nests, but the Son of Man has nowhere to lay his head" (Luke 9:58). On other occasions he uses the phrase when referring to his future fate: "The Son of Man will be handed over to the hands of others, and they will kill him, and after being killed he will arise after three days" (Mark 8:31).

In yet other instances there is nothing to indicate that when speaking about the Son of Man Jesus is referring to himself. This is true, for example, in Mark 8:38, already quoted above: "Whoever is ashamed of me and of my words in this adulterous and sinful generation, of that one will the Son of Man be ashamed when he comes in the glory of his Father with the holy angels." If you did not already think that Jesus was the Son of Man, you certainly would not think so from this kind of statement; on the contrary, Jesus seems to be referring to someone else.

Given these different Son of Man sayings, how can we decide how the historical Jesus actually used the term (as opposed to the Gospels or the storytellers from whom they learned these accounts)? This is where the criterion of dissimilarity can come into play. The early Christians believed that Jesus himself was the Son of Man, the cosmic judge of the earth who would return in glory (see, for example, Revelation 1:13). The sayings in which Jesus talks about himself as the Son of Man cannot pass the criterion of dissimilarity. But the sayings in which Jesus seems to be talking about someone else do pass the criterion: surely Christians who thought Jesus was the Son of Man would not make up sayings that appear to differentiate between him and the Son of Man.

The sayings that make this differentiation are always ones that predict what will happen in the future, when the Son of Man comes in judgment on the earth. These sayings are also multiply attested in early sources, as we saw earlier. Conclusion: Jesus appears to have talked about a future Son of Man who would bring in God's kingdom at the end of this age. Later Christians who thought that Jesus himself was that one took his sayings and manufactured traditions in which he spoke of himself in this way. This latter kind of saying, therefore, probably does not go back to Jesus. It is the future Son of Man sayings that do.

The Future Judgment

Jesus issues dire warnings about what will happen with the coming of the Son of Man in Mark, Q, M, and L (see, for example, Matthew 13:40–43; Mark 13:24–27; Luke 17:24; 21:34–36). Thus, for example, in the apocalyptic prediction of Matthew 13:47–50 we read the following (this has an independent parallel in the Gospel of Thomas):

> Again, the kingdom of heaven is like a net which was thrown into the sea and gathered fish of every kind. When it was full, they hauled it ashore, and sitting down chose the good fish and put them into containers, but the bad fish they threw away. That's how it will be at the completion of the age. The angels will come and separate the evil from the midst of the righteous, and cast them into the fiery furnace. There people will weep and gnash their teeth.

And so there will be a day of reckoning for all people when this age is "completed." One of Jesus's characteristic teachings is that there will be a massive reversal of fortunes when the end comes. Those who are rich and powerful now will be humbled then; those who are lowly and oppressed now will then be exalted. The apocalyptic logic of this view is clear: it is only by siding with the forces of evil that people in power have succeeded in this life; and by siding with God other people have been persecuted and rendered powerless. But when the Son of Man arrives, all that will be reversed so that anyone who has given up everything for the sake of that coming kingdom will be rewarded: the first will become last and the last first. And so we see from a saying in Mark and another in L:

> Truly I tell you, there is no one who has left a house or
> brothers or sisters or mother or father or children or lands for
> my sake and the sake of the good news, who will not receive
> them all back a hundred fold in this present time—houses,
> brothers, sisters, mothers, children, and lands, along with
> persecutions—and in the age that is coming, life that never
> ends. But many who are first will be last and the last will be
> first. (Mark 10:29–31)

> And people will come from east and west and from north and
> south and recline in the kingdom of God; and behold, those
> who are last will be first and the first will be last. (Luke 13:29–
> 30; this may be Q—cf. Matthew 20:16)

This coming judgment will not simply involve humans: it will have a cosmic dimension. This entire world has grown corrupt, and so it will be destroyed to make way for the coming of the kingdom.

> And in those days, after that affliction, the sun will grow
> dark and the moon will not give its light, and the stars will
> be falling from heaven, and the powers in the sky will be
> shaken; and then they will see the Son of Man coming on
> the clouds with great power and glory. And then he will
> send forth his angels and he will gather his elect from the
> four winds, from the end of earth to the end of heaven.
> (Mark 13:24–27)

Preparation for the End: Keeping the Torah and Living Ethically

How was one to prepare for this coming end? We saw in Jesus's earliest recorded words that his followers were to "repent" in light of the coming kingdom. This meant that, in particular, they were to change their ways and begin doing what God wanted them to do. As a good Jewish teacher, Jesus was completely unambiguous about how one knows what God wants people to do. It is spelled out in the Torah. The Law was a central component of Jesus's teaching, as can be seen from the fact that he focused on the Law, and the correct interpretation of the Law, in multiple independent sources, both early and late.

From Mark: When a man runs up to Jesus and asks him what he must do to "inherit eternal life," Jesus's immediate response is to list some of the Ten Commandments. (In Matthew's version of this story, he actually tells the man, "If you want to enter into life, keep the commandments" (Mark 10:17–22; Matthew 19:16–22; see also Luke 18:18–23).

From Q: Jesus states that it is easier for heaven and earth to pass away than for a single dot of the Law to pass away (Luke 16:16; Matthew 5:18).

From M: Jesus states that he came to fulfill the Law and that his followers must keep the Law even better than the scribes and Pharisees if they want to enter into the kingdom of heaven (Matthew 5:17, 19–20).

From John: Jesus argues with his opponents about the Law and points out to them that "the scripture cannot be broken" (John 10:34–35).

I should stress that some of these multiply attested sayings appear to pass the criterion of dissimilarity. For example, in the first passage mentioned (Mark 10:17–27), when a rich man asks Jesus how to have eternal life, he tells him to "keep the commandments." Is this what early Christians thought, that it was by keeping the Law that a person would inherit eternal life? Quite the contrary, this is a view that the vast majority of Christians rejected. The early Christians maintained that a person had to believe in the death and resurrection of Jesus for eternal life. Some early Christians—an increasingly greater number with the passage of time—argued precisely *against* the idea that keeping the Law could bring eternal life. If it could, then what was the purpose of Christ and his death? No, it was not the Law but Jesus who could bring salvation. So why is Jesus portrayed in this passage as saying that salvation comes to those who keep the Law? Because that is something that he actually said.

What, more specifically, did Jesus teach about the Law? Perhaps it is easiest to explain his views by setting them in contrast with other perspectives that we know something about. Unlike certain Pharisees, Jesus did not think that what really mattered before God was the scrupulous observance of the laws in all their details. Going out of one's way to avoid doing anything questionable on the Sabbath was of very little importance to him. That is why he constantly had confrontations with Pharisees on the issue. Unlike some Sadducees, Jesus did not think that it was of the utmost importance to adhere strictly to the rules for worship in the Temple through the divinely ordained sacrifices. In fact, as we will see, his opposition to the Temple and its cult eventually led to his death. Unlike some Essenes, he did not think that people should seek to maintain their own ritual purity in isolation from others in order to find God's ultimate approval. As we will see in a moment, his reputation was tarnished among people like this, as he associated precisely with the impure.

What did matter for Jesus—as for some other Jews from his time about whom we are less well informed (see, for example, Mark 12:32–34)—were the commandments of God that formed, in his opinion, the very heart of the Law. These were the commandments to love God above all else (as in Deuteronomy 4:4–6) and to love one's neighbor as oneself (as in Leviticus 19:18).

This emphasis on the dual commandments to love is found in our earliest surviving Gospel, in a passage that deserves to be quoted at length:

> And one of the scribes who came up heard them arguing, and noticing that [Jesus] was giving good answers, he asked him, "What is first among all the commandments?" Jesus answered, "The first of all is this: 'Hear, O Israel, the Lord our God is one Lord, and you shall love the Lord your God with your whole heart and your whole soul and your whole understanding and your whole strength' [Deuteronomy 6:4–5]. This is the second: 'You shall love your neighbor as yourself' [Leviticus 19:18]. There is no other commandment greater than these." And the scribe said to him, "You are right, teacher; you speak the truth, because 'He is one and there is none other than him,' and 'to love him with all one's heart and understanding and strength' and 'to love one's neighbor as oneself' is much more than all of the burnt offerings and sacrifices." And when Jesus saw that he replied intelligently, he said, "You are not far from the kingdom of God." (Mark 12:23–34)

Notice: the kingdom of God again. The way to attain the kingdom, for Jesus, was by following the heart of the Law, which was the requirement to love God above all else and to love other people as much as (or in the same way as) one loved oneself.

The real, social, and practical implications of this teaching can be seen in a passage now found in the Gospel of Matthew, which passes our criterion of dissimilarity. At the end of Matthew 25 we find Jesus's famous description of the final judgment, in which the "Son of Man comes in his glory, and all the angels with him, and he sits on his glorious throne" (Matthew 25:31). All the nations appear before the Son of Man, and he separates them into two groups, as a shepherd would separate the sheep from the goats. He welcomes those on his right hand, the "sheep," and invites them to come and "inherit the kingdom prepared for you from the foundation of the earth." Why are they entitled to the kingdom? Because, says the king, "I was hungry and you gave me food, I was thirsty and you gave me drink, I was a stranger and you welcomed me, I was naked and you clothed me, I was sick and you visited me, I was in prison and you came to me." These righteous ones, though, don't understand since they had never laid eyes on this glorious divine figure, let alone done anything for him. And so they ask, "When did we see you hungry and feed you, or thirsty and give you drink? And when did we see you a stranger and welcome you . . . ?" And the king replies to them, "As you did it to one of the least of these, my brothers, you did it to me" (Matthew 25:34–40).

He then turns to the group on his left, the "goats," and curses them, telling them to "depart into the eternal fire prepared for the Devil and his angels." Why? Because "I was hungry and you gave me no food, I was thirsty and you gave me no drink, I was a stranger and you did not welcome me, naked and you did not clothe me, sick and in prison and you did not visit me." They, though, are equally surprised for they too have never seen this king of kings. But he then informs them, "Truly I say to you, insofar as you did not do it to the least of these, my brothers, neither did you do it to me." And he then sends them "away into eternal punishment," whereas the righteous enter "into eternal life" (Matthew 25:41–46).

What is striking about this story, when considered in light of the criterion of dissimilarity, is that there is nothing distinctively Christian about it. That is, the future judgment is based, not on belief in Jesus's death and resurrection, but on doing good things for those in need. Later Christians—including most notably Paul (see, for example, 1 Thessalonians 4:14–18) but also the writers of the Gospels—maintained that it was belief in Jesus that would bring a person into the coming kingdom. But nothing in this passage even hints at the need to believe in Jesus per se: these people didn't even know him. What matters is helping the poor, oppressed, and needy. It does not seem likely that a Christian would formulate a passage in just this way.

The conclusion? The sayings of the passage probably go back to Jesus. And their message is clear. Anyone who wants to enter into the future kingdom of God must follow the heart of the Torah and do what God commands, when he tells his people to love others as themselves.

Jesus is often thought of as a great moral teacher, and I think that is right. But it is also important to understand *why* he insisted on a moral lifestyle guided by the dictates of love. It is not for the reasons that people offer today for being moral. Today many people think that we should behave ethically for the good of society so that we can all get along in the long haul. For Jesus, however, there was not going to *be* a long haul. The end was coming soon, and people needed to prepare for it. The ethics of Jesus's teaching were not designed simply to make society better. They were designed to convince people to behave in appropriate ways so that when the Son of Man came, they would be among the elect and brought into the kingdom instead of being destined for either eternal torment or annihilation. Jesus's ethics were driven by an apocalyptic agenda, and anyone who transplants them into a different, nonapocalyptic setting has ripped them out of their own context and pretended that their original context is of no significance to their meaning.

The Imminence of the End

There should be little doubt that Jesus taught that the end of the age, with the appearance of the Son of Man, would occur shortly, within his own generation. As we have seen, in our earliest Gospels he explicitly declares that the kingdom will arrive before some of his disciples "taste death" (Mark 9:1). Elsewhere he indicates that the great cataclysmic events of the end will happen before "this generation" passes away (Mark 13:30). That is why, throughout our early traditions—Mark, Q, M, L—Jesus urges his hearers constantly to "watch" and "be ready." These exhortations suggest that no one could know exactly when the end would come but that it would be very soon and so people should be on their guard. And so, from our earliest Gospel:

> Be awake, keep alert. For you don't know when that time is. It is like a man on a journey, who leaves his house and gives his slaves authority over their own work, and orders the doorkeeper to watch. Watch therefore—for you don't know when the master of the house is coming, whether in the evening, at midnight, at the crack of dawn, or in the morning—lest when he comes suddenly he finds you sleeping. But what I say to you I say to everyone: Watch! (Mark 13:33–37)

Similar teachings can be found in Matthew 24:43–44, 48–50; 25:13; Luke 12:36, 39–40, 45–56. The end was coming soon, and people needed to be prepared.

At the same time, Jesus insisted that in a small way, the kingdom of God was already present, in the here and now. This does not contradict the view that it would come with the arrival of the Son of Man. It is instead an extension of Jesus's teaching about the future kingdom. Those who followed Jesus and did what he said were already experiencing some of what life would be like in the kingdom. In the kingdom there would be no more war, and so Jesus's followers were to be peacemakers now. In the kingdom there would be no more hatred, and so his followers were to love everyone now. In the kingdom there would be no injustice or oppression, so his followers were to fight for the rights of the oppressed now. In the kingdom there would be no hunger, thirst, or poverty, and so his followers were to minister to the poor and homeless now. In the kingdom there would be no illness, and so Jesus's followers were to tend to the sick now.

When his followers did what Jesus commanded them to do, based on his reading of the meaning of the Torah, they already began to implement the ideals of the kingdom in the present. That is why the kingdom, for Jesus, was like a tiny mustard seed. Even though it was the smallest of all seeds, said Jesus, when planted it would grow into an enormous bush (Mark 4:30–32). The kingdom was like that: a small inauspicious beginning in the ministry of Jesus and the lives of his followers that would mushroom fantastically when the Son of Man arrived, bringing in the kingdom for real at the end of the age.

The Apocalyptic Activities of Jesus

NOW THAT WE HAVE seen a brief overview of what Jesus proclaimed during his public ministry, what can we say about his activities? What did he do?

Jesus's Reputation as a Miracle Worker

Any attempt to establish beyond reasonable doubt what Jesus did during his ministry is inevitably frustrated by the nature of the accounts that have come down to us. On page after page of the Gospels we are confronted with reports of the miraculous, as Jesus defies nature, heals the sick, casts out demons, and raises the dead. What is the historian to make of all these miracles?

The short answer is that the historian cannot do anything with them. I have spelled out the reasons at greater length in another context and do not need to belabor the point here.[3] Suffice it to say that if historians want to know what Jesus probably did, the miracles will not make the list since by their very nature—and definition—they are the most improbable of all occurrences. Some would say, of course, that they are literally impossible; otherwise we would not think of them as miracles. I do not need to enter into that question here but can simply say that even though the majority of Jesus's activities in the Gospels involve the miraculous, these stories do not provide much grist for the historians' mill.

But in an indirect way, they do provide some limited grist. Even though historians—when speaking as historians (as opposed, for example, to historians speaking as believers)—cannot say that Jesus really did, for example, heal the sick and cast out demons, they can say that he had the reputation of having done so. There is nothing improbable about someone having a reputation as a miracle worker. There are plenty of people in our own day with just that reputation, deserved or not. But the important point for this part of our discussion is that Jesus was widely thought to have been a healer and an exorcist, and that reputation makes particular sense in an apocalyptic setting.

Like other apocalypticists, Jesus believed that there were forces of evil in this world that were creating pain and misery. This was seen particularly in the lives of people who were crippled, terminally ill, or possessed by demons. (I'm not saying they were *really* possessed by demons; I'm saying that this is how they were perceived at the time.) Jesus set himself and his message against the forces of evil in this world, as he proclaimed there was an age coming in which there would be no more pain, misery, or suffering—and no more Devil and demons to ruin people's lives. Moreover, he claimed that those who followed him were already receiving a foretaste of what that kingdom would be like. And so it is no surprise that he was associated with the practices of healing and exorcism, precisely in that apocalyptic context. He was already bringing the kingdom to earth in his public ministry. The healing and exorcism stories, then, are to be understood apocalyptically, not necessarily as things that happened, but as a direct reflection of Jesus's own proclamation of the coming kingdom of God.

The Associates of Jesus

Jesus's "good" reputation derived from the traditions that he could do miracles for the benefit of those in need. But his "bad" reputation proceeded from the people with whom he was known to associate—the poor, the outcast, the sinners. Other religious leaders apparently mocked him for preferring the company of lowlifes to that of the pious and upright. And so we find in a number of early traditions the claim that Jesus associated with "tax collectors and sinners" (Mark 2:15–16; Q [Matthew 11:19; Luke 7:29]; M [Matthew 21:31–32]; L [Luke 15:1]). It seems unlikely that Jesus's later followers would make up the claim that his friends were chiefly outcasts and prostitutes, so this may indeed have been his reputation.

The term *tax collectors* refers to employees of the large tax-collecting corporations that raised tribute for Rome from the hard-pressed workers of Galilee. As a group, the tax collectors were despised as collaborators with the Romans and as greedy, moneygrubbing, and dishonest—in part because their own salaries depended on raising more funds than were handed over to the authorities. The term *sinners* refers to any of the common people who simply did not make a great effort to keep strictly the laws of the Jews. Unlike other religious leaders—say, from among the Pharisees, Sadducees, or Essenes—Jesus associated with such people.

And it is not hard to understand why, given his apocalyptic message. Jesus proclaimed that in the coming kingdom all social roles would be reversed, that the high and mighty would be taken out of power and the lowly and oppressed would be given places of prominence. Moreover, he declared that the kingdom was already making its presence known in the here and now. And so he associated with the lowlifes to show that it was they who would inherit

the kingdom. The kingdom would come not to the stellar exem-
plars of Jewish piety but to the outcasts who were looked down
upon by those in power. It is no wonder that Jesus was not popular
with other religious leaders of his day.

One group that Jesus associated with in particular was the
"twelve," an inner circle of disciples who were evidently handpicked
by Jesus. The existence of this group of twelve is extremely well attested in our early sources. It is striking that all three synoptic Gospels speak of the twelve and list their names, but the names differ
from one list to the next (Mark 3:14–19; Matthew 10:1–4; Luke
6:12–16). This must show that everyone knew there were twelve in
the group, but not everyone knew who the twelve were. The group
is also explicitly mentioned in Paul (1 Corinthians 15:5), John (6:67;
20:24), and Acts (6:2).

There is one saying of Jesus involving the twelve that almost
certainly passes the criterion of dissimilarity. This is the Q saying I
mentioned earlier, given in Matthew as follows:

"Truly I say to you, that you who have followed me, in the new
world, when the Son of Man is sitting on the throne of his glory,
you will be seated—even you—on twelve thrones ruling the twelve
tribes of Israel" (Matthew 19:28).

That this saying probably goes back to Jesus himself is suggested
by the fact that it is delivered to all twelve disciples, including, of
course, Judas Iscariot. No one living after Jesus's death, who knew
that he had been betrayed by one of his own (as reported in all our
early sources), would have made up a saying in which the betrayer
would be one of the rulers of the future kingdom. The saying, then,
was generated before the events leading up to Jesus's death. That is
to say, it appears to be something that Jesus actually said.

One reason this matters is that the saying reveals the apocalyptic
significance of Jesus's decision to call twelve, and specifically twelve,
disciples. Why not nine or fourteen? For Jesus the number twelve
mattered, probably because in ancient Israel the people of God were

formed into twelve tribes. And so too, for him, in the future kingdom there would be twelve tribes, headed not by the patriarchs of
old but by the twelve men he had chosen to be his disciples. When
Jesus chose an inner group of twelve it was an apocalyptic statement
to the world that those who followed him would be the ones who
would enter into the future kingdom and that those closest to him
would be the rulers of the kingdom.

And who would rule over them? Jesus himself was their master
now. Who would be the ruler of that future kingdom, where the
twelve sat on twelve thrones ruling the twelve tribes? Since he
"ruled" them now, he would almost certainly still rule them then.
What this means is that Jesus probably taught his closest followers that he would be the king of the coming kingdom of God. In
other words, at least to those of his inner circle, Jesus appears to
have proclaimed that he really was the future messiah, not in the
sense that he would raise an army to drive out the Romans, but
in the sense that when the Son of Man brought the kingdom to
earth, he, Jesus, would be anointed its ruler. No wonder his disciples considered him the messiah. He appears to have told them
that himself.

The Opponents of Jesus

It is thoroughly attested throughout our early traditions that Jesus
was in constant conflict with other Jewish teachers of his day. And
so, during his public ministry in Galilee, he is shown as raising
the ire of Pharisees, who roundly attacked him for not keeping the
Jewish Law to their satisfaction. These confrontations should not
be read as meaning that Jesus had abandoned Judaism. Far from it.
The controversies involved instead the proper *interpretation* of Judaism. Jesus stood over against the Pharisees and their oral law, as did
many other Jews of the time. In Jesus's view, a strict observation of
Pharisaic law was not what God wanted. He wanted his people to

keep the essence of the law in the commandment to love God above all else and to love one's neighbor as oneself.

We do not have any indication that Jesus entered into direct conflict with the Essenes, although it should be clear that his interpretation of the apocalyptic realities that were bearing down on the world was very different from theirs. Whereas they believed in separating themselves from the rest of society so as to maintain their personal and communal purity, Jesus believed in spending time with the impure, the "tax collectors and sinners," who would be the ones to be brought into the kingdom. Jesus's views would have been anathema to the Qumran community.

One other area of opposition from Jesus's public ministry involves not a Jewish group but a widespread social entity: the family. As odd as this may seem today to modern proponents of "family values," who often cite Jesus as one who was simpatico with their views, Jesus appears to have opposed the idea of the family and to have been in conflict with members of his own family. This opposition to family, we will see, is rooted in Jesus's apocalyptic proclamation.

Jesus's opposition to the family unit is made clear in his requirement that his followers leave home for the sake of the coming kingdom. Doing so would earn them a reward:

> Truly I tell you, there is no one who has left a house or brothers or sisters or mother or father or children or lands for my sake and the sake of the good news, who will not receive them all back a hundred fold in this present time—houses, brothers, sisters, mothers, children, and lands, along with persecutions—and in the age that is coming, life that never ends. But many who are first will be last and the last will be first. (Mark 10.29–31)

His followers are to be concerned for the coming kingdom, not for their families. This is a hard saying in Jesus's historical context.

The men who became his followers by leaving their homes, in most or all instances, would have been the principal breadwinners of their households. By leaving their families high and dry, they almost certainly created enormous hardship, possibly even starvation. But it was worth it, in Jesus's view. The kingdom demanded it. No family tie was more important than the kingdom; siblings, spouses, and children were of no importance in comparison.

That is why Jesus is reported as saying (this comes from Q): "If anyone comes to me and does not hate his own father and mother and wife and children and brothers and sisters and even his own life, he is not able to be my disciple" (Luke 14:26; Matthew 10:37).[4] A person must "hate" his or her family? The same word is used, strikingly, in the saying independently preserved in the Gospel of Thomas: "The one who does not hate his father and mother will not be worthy to be my disciple" (Gospel of Thomas 55). If we understand *hate* here to mean something like "despise in comparison to" or "have nothing to do with," then the saying makes sense.

And it helps explain Jesus's own reaction to his own family. For there are clear signs not only that Jesus's family rejected his message during his public ministry but that he in turn spurned them publicly (independently attested in Mark 3:31–34 and Gospel of Thomas 99). Jesus clearly saw the familial rifts that would be created when someone became committed to his message of the coming kingdom:

> You think that I have come to bring peace on earth; not peace, I tell you, but division. For from now on there will be five people in one house, divided among themselves: three against two and two against three; a father will be divided against his son and a son against his father, a mother against her daughter and a daughter against her mother; a mother-in-law against her daughter-in-law and a daughter-in-law against her mother-in-law. (Luke 12:51–53; Matthew 10:34–46; independently attested in Gospel of Thomas 16)

And family tensions would be heightened immediately before the end of the age, when "a brother will betray his brother to death, and a father his child, and children will rise up against their parents and kill them" (Mark 13:12).

These antifamily traditions are too widely attested in our sources to be ignored (they are found in Mark, Q, and Thomas, for example), and they show that Jesus did not support what we today might think of as family values. But why not? Evidently because, as I have already emphasized, he was not teaching about the good society and about how to maintain it. The end was coming soon, and the present social order was being called radically into question. What mattered was not ultimately the strong family ties and social institutions of this world. What mattered was the new thing that was coming, the future kingdom. It was impossible to promote this teaching while trying to retain the present social structure. That would be like trying to put new wine into old wineskins or trying to sew a new piece of cloth to an old garment. As any wine master or seamstress can tell you, it just won't work. The wineskins will burst and the garment will tear. New wine and new cloth require new wineskins and new garments. The old is passing away, and the new is almost here (Mark 2:18–22; Gospel of Thomas 47).

Jesus and the Temple

In addition to being opposed to other Jewish leaders and to the institution of the family, Jesus is portrayed in our early traditions as being in severe opposition to one of the central institutions of Jewish religious life, the Temple in Jerusalem. Throughout our Gospel traditions we find multiple, independent declarations on the lips of Jesus that the Temple will be destroyed in a divine act of judgment. As we have seen, the Temple was the locus of all religious practice and authority for most Jews in Jesus's day. It was there, and there alone, that the sacrifices could be made to God as commanded in the Torah. And since the Temple service was such an enormous affair, the Temple stood at the center of all political, economic, and social life in Jerusalem, the capital city of Judea.

At different periods of ancient history, however, various Jewish prophets believed that the Temple had become corrupted by those who were in charge of it. Some six centuries before Jesus, for example, this was the view of the prophet Jeremiah, whose many rants against the Temple and its leaders led to his abuse and mistreatment by the local authorities (see especially Jeremiah 7). It was also the view of the Essenes living just a few years before Jesus, who separated themselves from the religious life of Jews in Jerusalem, in no small measure because they believed the Temple cult had become defiled and impure. And it was the view of other apocalyptic prophets from the days after Jesus, including one discussed by the Jewish historian Josephus. This was a man who was also called, remarkably enough, Jesus, although this one was the son of an otherwise unknown Ananias. Some thirty years after Jesus's death, this other Jesus proclaimed that God would soon destroy the city of Jerusalem and the Temple. The Jewish leaders arrested him and placed him on trial as a troublemaker. They had him scourged and released, but he continued making his woeful declarations against the Temple until he was accidentally killed by a catapulted stone during the siege of Jerusalem in the Jewish uprising against Rome in 66–70 CE.

Jesus too is recorded as predicting the destruction of the Temple. Most famously, this is found in an important collection of his sayings in our earliest Gospel: "And as [Jesus] was coming out of the Temple, one of his disciples said to him, 'Teacher: see what great stones and what great buildings are here.' And Jesus said to him, 'Do you see these great buildings? Not one stone will be left upon another that will not be destroyed'" (Mark 13:2).

In later traditions Jesus himself is said to have threatened to destroy the place. For example, at his trial false witnesses reputedly claimed, "We have heard him saying, 'I will destroy this Temple that is made with hands and after three days build another made without hands'" (Mark 14:58), and on the cross he was allegedly mocked: "Look at the one who would destroy the Temple and re-build it in three days!" (Mark 15:29) Something similar is inde-pendently stated in John, where Jesus tells his Jewish opponents, "Destroy this Temple and I will raise it up in three days" (John 2:19). And from an unrelated source, a speech found in the book of Acts, at the martyrdom of Stephen, false witnesses again arise to say that they heard Stephen claim that "this Jesus the Nazarene will destroy this place and revamp the customs that Moses gave to us." Even the Gospel of Thomas chimes in with a similar saying, as Jesus there says, "I will destroy this house and no one will be able to rebuild it" (Gospel of Thomas 71).

Thus the tradition that Jesus spoke about the destruction of the Temple is widespread. The idea that he would personally destroy the Temple does not, of course, pass the criterion of dissimilar-ity: Christians who considered him the all-powerful Lord may well have given the sayings that twist in order to show that after his death, he "got even" with Jews by destroying their Temple. Neither does it do well by the criterion of contextual credibility: it is hard to imagine Jesus as a one-man wrecking crew able to demolish entire buildings. Similarly problematic is the notion, found only in John, that when Jesus talked about the Temple being destroyed and raised in three days, he was actually speaking of his body (John 2:21).

Did Jesus then speak at all about the coming destruction of the Temple? One might be tempted to push the criterion of dissimilarity a bit further and claim that since the Temple was in fact destroyed by the Romans in 70 CE, none of the predictions of Jesus can be safely trusted as actually going back to him—that is, that later Christians put predictions of its destruction on his lips to show his prophetic powers. Most scholars, though, consider this an extreme view since the predictions of the destruction on one level or another pass all of our criteria: (a) they are multiply attested (Mark, John, Acts, and

Thomas); (b) in one respect at least, the earliest form of these say-ings appears to pass the criterion of dissimilarity since Jesus's claim in Mark that not one stone will be left upon another did not in fact come true, as you can see yourself by visiting the Western Wall in Je-rusalem today; if anyone actually knew the details of the destruction, they wouldn't have invented this verse; and (c) just as important, the sayings are contextually credible. For we know of other prophetic fig-ures throughout the history of Israel who maintained that the Jewish people had so strayed from God that he would enter into judgment against them by destroying their central place of worship. Jesus too may well have predicted some such destruction when the Son of Man arrived in judgment on those who stood opposed to God.

That, of course, is a radical teaching, that the Temple of God and the sacrifices taking place in it, sacrifices prescribed by the Law of Moses itself, are in fact opposed to God. It is no wonder that the Jewish leaders in Jerusalem took offense and saw Jesus as a potential troublemaker.

The offense may have been sparked by one of the best attested incidents in Jesus's life. In the synoptic Gospels, Jesus spends his entire preaching ministry in Galilee, and then during the last week of his life he makes a pilgrimage to Jerusalem to celebrate the Pass-over feast. This is completely plausible, historically. The trip can be understood in light of Jesus's apocalyptic mission. He appears to have thought that the end was coming soon and that Jews needed to repent of their sins in preparation for the coming of the Son of Man. After taking his message around the countryside of his home-land, Galilee, he came to Jerusalem, also to proclaim his message, as our Gospels agree in saying he did, once he arrived in the city. Why Jerusalem? It was the heart of Judaism. Why at Passover? That was the one time of year when there were the biggest crowds in the city, as the place swelled in size with pilgrims arriving from around the world to celebrate the feast. This was the best venue for Jesus to make his apocalyptic message known.

When Jesus arrived in town, according to our early reports, he entered the Temple precincts and caused a disturbance. Our earliest Gospel, Mark, indicates that it was a massive disturbance, that Jesus single-handedly shut down the Temple operations (see Mark 11:15–16). That is completely implausible; the Temple complex was immense, encompassing an area roughly 500 yards by 325 yards, large enough to accommodate twenty-five American football fields, including the end zones. There would have been hundreds of priests doing their work and many hundreds of Jews participating. That one man could bring the entire operation to a grinding halt by turning over a few tables and uttering harsh words defies the imagination.

But Jesus may well have caused a small disturbance there, as is multiply attested (Mark and John) since this tradition coincides so well with his proclamations about the corruption of the Temple and its coming destruction. And it explains especially well why the local authorities, the Sadducees and the chief priests in charge of the place, decided to have him rounded up as a troublemaker.

The early accounts indicate that Jesus drove out those who were selling sacrificial animals and overturned the tables of those exchanging money, quoting the words of Jeremiah that I alluded to earlier: "Is it not written, 'My house will be called a house of prayer for all the nations'? But you have made it into a den of thieves" (Mark 11:17). These sellers and money changers have had a bad reputation among Christian readers of these accounts over the years, but their importance to the Temple cult should be obvious. If Jews were coming to the Passover from around the world, they could not very well bring sacrificial animals with them on their long journeys. The Temple staff had to make animals available on-site. But it would not make sense for Jews to purchase these animals with Roman currency. Roman coins had an image of the Caesar on them, and images were not allowed, especially in the Temple. And so of course there needed to be a currency exchange. This allowed the sacrificial animals to be purchased with Temple coinage.

Jesus apparently took umbrage at the operation and reacted violently to it. We do not know why. Possibly he simply saw it as corrupt, much as the Essenes did, who refused to participate in the worship in the Temple. Or maybe he could not stand the idea of someone making a profit out of the worship of God. Or possibly (these are not mutually exclusive options) Jesus's actions were meant to be a symbolic gesture.[5] If, as seems likely, Jesus predicted the destruction of the Temple in the coming judgment, he may have overturned the tables and caused a ruckus as a kind of enacted parable of his apocalyptic message, where his actions were meant to be a metaphor for what would soon happen to the place, a symbolic illustration of his proclamation of the destruction that would affect not only such enemies of God as the Romans but even the religious institutions and leaders of his own people.

This was a radical message indeed, and the leaders themselves appear to have gotten the point. According to our early traditions, they kept their eye on Jesus over the course of the following week, and as he started to amass crowds of Jews listening to his message, they arranged to have him arrested and taken from the public view, possibly to prevent any uprisings during the incendiary times of the Jewish Passover feast.

The Death of Jesus

THE LAST DAYS AND hours of Jesus receive far more attention in our early sources than any other period of his life. Our first Gospel, Mark, devotes ten chapters to Jesus's ministry in Galilee (we're not told how long it lasts), and the final six to just his last week. Our last canonical account, John, gives eleven chapters over to a three-year ministry and fully ten to the last week. Unfortunately, a good deal of the material in these chapters does not readily pass our criteria. What we can say is that Jesus was probably betrayed to the Jewish authorities by one of his own followers; these authorities delivered him over to the Roman governor, Pilate, who was in town to keep the peace during the festival; after what was almost certainly a rather brief trial, Pilate ordered him crucified. All of these data make sense when seen in light of Jesus's apocalyptic proclamation.

The early accounts of Matthew, Mark, and Luke agree that Jesus came to Jerusalem a week before the Passover itself. This makes sense, as it was customary: one needed to go through certain rituals of purification before celebrating the festival, and that required attendance in the Temple a week in advance. Jesus reportedly spent most of the week making his apocalyptic proclamation to the gathering crowds, and it is during these days that he is said to have delivered a particularly straightforward message of the coming apocalypse (for example, Mark 13). According to these accounts—unlike John, as we have seen—Jesus celebrated the Passover feast with his disciples, and it is then that he is alleged to have instituted the Lord's Supper (Mark 14). Even though the event is narrated as well by Paul, it is difficult to see how it can pass our criterion of dissimilarity for Jesus predicts in graphic detail how his body will be broken and his blood shed for the sake of others—a decidedly Christian theme. It is not implausible, however, to think that Jesus suspected that his time was up. It does not take a revelation from God to realize what happens when one speaks out violently against the ruling authorities in this kind of inflammatory context, and there was a long history of Jewish prophets having met their demise for crossing the lines of civil discourse.

There are solid reasons for thinking that Jesus really was betrayed by one of his own followers, Judas Iscariot. It is, of course, recorded in multiple independent traditions: Mark, M, John, and the book of Acts (thus Mark 14:10–11; 43–50; Matthew 27:3–10; John 18:1–11; Acts 1:15–20). Moreover, the tradition seems to pass the criterion of dissimilarity, as it does not seem to be the sort of thing that a later Christian would make up. Jesus had no more authority over his closest followers than *that?*

We are completely handicapped in knowing why Judas would have done such a thing, even though there have been a plethora of suggestions over the years.[6] Maybe he did it for the money. Maybe he had a mean streak (inspired by the Devil, to use the theological language of the New Testament). Maybe he was disenchanted with Jesus's refusal to assume the public role of the messiah. Maybe he thought he could force Jesus's hand to compel him to call out for public support. No one really knows.

A more interesting question, in some ways, is, What did Judas actually betray? In the Gospels, of course, he simply betrays Jesus's whereabouts so that the authorities can arrest him when no one is around. That may be the simplest answer, but it does make one wonder: Why couldn't the authorities simply have Jesus followed?

Another possibility presents itself, however. I have discussed this issue at length elsewhere and can simply summarize it here.[7] What is very strange about the Gospel stories of Jesus's death is that Pilate condemns him to crucifixion for calling himself the king of the Jews. This is multiply attested in all the traditions, and it passes the criterion of dissimilarity because this is not a title that, so far as we can tell, the early Christians ever used of Jesus. His followers called him the Son of God, the Son of Man, the Lord, the messiah, and lots of other things but not, in the New Testament at least, the king of the Jews. And so they would not have made that up as the charge against him, which means that it appears really to have been the crime.

But the problem is that during his public ministry Jesus is never portrayed as calling himself the king of the Jews. So why was he executed for calling himself something that he never called himself? The solution may be the one that I broached earlier, when speaking about Jesus's anticipation that the twelve disciples (including Judas) would sit on thrones as rulers in the future kingdom of God. There I suggested that just as Jesus was the master of the twelve now, in this age, so too he would be their master then, in the age to come. That is to say, that he would be the future king of the coming kingdom. This is not something that he openly proclaimed, so far as we can tell. But it does appear to be what he taught his disciples.

What then did Judas betray that allowed the authorities to arrest Jesus? Possibly this insider information. Jesus was calling himself the future king. Jesus was not executed for calling himself the Son of God or the Son of Man or the Lord or even God. He was executed for calling himself the messiah, the anointed one of God, the king of the Jews. And Judas may well have been the one who let the authorities know.

It makes sense that Jesus would have been arrested by the Jewish authorities, as they had control over all local civic affairs. Accounts of Jesus's trial before the Sanhedrin appear in the Gospels, but little there can be trusted as historically reliable. The only ones present were the Jewish leaders and Jesus, none of his followers and no one taking notes. It seems unlikely that the leaders themselves would tell later Christians what happened at the time (if they remembered). And Jesus himself could not have told, since he was jailed and then executed the next morning. What is clear is that the Jewish authorities did not try Jesus according to Jewish law but instead handed him over to Pilate.

We also do not know exactly what happened at the trial with Pilate. Again, there are no reliable sources. What we do know, as I indicated, is that Jesus was charged with calling himself the king of the Jews. That was a political charge, and of course Pilate was interested only in the political issues. He could not have cared less about disputes among the Jews about their own religious traditions. Since this is the charge that led to Jesus's execution, it is not difficult to imagine what may have happened at the trial. Pilate had been informed that Jesus considered himself a king. This was a treasonous offense. Only the Romans could appoint a king, and Jesus was certainly not chosen to rule over Israel. He was claiming an office that was not his to claim, and for him to assume the role of king he would first need to overthrow the Romans themselves.

Jesus, of course, did not understand his kingship in this way. He was an apocalypticist who believed that God would soon intervene in the course of human affairs to destroy the Romans, and everyone else opposed to him, before setting up his kingdom on earth. And then Jesus would be the one awarded the throne. Still, it may simply be that Pilate interrogated him briefly, asking him what he had to say to the charge. Jesus could hardly deny that he was the king of the Jews. He thought he was. So he either refused to answer the charge or answered it in the affirmative.

In either case, that was all Pilate needed. He had other things on his hands and other demands on his time. As governor, he had the power of life and death—no need to appeal to Roman federal law, which for the most part did not exist. If there were troublemakers, the easiest thing to do was simply to dispose of them. And so he did. He ordered Jesus to be crucified. The whole trial may have lasted no more than a couple of minutes. And the order was carried out immediately. The soldiers reportedly flogged Jesus and led him off to be executed, presumably outside the city walls. Before anyone knew it, the apocalyptic preacher was on a cross. According to our earliest account, he was dead within six hours.

CONCLUSION

Jesus and the Mythicists

Tᴴɪꜱ ᴘᴀꜱᴛ Aᴘʀɪʟ I was honored at the national meeting of the
American Humanist Association, where I received the Religious
Liberty Award. I was only vaguely aware of the association before
attending this meeting in Cambridge, Massachusetts. Four or five
hundred humanists meet every year to discuss matters of mutual interest, attending sessions and workshops on issues related to the need
to promote humanist objectives and ideals throughout society. The
group uses the term *humanist* as a positive moniker. They celebrate
what is good about being human. But a negative implication runs
beneath the surface of the self-description and is very much on the
surface in the sessions of the meeting and in almost every conversation happening there. This is a celebration of being human *without
God*. *Humanist* is understood to stand over against *theist*. This is a
gathering of nonbelievers who believe in the power of humanity to
make society and individual lives happy, fulfilling, successful, and
meaningful. And the group is made up almost exclusively of agnostics and atheists.

Even though I had earlier been in the dark about the group and its goals, I completely agree with its ideals. I am an agnostic myself, and I certainly believe that it is both desirable and possible to have a happy, fulfilling, meaningful life without Christian faith or any other kind of faith. I suppose I am a living testament to that possibility. My life is absolutely fantastic, and I could not wish for anything better, other than possibly more of the same.

But what struck me most about the meeting was precisely how religious it was. Every year I attend meetings of the Society of Biblical Literature, conferences on early Christian studies, and the like. I have never, in my recollection, been to a meeting that was so full of talk about personal religion as the American Humanist Association, a group dedicated to life without religion.

I suppose there was so much talk about religious belief because it is almost impossible in our society to talk about meaning and fulfillment without reference to religion, and humanists feel a need to set themselves over against that dominant discourse. And so at their annual meetings one finds workshops and sessions dealing with such matters as how to talk to one's family when one has left the faith, how to deal with religion in the schools (school prayer, creationism, and so forth), how to engage in the practice of meditation outside religious structures (for example, Buddhist), and so on. All of these situate humanism in relation to something else, as is clear as well when humanists describe their personal beliefs in negative terms: "agnosticism" (one who does not know whether there is a God) or "atheism" (one who does not believe in God). Even the association's self-description on their website involves a contrast with others in society: "Humanism is a progressive philosophy of life that, without theism and other supernatural beliefs, affirms our ability and responsibility to lead ethical lives of personal fulfillment that aspire to the greater good of humanity."

As surprised as I was at the meeting of humanists to hear so much about religion, what I was not surprised to learn was that a

334   DID JESUS EXIST?

good number of the people there—at least the ones I talked to—are either mythicists or are leaning toward mythicism. Their favorite authors are such figures as Robert Price, Earl Doherty, and some of the others I have mentioned in these pages. And many of them were completely taken aback when they learned that I have a different view, that I think that there certainly was a Jesus of Nazareth who existed in history, who was crucified under Pontius Pilate, and about whom we can say a good deal as a historical figure.

The Problem of the Historical Jesus

IN MY VIEW MYTHICISTS are, somewhat ironically, doing a disservice to the humanists for whom they are writing. By staking out a position that is accepted by almost no one else, they open themselves up to mockery and to charges of intellectual dishonesty. But to accomplish their goals (about which I will say more in a moment), this is completely unnecessary. Of course, for mythicists, it goes without saying, belief in Jesus is a problem. But the real problem with Jesus is not that he is a myth invented by early Christians—that is, that he never appeared as a real figure on the stage of history. The problem with Jesus is just the opposite. As Albert Schweitzer realized long ago, the problem with the historical Jesus is that he was far *too* historical.

Most televangelists, popular Christian preacher icons, and heads of those corporations that we call megachurches share an unreflective modern view of Jesus—that he translates easily and almost automatically into a modern idiom. The fact is, however, that Jesus was not a person of the twenty-first century who spoke the language of contemporary Christian America (or England or Germany or anywhere else). Jesus was inescapably and ineluctably a Jew living in first-century Palestine. He was not like us, and if we make him like us we transform the historical Jesus into a creature that we have invented for ourselves and for our own purposes.

Jesus would not recognize himself in the preaching of most of his followers today. He knew nothing of our world. He was not a capitalist. He did not believe in free enterprise. He did not support the acquisition of wealth or the good things in life. He did not believe in massive education. He had never heard of democracy. He had nothing to do with going to church on Sunday. He knew nothing of social security, food stamps, welfare, American exceptionalism, unemployment numbers, or immigration. He had no views on tax reform, health care (apart from wanting to heal leprosy), or the welfare state. So far as we know, he expressed no opinion on the ethical issues that plague us today: abortion and reproductive rights, gay marriage, euthanasia, or bombing Iraq. His world was not ours, his concerns were not ours, and—most striking of all—his beliefs were not ours.

Jesus was a first-century Jew, and when we try to make him into a twenty-first-century American we distort everything he was and everything he stood for. Jesus himself was a complete supernaturalist. He believed in the Devil and demons and the forces of evil at work in this world. He knew little—possibly almost nothing—about the workings of the Roman Empire. But what little he knew, he considered evil. He may have considered all government evil unless it was a (future) theocracy to be run by God himself through his messiah. He certainly was no proponent of our political views, whatever our views happen to be.

These forces of evil were asserting their control over the world with increasing vehemence. But Jesus thought that God would soon intervene and destroy them all to bring in his good kingdom on earth. This would not come from human effort—expanding democracy, building up national defense, improving the educational system, winning the war on drugs, and so on. Human effort counted for nothing. It would come from God, when he sent a cosmic judge to destroy the present order and to establish God's kingdom here on earth. This was no metaphor for Jesus. He believed it was going to happen. And happen soon. Within a few years.

Jesus was mistaken about that. He was mistaken about a lot of things. People don't want to hear that, but it's true. Jesus was a man of his own time. And just as all men and women of their own time are wrong about so many things, so too was Jesus. And so too are we.

The problem then with Jesus is that he cannot be removed from his time and transplanted into our own without simply creating him anew. When we create him anew we no longer have the Jesus of history but the Jesus of our own imagination, a monstrous invention created to serve our own purposes. But Jesus is not so easily moved and changed. He is powerfully resistant. He remains always in his own time. As Jesus fads come and go, as new Jesuses come to be invented and then pass away, as newer Jesuses come to take the place of the old, the real, historical Jesus continues to exist, back there in the past, the apocalyptic prophet who expected that a cataclysmic break would occur within his generation when God would destroy the forces of evil, bring in his kingdom, and install Jesus himself on the throne. This is the historical Jesus. And he is obviously far too historical for modern tastes. That is why so many Christians today try to reform him.

The Mythicist Agenda

In my view humanists, agnostics, atheists, mythicists, and anyone else who does not advocate belief in Jesus would be better served to stress that the Jesus of history is not the Jesus of modern Christianity than to insist—wrongly and counterproductively—that Jesus never existed. Jesus did exist. He simply was not the person that most modern believers today think he was.

Why then do mythicists claim he did not exist? I am not asking what evidence mythicists offer for Jesus's nonexistence. I have already considered the evidence and shown why it is problematic. I am asking the deeper question: What is driving the mythicists' agenda? Why do they work so hard at showing that Jesus never really lived? I do not have a definitive answer to that question, but I do have a guess.

It is no accident that virtually all mythicists (in fact, all of them, to my knowledge) are either atheists or agnostics. The ones I know anything about are quite virulently, even militantly, atheist. On the surface that may make sense: who *else* would be invested in showing Jesus never existed? But when you think about it for a moment, it is not entirely logical. Whether or not Jesus existed is completely irrelevant to the question of whether God exists. So why would virulent atheists (or agnostics) be so invested in showing that Jesus did not exist?

It is important to realize the obvious fact that the mythicists all live in a Christian world for which Christianity is the religion of choice for the vast bulk of the population. Of course we have large numbers of Jews and Muslims among us and scattered Buddhists, Hindus, and other major faith traditions in our culture. But by and large the people we meet who are avidly religious are Christian. And mythicists are avidly antireligious. To debunk religion, then, one needs to undermine specifically the Christian form of religion. And what easier way is there to undermine Christianity than to claim that the figure at the heart of Christian worship and devotion never even existed but was invented, made up, created? If Christianity is based on Jesus, and Jesus never existed, where does that leave the religion of billions of the world's population? It leaves it in total shambles, at least in the thinking of the mythicists. (One could easily argue that Christianity would survive quite well without a historical figure of Jesus, but that would be a different story and a different book.)

What this means is that, ironically, just as the secular humanists spend so much time at their annual meetings talking about religion, so too the mythicists who are so intent on showing that the historical Jesus never existed are not being driven by a historical concern.

Their agenda is religious, and they are complicit in a religious ideology. They are not doing history; they are doing theology.

To be sure, they are doing their theology in order to oppose traditional religion. But the opposition is driven not by historical concerns but by religious ones.

But why would mythicists be so violently opposed to traditional religion? My sense is that it is because they believe that historic Christianity—the form of religion best known in the mythicists' environment—has done and continues to do more harm than good in the world. They look at our educational systems and see fervent Christians working hard to promote ignorance over knowledge, for example, in the insistence that evolution is merely a theory and that creationism should be taught in the schools. They look at our society and see what incredible damage religion has done to human lives: from the sponsorship of slavery to the refusal to grant women reproductive rights to the denial of the possibility of gay love and marriage. They look at the political scene and see what awful political power the religious right yields: from imposing certain sets of religious beliefs on our society or in our schools to electing only those political figures who support certain religious agendas, no matter how hateful they may be toward other (poor, or non-American) human beings and how ignorant they may be about the world at large.

I have to admit that I have a good deal of sympathy with these concerns. But I am also a historian who thinks that it is important not to promote revisionist versions of the past for ideological reasons rooted in nonhistorical agendas. The writing of history should be done by following strict historical protocols. It is not simply a means of promoting a set of personal likes and dislikes.

I should also say that even though I happen to share some of the biases of many of the mythicists when it comes to harm that has been done over the years in the name of Christ (not just in crusades and inquisitions, but in our own society, right here, right now), I also see that a tremendous amount of good has been done in his name, and continues to be done, by well-meaning and hardworking Christian men and women who do untold good in the world on both massive and individual scales.

But neither issue—the good done in the name of Christ or the evil—is of any relevance to me as a historian when I try to reconstruct what actually happened in the past. I refuse to sacrifice the past in order to promote the worthy cause of my own social and political agendas. No one else should either. Jesus did exist, whether we like it or not.

BIBLIOGRAPHY

I HAVE GIVEN HERE TWO separate bibliographies that may be useful for the nonprofessional: one of mythicist literature, the other of scholarship on the historical Jesus.

Mythicist Literature

This list is not meant to be exhaustive. Instead, it comprises some of the best-known and most influential mythicist literature produced, especially (but not exclusively) in recent years. I have included only books in English.

Acharya, S (a.k.a. D. M. Murdock). *The Christ Conspiracy: The Greatest Story Ever Sold.* Kempton, IL: Adventures Unlimited, 1999.
Carrier, Richard. *Not the Impossible Faith: Why Christianity Didn't Need a Miracle to Succeed.* N.p.: Lulu Press, 2009.

Doherty, Earl. *Jesus: Neither God nor Man: The Case for a Mythical Jesus.* Ottawa, ON: Age of Reason Publications, 2009.

———. *The Jesus Puzzle: Did Christianity Begin with a Mythical Christ?* Ottawa, ON: Age of Reason Publications, 1999.

Drews, Arthur. *The Witnesses to the Historicity of Jesus Christ.* Trans. Joseph McCabe. London: Watts & Co., 1912.

Freke, Timothy, and Peter Gandy. *The Jesus Mysteries: Was the "Original Jesus" a Pagan God?* New York: Three Rivers Press, 1999.

Graves, Kersey. *The World's Sixteen Crucified Saviors: Christianity Before Christ.* New York: Cosimo Classics, 2007. First published in 1875.

Harpur, Tom. *The Pagan Christ: Recovering the Lost Light.* New York: Walker & Co., 2004.

Hoffmann, R. Joseph, ed. *Sources of the Jesus Tradition: Separating History from Myth.* Amherst, NY: Prometheus Books, 2010.

Jackson, John G. *Pagan Origins of the Christ Myth.* Austin: American Atheist Press, 1988. First published in 1941.

Leidner, Harold. *The Fabrication of the Christ Myth.* Tampa, FL: Survey Books, 2000.

Price, Robert. *The Christ-Myth Theory and Its Problems.* Cranford, NJ: American Atheist Press, 2011.

———. *The Incredible Shrinking Son of Man: How Reliable Is the Gospel Tradition?* Amherst, NY: Prometheus Books, 2003.

———. *Jesus Is Dead.* Cranford, NJ: American Atheist Press, 2007.

Robertson, Archibald. *Jesus: Myth or History?* London: Watts & Co., 1946.

Robertson, John M. *Christianity and Mythology.* London: Watts & Co., 1910.

———. *Jesus and Judas: A Textual and Historical Investigation.* London: Watts & Co., 1927.

———. *The Jesus Problem: A Restatement of the Myth Theory.* London: Watts & Co., 1917.

Salm, René. *The Myth of Nazareth: The Invented Town of Jesus.* Cranford, NJ: American Atheist Press, 2008.

Thompson, Thomas L. *The Messiah Myth: The Near Eastern Roots of Jesus and David.* New York: Basic Books, 2005.

Wells, George A. *Cutting Jesus Down to Size: What Higher Criticism Has Achieved and Where It Leaves Christianity.* Chicago: Open Court Press, 2009.

————. *Did Jesus Exist?* 2nd ed. Amherst, NY: Prometheus Books, 1986. First published in 1975.

————. *The Historical Evidence for Jesus.* Amherst, NY: Prometheus Books, 1988.

————. "Is There Independent Confirmation of What the Gospels Say of Jesus?" *Free Inquiry* 31 (2011): 19–25.

————. *The Jesus Legend.* Peru, IL: Carus, 1996.

————. *The Jesus Myth.* Chicago: Open Court, 1999.

Zindler, Frank R. *Through Atheist Eyes: Scenes from a World That Won't Reason.* Cranford, NJ: American Atheist Press, 2011.

Studies of the Historical Jesus (and Related Topics)

The following list is highly selective. I've included only a few of the books that in my opinion are among the most important and interesting studies of the past thirty or forty years that are accessible to nonspecialists. For a full annotated bibliography, which is now fifteen years old, see Craig A. Evans, *Life of Jesus Research: An Annotated Bibliography,* rev. ed., New Testament Tools and Studies 24 (Leiden: Brill, 1996). Evans's bibliography includes 2045 entries of significant books and articles—and even this is nowhere near exhaustive.

Allison, Dale. *Jesus of Nazareth: Millenarian Prophet.* Minneapolis: Fortress Press, 1998.

Borg, Marcus J. *Conflict, Holiness, and Politics in the Teachings of Jesus.* New York: E. Mellen Press, 1984.

————. *Jesus, the New Vision: The Spirit, Culture, and the Life of Discipleship.* San Francisco: Harper & Row, 1987.

Brandon, S. G. F. *Jesus and the Zealots: A Study of the Political Factor in Primitive Christianity.* New York: Scribner, 1967.

Charlesworth, James. *Jesus Within Judaism: New Light from Exciting Archaeological Discoveries.* New York: Doubleday, 1988.

Crossan, John Dominic. *The Historical Jesus: The Life of a Mediterranean Jewish Peasant.* San Francisco: Harper San Francisco, 1991.

———. *Jesus: A Revolutionary Biography*. San Francisco: Harper San Francisco, 1994.

———. *Who Killed Jesus? Exposing the Roots of Anti-Semitism in the Gospel Story of the Death of Jesus*. San Francisco: Harper San Francisco, 1995.

Downing, F. Gerald. *Christ and the Cynics: Jesus and Other Radical Preachers in First-Century Tradition*. Sheffield, Eng.: JSOT Press, 1988.

Ehrman, Bart D. *Jesus: Apocalyptic Prophet of the New Millennium*. New York: Oxford Univ. Press, 1999.

———. *The New Testament: A Historical Introduction to the Early Christian Writings*. 5th edition. New York: Oxford Univ. Press, 2011.

Fredriksen, Paula. *From Jesus to Christ: The Origins of the New Testament Images of Jesus*. New Haven, CT: Yale Univ. Press, 1988.

———. *Jesus of Nazareth: King of the Jews*. New York: Vintage, 1999.

Funk, Robert W. *Honest to Jesus: Jesus for a New Millennium*. San Francisco: Harper San Francisco, 1996.

Funk, Robert W., and the Jesus Seminar. *The Acts of Jesus: The Search for the Authentic Deeds of Jesus*. San Francisco: Harper San Francisco, 1998.

Funk, Robert W., Roy W. Hoover, and the Jesus Seminar. *The Five Gospels: The Search for the Authentic Words of Jesus*. New York: Macmillan, 1993.

Goldstein, Morris. *Jesus in the Jewish Tradition*. New York: Macmillan, 1950.

Goodacre, Mark. *The Case Against Q: Studies in Markan Priority and the Synoptic Problem*. Harrisburg, PA: Trinity Press International, 2002.

Harvey, Anthony E. *Jesus and the Constraints of History*. London: Duckworth, 1982.

Herberg, R. Travers. *Christianity in Talmud and Midrash*. New York: Ktav, 1903.

Horsley, Richard A. *Jesus and the Spiral of Violence: Popular Jewish Resistance in Roman Palestine*. Minneapolis: Fortress Press, 1987.

Johnson, Luke Timothy. *The Real Jesus: The Misguided Quest for the Historical Jesus and the Truth of the Traditional Gospels*. San Francisco: Harper San Francisco, 1996.

Kloppenborg, John. *The Formation of Q: Trajectories in Ancient Wisdom Collections*. Philadelphia: Fortress Press, 1987.

Marshall, I. Howard. *I Believe in the Historical Jesus*. Grand Rapids, MI: Eerdmans, 1977.

Meier, John. *A Marginal Jew: Rethinking the Historical Jesus.* 4 vols. New York: Doubleday, 1991, 1994, 2001, 2009.

Merz, Annette, and Gerd Theissen. *The Historical Jesus: A Comprehensive Guide.* Minneapolis: Fortress Press, 1998.

Sanders, E. P. *The Historical Figure of Jesus.* London: Allen Lane/Penguin Press, 1993.

————. *Jesus and Judaism.* Philadelphia: Fortress Press, 1985.

————. *Judaism: Practice and Belief, 63 BCE–66 CE.* London: SCM Press and Philadelphia: Trinity Press International, 1992.

Schüssler Fiorenza, Elisabeth. *In Memory of Her: A Feminist Theological Reconstruction of Christian Origins.* New York: Crossroad, 1983.

Schweitzer, Albert. *The Quest of the Historical Jesus: A Critical Study of Its Progress from Reimarus to Wrede.* Minneapolis: Fortress Press, 2001. First published in German in 1906.

Segal, Alan F. *Two Powers in Heaven: Early Rabbinic Reports About Christianity and Gnosticism.* Leiden: Brill, 1977.

Smith, Jonathan Z. *Drudgery Divine: On the Comparison of Early Christianities and the Religions of Late Antiquity.* Chicago: Univ. of Chicago Press, 1990.

Smith, Morton. *Jesus the Magician.* San Francisco: Harper & Row, 1978.

Stanton, Graham. *The Gospels and Jesus.* Oxford: Oxford Univ. Press, 1989.

Strauss, David Friedrich. *The Life of Jesus Critically Examined.* Philadelphia: Fortress Press, 1972. First published in German in 1835–36.

Vermès, Géza. *Jesus in His Jewish Context.* Minneapolis: Fortress Press, 2003.

————. *Jesus in the Jewish World.* London: SCM Press, 2011.

————. *Jesus the Jew: A Historian's Reading of the Gospels.* London: Collins, 1973.

Wright, N. T. *Jesus and the Victory of God.* Minneapolis: Fortress Press, 1996.

NOTES

Chapter 1: An Introduction to the Mythical View of Jesus

1. Earl Doherty, *Jesus: Neither God nor Man: The Case for a Mythical Jesus* (Ottawa, ON: Age of Reason Publications, 2009), vii–viii. This is a much-expanded and somewhat revised edition of Doherty's earlier book, which is sometimes looked upon as a modern classic in the field of mythicism, *The Jesus Puzzle: Did Christianity Begin with a Mythical Christ?* (Ottawa, ON: Age of Reason Publications, 1999).

2. Albert Schweitzer, *The Quest of the Historical Jesus,* ed. John Bowden (1906; repr., Minneapolis: Fortress Press, 2001), 478. Quoted with approbation by Tom Harpur, *The Pagan Christ* (New York: Walker & Co., 2004), 166. Harpur realizes that Schweitzer does not mean that Jesus never existed, even though the way he cites the passage may well leave the unwary reader with that impression.

3. For fuller summaries of these early works, see Schweitzer, *Quest,* chaps. 22 and 23 (he added these chapters on mythicists only after the success of his first edition) and the brief but helpful overview of Archibald Robertson, *Jesus: Myth or History?* (London: Watts & Co., 1946). See

also Jonathan Z. Smith, *Drudgery Divine* (Chicago: Univ. of Chicago Press, 1990), chap. 1.

4. See Schweitzer, *Quest,* chap. 11.

5. J. M. Robertson, *Christianity and Mythology,* 2nd ed. (London: Watts & Co., 1910).

6. See Schweitzer, *Quest,* 381–89.

7. Robert Price, *The Incredible Shrinking Son of Man: How Reliable Is the Gospel Tradition?* (Amherst, NY: Prometheus Books, 2003); Price, *The Christ-Myth Theory and Its Problems* (Cranford, NJ: American Atheist Press, 2011).

8. Frank Zindler, *Religions and Scriptures,* vol. 1 of *Through Atheist Eyes: Scenes from a World That Won't Reason* (Cranford, NJ: American Atheist Press, 2011).

9. Thomas L. Thompson, *The Messiah Myth: The Near Eastern Roots of Jesus and David* (New York: Basic Books, 2005).

10. A. Robertson, *Jesus: Myth or History?,* 107.

11. George A. Wells, *Did Jesus Exist?,* 2nd ed. (Amherst, NY: Prometheus Books, 1986). See also the following of his writings, most of which do not significantly alter or advance his argument (but see note 20): *The Historical Evidence for Jesus* (Amherst, NY: Prometheus Books, 1988); *The Jesus Legend* (Peru, IL: Carus, 1996); *Cutting Jesus Down to Size: What Higher Criticism Has Achieved and Where It Leaves Christianity* (Chicago: Open Court, 2009); "Is There Independent Confirmation of What the Gospels Say of Jesus?" *Free Inquiry* 31 (2011): 19–25.

12. A. Robertson, *Jesus: Myth or History?,* x.

13. John P. Meier, *A Marginal Jew: Rethinking the Historical Jesus* (New York: Doubleday, 1991), 1:87.

14. I. Howard Marshall does devote a longer footnote to the question, *I Believe in the Historical Jesus* (Grand Rapids: Eerdmans, 1977).

15. Mythicists are taken seriously by the two German New Testament scholars Gerd Theissen and Annette Merz, *The Historical Jesus: A Comprehensive Guide* (Minneapolis: Fortress Press, 1998), 122–23.

16. D. M. Murdock, *The Christ Conspiracy: The Greatest Story Ever Sold* (Kempton, IL: Adventures Unlimited, 1999).

17. Murdock, *Christ Conspiracy,* 21.

18. Murdock, *Christ Conspiracy,* 154.

19. Timothy Freke and Peter Gandy, *The Jesus Mysteries: Was the "Original Jesus" a Pagan God?* (New York: Three Rivers Press, 1999), 2.

20. For a good, direct, and recent statement of the mythicist view, see George A. Wells, "Independent Confirmation." As will be clear, in one important respect Wells differs from most other mythicists: rather than tracing the invention of the historical Jesus back to the myths about the pagan gods, Wells thinks that it derived from Jewish wisdom traditions, in which God's wisdom was thought to have been a personalized being who was with him at the creation and then came to visit humans (see, for example, Proverbs 8).

Chapter 2: Non-Christian Sources for the Life of Jesus

1. Robert Price, *The Christ-Myth Theory and Its Problems* (Cranford, NJ: American Atheist Press, 2011), 15.

2. Price, *Christ-Myth Theory,* 25, emphasis his.

3. The only indication in the New Testament Gospels that Jesus could write is in the famous story of the woman taken in adultery in John 8, where he writes on the ground while dealing with the woman's accusers (in the context of saying, "Let the one without sin among you be the first to cast a stone at her"). Unfortunately, this passage was not originally in the Gospel of John but was added later. See my discussion in Bart D. Ehrman, *Misquoting Jesus: The Story Behind Who Changed the Bible and Why* (San Francisco: Harper San Francisco, 2005), 63–65. There are only a couple of later legends of Jesus writing, including the famous exchange of letters that he has with King Abgar of Edessa, who sent him a request to be healed, to which Jesus graciously replied in writing. I include a translation of both letters in the book I published with my colleague Zlatko Plese, *The Apocryphal Gospels: Texts and Translations* (New York: Oxford Univ. Press, 2011), 413–17.

4. Throughout this book I will be using the term *pagan* in the non-derogatory sense used by historians to refer to anyone who subscribed to any of the many polytheistic religions of antiquity—that is, anyone who was neither Jewish nor Christian. The term when used by historians does not have any negative connotations.

5. See the article on "Pontius Pilate" by Daniel Schwartz in the *An-*

chor Bible Dictionary, ed. David Noel Friedman (New York: Doubleday, 1992), 5:395–401.

6. William Harris, *Ancient Literacy* (Cambridge, MA: Harvard Univ. Press, 1989).

7. Catherine Hezser, *Jewish Literacy in Roman Palestine* (Tübingen: Mohr Siebeck, 2001).

8. On the question of the sources of the Gospels, see my fuller discussion in Bart D. Ehrman, *The New Testament: A Historical Introduction to the Early Christian Writings,* 5th ed. (New York: Oxford Univ. Press, 2011), chaps. 8 and 12.

9. For a collection of them, see Ehrman and Plese, *Apocryphal Gospels.*

10. See the discussion in Hezser, *Jewish Literacy,* esp. 422–26.

11. For an accessible translation of this letter, along with translations of the other Roman sources that I mention in this chapter, see Robert M. Grant, *Second-Century Christianity: A Collection of Fragments,* 2nd ed. (Louisville: Westminster John Knox Press, 2003), 3–12.

12. Representative of this view is Tom Harpur, *The Pagan Christ* (New York: Walker & Co., 2004), 162.

13. There is a large literature on Josephus. Of particular use for the topics I will be dealing with in this book, see Steve Mason, *Josephus and the New Testament,* 2nd ed. (Grand Rapids: Baker Academic, 2002).

14. See the discussion in John P. Meier, *A Marginal Jew: Reconsidering the Historical Jesus* (New York: Doubleday, 1991), 59–69.

15. See Meier, *Marginal Jew,* 59–69.

16. Doherty, *Jesus: Neither God nor Man,* 534; his entire discussion can be found on 533–86.

17. Doherty, *Jesus: Neither God nor Man,* 535.

18. For two of the more important studies of the apologists, see R. M. Grant, *Greek Apologists of the Second Century* (Louisville, KY: Westminster John Knox Press, 1988), and Eugene Gallagher, *Divine Man or Magician? Celsus and Origen on Jesus* (Atlanta: Scholars Press, 1982).

19. Doherty, *Jesus: Neither God nor Man,* 562.

20. Ken Olson, "Eusebius and the *Testimonium Flavianum,*" *Catholic Biblical Quarterly* 61 (1999): 305–22.

21. J. Carleton Paget, "Some Observations on Josephus and Christianity," *Journal of Theological Studies* 52, no. 2 (2001): 539–624; Alice Whealey, "Josephus, Eusebius of Caesarea, and the *Testimonium Flavianum,*" in

Josephus und das Neue Testament, ed. Christfried Böttrich and Jens Herzer (Tübingen: Mohr Siebeck, 2007), 73–116.

22. Final judgment on the authenticity of the *Testimonium* will ultimately depend, in the short term, on the strength of the argument that Olson can make in his doctoral dissertation and especially on the critical reaction to it by experts on both Josephus and Eusebius. However that debate resolves itself, it should be obvious that my case for the historicity of Jesus does not depend on the reliability of Josephus's testimony, even though I take the passage to be, at its core, authentic.

23. The most conservative estimates put the population under one million. See Magen Broshi, *Bread, Wine, Walls, and Scrolls* (Sheffield, Eng.: Sheffield Academic Press, 2002).

24. Here I am simply summarizing my discussion in *Jesus: Apocalyptic Prophet of the New Millennium* (Oxford: Oxford Univ. Press, 1999), 62–63. For fuller discussions, see the classic studies of R. Travers Herford, *Christianity in Talmud and Midrash* (New York: Ktav, 1903), and Morris Goldstein, *Jesus in the Jewish Tradition* (New York: Macmillan, 1950).

Chapter 3: The Gospels as Historical Sources

1. See my college-level textbook, *The New Testament: A Historical Introduction to the Early Christian Writings,* 5th ed. (New York: Oxford Univ. Press, 2011), chap. 8, and the bibliography that I offer there.

2. See Robert Kysar, *John the Maverick Gospel,* 3rd ed. (Louisville, KY: Westminster John Knox Press, 2007).

3. Some scholars think that John knew and used the synoptic Gospels, but I think this is unlikely. Even if he did, he includes many stories unrelated to those of the synoptics, and in these at least there certainly cannot have been any dependence. On the entire question, see D. Moody Smith, *John Among the Gospels,* 2nd ed. (Columbia: Univ. of South Carolina Press, 2001).

4. For a new translation of the Gospel of Thomas by Zlatko Plese, see Bart Ehrman and Zlatko Plese, *The Apocryphal Gospels: Texts and Translations* (New York: Oxford Univ. Press, 2011), 310–35; for a discussion of the contents and character of the Gospel, see my book *Lost Chris-*

tianities: The Battle for Scripture and the Faiths We Never Knew (New York: Oxford Univ. Press, 2003), chap. 3.

5. For translation of the Gospel of Peter, see Ehrman and Plese, *Apocryphal Gospels,* 371–87; for discussion of its contents and character, see Ehrman, *Lost Christianities,* chap. 1.

6. For a full commentary on the Gospel of Peter, see Paul Foster, *The Gospel of Peter* (Leiden: Brill, 2010).

7. Translation and brief discussion of Papyrus Egerton 2 in Ehrman and Plese, *Apocryphal Gospels,* 245–53.

8. This is a highly fragmentary account in which Jesus is beside the Jordan River, in which he may be described as performing a miracle, possibly to illustrate his parable about the miraculous growth of seeds.

9. See Ehrman, *New Testament,* chap. 8.

10. For a spirited attempt to dispense with Q and to argue that Matthew was the source of Luke, see Mark Goodacre, *The Case Against Q: Studies in Markan Priority and the Synoptic Problem* (Harrisburg, PA: Trinity Press International, 2002). As lively as the argument of the book is, it has failed to convince most of the scholars working in the field.

11. Joel Marcus, *Mark: A New Translation with Introduction and Commentary,* 2 vols., Anchor Bible Commentary (New York: Doubleday, 2000–2009).

12. I give some of the evidence, with bibliography, in *New Testament,* chap. 12.

13. April D. DeConick, *The Original Gospel of Thomas in Translation* (London: T & T Clark, 2006). For the Gospel of Peter, see the less convincing argument of John Dominic Crossan, *The Cross That Spoke: The Origins of the Passion Narrative* (San Francisco: Harper San Francisco, 1988). Even if one does not accept the extreme views of Crossan about a Cross Gospel that originated before even Mark, which was used by all four of the New Testament Gospel writers, a good case can still be made that the Gospel of Peter is based on written sources.

14. See Edgar McKnight, *What Is Form Criticism?* (Philadelphia: Fortress Press, 1969).

Chapter 4: Evidence for Jesus from Outside the Gospels

1. For an introduction to Papias and a translation of all his surviving literary remains, see Bart D. Ehrman, *The Apostolic Fathers,* Loeb Classical Library (Cambridge, MA: Harvard Univ. Press, 2003), 2:86–119.

2. This and the following excerpts of Papias are taken from Ehrman, *Apostolic Fathers,* 85–119.

3. See John 7:53–8:11.

4. See my discussion in *Jesus, Interrupted: Revealing the Hidden Contradictions in the Bible (and Why We Don't Know About Them)* (San Francisco: HarperOne, 2009), 107–10.

5. See Ehrman, *Jesus, Interrupted,* 107–10.

6. For introductions and translations, see Ehrman, *Apostolic Fathers,* 1:203–321.

7. I have taken translations from Ehrman, *Apostolic Fathers,* 203–321.

8. See Ehrman, *Apostolic Fathers,* 1:23–25.

9. This is the oldest form of the baptism scene found in the Gospel of Luke; see my discussion in Bart Ehrman, *The Orthodox Corruption of Scripture,* 2nd ed. (New York: Oxford Univ. Press, 2011), 73–79.

10. See my fuller study, *Forged: Writing in the Name of God: Why the Bible's Authors Are Not Who We Think They Are* (San Francisco: HarperOne, 2011), 79–114.

11. See Ehrman, *Forged,* 43–78.

12. See chap. 3. To recall: the seven independent Gospel witnesses are Mark, parts of Matthew, parts of Luke, John (in whole or in part), the Gospel of Peter, the Gospel of Thomas (in whole or in part), and Papyrus Egerton 2 (in whole or in part).

13. Wells, *Did Jesus Exist?,* 28.

14. See Joel Marcus, *Mark 8–16: A New Translation with Introduction and Commentary,* Anchor Bible 27 (New Haven, CT: Yale Univ. Press, 2009), 705–7.

15. See Victor Paul Furnish, *Jesus According to Paul* (Cambridge: Cambridge Univ. Press, 1993).

16. One place where it is sometimes thought that Paul is quoting a prophecy instead of a saying of the historical Jesus is in 1 Corinthians 14:34–37, where he instructs women to be silent in the churches because this is "a command of the Lord." The problem in this passage is that

there are solid reasons, including some manuscript evidence, to suggest that the injunction for women not to speak was not originally part of 1 Corinthians but was added by later scribes. In that case, the command of the Lord would have to do with the passage before 14:34, where Paul urges order in the worship services instead of allowing chaos to reign, as it appears to have been doing in Corinth. One can easily imagine a teaching of Jesus where he instructed his disciples to be harmonious, unified, and orderly rather than self-aggrandizing and disruptive. Some such saying rather than a Christian prophecy may well lie behind Paul's injunction.

17. I am drawing these examples from Wells, *Did Jesus Exist?,* 19.

18. George A. Wells, *The Jesus Legend* (Peru, IL: Carus, 1996), 14.

19. George A. Wells, "Is There Independent Confirmation of What the Gospels Say of Jesus," *Free Inquiry* 31 (2011): 22.

Chapter 5: Two Key Data for the Historicity of Jesus

1. Earlier in my career I played with the idea that Cephas and Peter were two different persons, but now I think that's a bit bizarre—as most of the critics of the idea have pointed out! The most compelling reason for identifying them as the same person is not simply John 1:42 but the historical fact that neither Cephas nor Peter was a personal name in the ancient world. *Peter* is the Greek word for "rock," which in Aramaic was *Cephas.* And so Jesus gave this person—his real name was Simon—a nickname, "the Rock." It seems highly unlikely that two different persons were given precisely the same nickname at the same time in history when this name did not previously exist.

2. For example, in Paul's two longest letters, Romans and 1 Corinthians, he uses the name Jesus by itself a total of one time. He frequently, however, speaks of "the Lord."

3. Robert Price, *Christ-Myth Theory,* 336.

4. J. M. Robertson, *Jesus and Judas: A Textual and Historical Investigation* (London: Watts & Co., 1927).

5. George A. Wells, *The Historical Evidence for Jesus* (Amherst, NY: Prometheus Books, 1988), 168.

6. Price, *Christ-Myth Theory,* 336–43.

7. Price, *Christ-Myth Theory,* 352.

8. Price, *Christ-Myth Theory,* 349.

9. Price here is building on the imaginative but wildly speculative and widely discredited views of Robert Eisenmann in his book *James, the Brother of Jesus* (New York: Viking, 1997). For sober evaluations of what scholars think about the Dead Sea Scrolls and their community, see the authoritative and justly acclaimed works of such scholars as Joseph Fitzmyer, *Responses to 101 Questions on the Dead Sea Scrolls* (New York: Paulist Press, 1992); Géza Vermès, *The Story of the Scrolls* (London: Penguin, 2010); and James Vanderkam, *The Dead Sea Scrolls Today* (Grand Rapids, MI: Eerdmans, 2010).

10. Translation of R. B. Wright, "Psalms of Solomon," in *The Old Testament Pseudepigrapha,* ed. James H. Charlesworth (New York: Doubleday, 1985), 2:667.

11. Translation of E. Isaac, in *Old Testament Pseudepigrapha,* ed. Charlesworth, 2:49.

12. See John Collins, *The Scepter and the Star: Messianism in Light of the Dead Sea Scrolls,* 2nd ed. (Grand Rapids: Eerdmans, 2010).

13. Richard Carrier, *Not the Impossible Faith: Why Christianity Didn't Need a Miracle to Succeed* (n.p.: Lulu Press, 2009), 34, emphasis his.

14. See John Collins, "Daniel, Book of," *Anchor Bible Dictionary,* ed. David Noel Friedman (New York: Doubleday, 1992), 2:29–37.

15. Louis Hartman, *The Book of Daniel: A New Translation with Introduction and Commentary,* Anchor Bible (New Haven, CT: Yale Univ. Press, 1978), 251.

16. Hartman, *Book of Daniel,* 252.

Chapter 6: The Mythicist Case

1. See Ehrman, *Misquoting Jesus: The Story Behind Who Changed the Bible and Why* (San Francisco: Harper San Francisco, 2005).

2. See Bart Ehrman, *Forged: Writing in the Name of God: Why the Bible's Authors Are Not Who We Think They Are* (San Francisco: HarperOne, 2010).

3. The difference, of course, is that no one would use the Hitler Diaries as historical sources for the life of Hitler, as my student Stephen Carl-

son has pointed out to me. But that is because we have so many other sources, including those used by Kujau to construct his forgeries. If we did not have these other sources, though, a careful study of his forgeries could help us reconstruct his sources, and to that extent the Hitler Diaries would be like the Gospels: they would be evidence of earlier historical accounts. But my main point is that what matters is not the name of a book's author (real or false) but the nature of its contents.

4. Luke indicates that Mary and Joseph returned to Nazareth after they had completed the necessary rites of purification. This is a reference to the law found in Leviticus 12, which indicates that thirty-two days after giving birth the woman was to make an offering to God for cleansing.

5. Bart Ehrman, *Jesus, Interrupted,* chap. 2.

6. See Ehrman, *Jesus, Interrupted,* 29–39.

7. Robert Price, *The Christ-Myth Theory and Its Problems* (Cranford, NJ: American Atheist Press, 2011); Price, *The Incredible Shrinking Son of Man* (Amherst, NY: Prometheus Books, 2003).

8. Albert Schweitzer, *The Quest of the Historical Jesus,* ed. John Bowden (1906; repr., Minneapolis: Fortress Press, 2001), chaps. 22 and 23.

9. Frank Zindler, "Where Jesus Never Walked," *Through Atheist Eyes,* vol. 1 (Cranford, NJ: American Atheist Press, 2011), 27–55. I do not mean to say that Zindler does not cite evidence for his view. He claims that the name Jesus in Mark 1:9 does not have the definite article, unlike the other eighty places it occurs in Mark, and therefore the verse does not appear to be written in Markan style. In response, I should say that (a) there are two other places in Mark where the name Jesus does not have the article; (b) if the problem with the entire verse is that the name Jesus does not have article, then if we posit a scribal change to the text, the more likely explanation is that a scribe inadvertently left out the article. Nazareth has nothing to do with it; and (c) there is not a single stitch of manuscript evidence to support his claim that the verse was interpolated into the Gospel. This latter point is worth stressing since it is the reason that no serious scholar of the textual tradition of Mark thinks that the verse is an interpolation.

10. George A. Wells, *Did Jesus Exist?,* 2nd ed. (Amherst, NY: Prometheus Books, 1986), 146.

11. René Salm, *The Myth of Nazareth* (Cranford, NJ: American Atheist Press, 2008).

12. Salm, *Myth of Nazareth*, xii.

13. As I have learned from my UNC colleague Jodi Magness, one of the premier archaeologists of Roman Palestine in the world today.

14. Stephen J. Pfann, Ross Voss, and Yehudah Rapuano, "Surveys and Excavations at the Nazareth Village Farm (1997–2002): Final Report," *Bulletin of the Anglo-Israel Archaeological Society* 25 (2007): 16–79.

15. René Salm, "A Response to 'Surveys and Excavations at the Nazareth Village Farm (1997–2002): Final Report,'" *Bulletin of the Anglo-Israel Archaeological Society* 26 (2008): 95–103. The responses were compelling (based in part on their communications with Alexandre): Stephen J. Pfann and Yehudah Rapuano, "On the Nazareth Village Farm Report: A Reply to Salm," *Bulletin of the Anglo-Israel Archaeological Society* 26 (2008): 105–8; and Ken Dark, "Nazareth Village Farm: A Reply to Salm," *Bulletin of the Anglo-Israel Archaeological Society* 26 (2008): 109–11.

16. Pfann and Rapuano, "Nazareth Village Farm Report," 108.

17. Pfann and Rapuano, "Nazareth Village Farm Report," 108.

18. Ken Dark, "Review of Salm, *Myth of Nazareth*," in the *Bulletin of the Anglo-Israel Archaeological Society* 26 (2008), 145.

19. Price, *Christ-Myth Theory*, 34.

20. Thomas L. Thompson, *The Messiah Myth: The Near Eastern Roots of Jesus and David* (New York: Basic Books, 2005).

21. A convenient abbreviated version of *The Life of Apollonius of Tyana* can be found in David Cartlidge and David Dungan, *Documents for the Study of the Gospels* (Minneapolis: Fortress Press, 1994).

22. Kersey Graves, *The World's Sixteen Crucified Saviors: Christianity Before Christ* (1875; repr., New York: Cosimo Classics, 2007), 29.

23. Graves, *Sixteen Crucified Saviors*, 30–31.

24. Frank Zindler, "How Jesus Got a Life," *Through Atheist Eyes: Scenes from a World That Won't Reason* (Cranford, NJ: American Atheist Press, 2011), 1:57–80.

25. Zindler, "How Jesus Got a Life," 66.

26. For interesting works of real scholarship, see Roger Beck, *The Religion of the Mithras Cult in the Roman Empire: Mysteries of the Unconquered Sun* (New York: Oxford Univ. Press, 2007), and the speculative but

fascinating work of David Ulansey, *The Origins of the Mithraic Mysteries: Cosmology and Salvation in the Ancient World* (New York: Oxford Univ. Press, 1991).

27. The literature on the mystery cults is extensive. For a most recent and accessible introduction by an authority in the field, see Hugh Bowden, *Mystery Cults of the Ancient World* (Princeton: Princeton Univ. Press, 2010).

28. Price, *Christ-Myth Theory,* 44–46.

Chapter 7: Mythicist Inventions

1. On Kersey Graves, see the previous chapter. For more recent discussions, see Robert Price, *Christ-Myth Theory,* 16. The details of the transformation from dying-rising god to the historical Jesus are worked out differently, of course, by different mythicist authors. As two popular examples, see Tom Harpur, *The Pagan Christ* (New York: Walker & Co., 2004), and Timothy Freke and Peter Gandy, *The Jesus Mysteries: Was the "Original Jesus" a Pagan God?* (New York: Three Rivers Press, 1999).

2. See the discussion, for example, in Jonathan Z. Smith, *Drudgery Divine: On the Comparison of Early Christianities and the Religions of Late Antiquity* (Chicago: Univ. of Chicago Press, 1990), chap. 4.

3. Tryggve N. D. Mettinger, *The Riddle of the Resurrection: "Dying and Rising Gods" in the Ancient Near East* (Stockholm: Almquist and Wiksell International, 2001), 217.

4. Mettinger, *Riddle of the Resurrection,* 219.

5. Mettinger, *Riddle of the Resurrection,* 221.

6. Jonathan Z. Smith, "Dying and Rising Gods," *Encyclopedia of Religion,* 2nd ed., ed. Lindsay Jones (Detroit: Macmillan, 2005), 4:2535–40.

7. J. Z. Smith, "Dying and Rising Gods," 2535.

8. J. Z. Smith, "Dying and Rising Gods," 2538.

9. Mark S. Smith, "The Death of 'Dying and Rising God' in the Biblical World: An Update, with Special Reference to Baal in the Baal Cycle," *Scandinavian Journal of the Old Testament* 12 (1998): 257–313.

10. M. S. Smith, "Death of 'Dying and Rising Gods,'" 288.

11. Most famous is Ralph Martin, *A Hymn of Christ: Philippians 2:5–11*

in Recent Interpretation and in the Setting of Early Christian Worship (Downers Grove, IL: Intervarsity Press, 1997). See also the useful collection of essays in Ralph Martin and Brian Dodd, eds., *Where Christology Began: Essays on Philippians 2* (Louisville, KY: Westminster John Knox Press, 1998).

12. Few scholars take the latter view, but one who does is Gordon Fee, *Paul's Letter to the Philippians,* New International Commentary on the Bible (Grand Rapids, MI: Eerdmans, 1995).

13. To get a sense of the richness of the interpretive tradition, see, for example, the commentary by John Reumann, *Philippians: A New Translation with Introduction and Commentary,* Yale Anchor Bible (New Haven, CT: Yale Univ. Press, 2008), 338–83.

14. For a brief statement of this view, see the essay by James D. G. Dunn, "Christ, Adam, and Preexistence," in *Where Christology Began,* ed. Martin and Dodd, 74–83.

15. See Alan Segal, *Two Powers in Heaven: Early Rabbinic Reports About Christianity and Gnosticism* (Leiden: Brill, 1977).

16. See "The Speeches of Acts" in chapter 4, above.

17. And, of course, in later Christian texts. It remains a significant question whether it is the view of the Philippians hymn. It is important to recognize that views of Jesus did not develop in a straight line in all early Christian communities at the same pace. Some communities began calling Jesus God before others did. But the development we clearly see in the Gospels (starting with Mark and ending with John) replicates the development that happened throughout Christendom at large, in different places and at different times, as Christians went from thinking that Jesus was exalted to be the Son of God at the resurrection (thus the speeches in Acts) to thinking that he was the Son of God at his baptism to thinking that he was Son of God from his birth to thinking that he had existed as Son of God even before his birth.

18. Wells, *The Historical Evidence for Jesus.*

19. Archibald Robertson, *Jesus: Myth or History?* (London: Watts & Co., 1946), 95.

20. Wells, *Did Jesus Exist?,* 39.

21. See my discussion in *Forged.*

22. See Wells, *Did Jesus Exist?,* 97.

23. Wells, *Did Jesus Exist?*, 18.

24. Wells, *The Historical Evidence for Jesus*, 33.

25. Doherty, *Jesus: Neither God nor Man*, 97.

26. For example, Earl Doherty, *The Jesus Puzzle: Did Christianity Begin with a Mythical Christ?* (Ottawa, ON: Age of Reason Publications, 1999), 5.

27. Doherty, *Jesus Puzzle*, 98.

28. Doherty, *Jesus: Neither God nor Man*, 101.

29. Wells, *Did Jesus Exist?*, 101; Wells, "Is There Independent Confirmation of What the Gospels Say of Jesus?" *Free Inquiry* 31 (2011): 23. For Wells, Mark was the first to combine the idea of an earthly Jesus who taught and did miracles with a passion narrative.

30. Doherty, *Jesus: Neither God nor Man*, xi.

31. See D. Moody Smith, *John Among the Gospels*, 2nd ed. (Columbia: Univ. of South Carolina Press, 2001).

32. See Robert Kysar, *John the Maverick Gospel*, 3rd ed. (Louisville, KY: Westminster John Knox Press, 2007).

33. See "The Aramaic Origins of (Some) Oral Traditions" in chap. 3 above.

Chapter 8: Finding the Jesus of History

1. See further my discussion in *Jesus: Apocalyptic Prophet of the New Millennium* (New York: Oxford Univ. Press, 1999), chap. 2, esp. n. 1.

2. An earlier assertion of this view can be found in Johannes Weiss, *Jesus' Proclamation of the Kingdom of God* (1892; repr., Chico, CA: Scholars Press, 1995).

3. For a full exposition of Judaism in the days of Jesus, see E. P. Sanders, *Judaism: Practice and Belief, 63 BCE–66 CE* (Philadelphia: Trinity Press International, 1992).

4. It needs to be remembered that when scholars use the term *pagan* it does not have derogatory connotations; it simply refers to people who held to polytheistic religious beliefs, who were not, therefore, either Jewish or Christian.

5. Josephus indicates that the Pharisees made up the largest group and that they numbered six thousand, the Essenes claimed four thousand, and the Sadducees had far fewer. These numbers should be considered

in light of the overall Jewish population at the time, which may have been as many as four million.

6. For further reading on the Essenes and the Dead Sea Scrolls, see James Vanderkam, *The Dead Sea Scrolls Today,* 2nd ed. (Grand Rapids: Eerdmans, 2010).

7. For fuller information, see my discussion in *Jesus: Apocalyptic Prophet.* For a comprehensive coverage of ancient Jewish and Christian apocalyptic thought, see John Collins, ed., *Encyclopedia of Apocalypticism: The Origins of Apocalypticism in Judaism and Christianity,* vol. 1 (New York: Continuum, 1998).

8. The story is found only in Matthew and Luke, so in that sense it is multiply attested, but the accounts disagree sharply in their depictions of the event.

9. See Jonathan Reed, *Archaeology and the Galilean Jesus: A Re-examination of the Evidence* (Harrisburg, PA: Trinity Press International, 2000).

Chapter 9: Jesus the Apocalyptic Prophet

1. Pharisees were known to be strong advocates of the apocalyptic doctrine of the resurrection of the dead at the end of the age, in contrast to the Sadducees. See, for example, Acts 23:6–8.

2. For portions of the following discussions I have relied heavily on my more extensive treatment in Bart Ehrman, *Jesus: Apocalyptic Prophet of the New Millennium* (Oxford: Oxford Univ. Press, 1999), chaps. 8–10.

3. See Ehrman, *Jesus: Apocalyptic Prophet,* 193–97.

4. I assume that the stronger word, "hate," is original to Jesus rather than "love more than," as in Matt. 10:37, and that the latter represents a change by Christians who recounted these words of Jesus and were taken aback by their harshness.

5. This is argued most convincingly in E. P. Sanders, *Jesus and Judaism* (Philadelphia: Fortress Press, 1985), 71–76.

6. See the discussion in my book *The Lost Gospel of Judas Iscariot: A New Look at Betrayer and Betrayed* (Oxford: Oxford Univ. Press, 2006), 166–69.

7. See Ehrman, *Lost Gospel of Judas,* chap. 10.